"Winners" and "Losers" in t̶h̶e̶ ̶o̶n̶g̶o̶i̶n̶g̶ Battle to Protect and Control the Spectacular Water Wilderness of Havasu Canyon

A historical analysis of the seemingly never-ending battle of the Havasupai tribe to regain and control much of its lost pre-European contact land and a new proposal to possibly further help them in this effort

by
Larry R. Stucki, Ph.D.
Summer 2020

Outskirts Press, Inc.
http://www.outskirtspress.com

Paperback ISBN: 978-1-9772-2935-9
Hardback ISBN: 978-1-9772-2974-8

Library of Congress Control Number: 2020911306

Cover Photo © 2020 Larry R. Stucki, Ph.D.. All Rights Reserved – Used With Permission.

Outskirts Press and the "OP" logo are trademarks belonging to Outskirts Press, Inc.

PRINTED IN THE UNITED STATES OF AMERICA

Contents

Preface

Just off the trail, near the scenic splendors of the waterfalls, above the grave of a small child, in 1973, I sadly observed a weather-battered doll lying in a decomposing crib. This grim reminder of the terrible price that the Havasupai people continued to pay for their wilderness isolation was not even noticed by the average backpacking tourist. In fact, conditions for the weekend backpacker were never better than during my 1977 and 1980 visits. The campground was less crowded than usual and the splendid waterfalls and "noble savages" of Supai had been saved "forever" from the evils of exploitation.

Few campers remember that their own ancestors often fled from the wilderness to the cities to escape from poverty or that today it is seldom the lifelong rural resident who advocates further expansion of our national wilderness areas. For city dwellers, a brief wilderness experience is a welcome change of pace especially when buffered by expensive boots, freeze dried foods, tents, sleeping bags, and other technological gadgets. However, most such adventurers after their brief encounter with the wilderness eagerly anticipate their reunion with the luxuries of urban living, an option that in 1977 no longer appeared to be available to most permanent residents of Supai… (Chapter 8:136)

Chapter 1

Few Americans realize that on January 3, 1975, Grand Canyon National Park lost what many of those who know the canyon most intimately have described as its former greatest scenic treasure. It was no mighty act of God that severed the spectacular falls of Havasu Creek from our National Park system but rather the simple stroke of President Gerald Ford's pen as he reluctantly signed Senate Bill 1296 into law.

To a small band of Native Americans, the return to their control of these waterfalls and vast amounts of the surrounding countryside signaled the beginning of a long dreamed of millennium. This action, they believed, would now free them from the 518-acre canyon "prison" in which they had been confined by the government since the establishment of their reservation in 1882.

In all of America north of Mexico there is no more isolated Native American village than Supai and this has often proven to be more of a curse to its permanent residents than a blessing. No major Interstate highway passes near the reservation and even the long, dreary access road from highway 66 ends at a desolate "hilltop" eight miles away from and half a mile above the village.[1] Thus, even today, Supai can be reached only by helicopter or a steep, dry, and often extremely hot, 8 mile foot and horse trail.

However, every summer, for thousands of hardy tourists who seek a temporary escape from the pressures of modern "civilized" life, the "wilderness" of Cataract Canyon becomes a "Shangri-La." Lured by full-color illustrated articles in such magazines and newspapers as the National Geographic, Arizona Highways, and the Arizona Republic; countless numbers of Boy Scouts, college students, and adventuresome couples and families have sought access to the pleasures and delights of this watery "paradise." But, in past years, with the exception of a few "hippies" who for a day or two wandered around the village of Supai trying to escape into "Indian brotherhood,"[2] most tourists made few attempts to socialize with the approximately three hundred[3] Havasupai living in the canyon during the summer months. In fact, many tourists before the major scenic areas were returned to Havasupai control, deeply resented being forced to pay the Havasupai a small fee for crossing their land on the way to the waterfalls and in previous years some individuals and groups deliberately hiked through the village at night or in the early morning hours to avoid paying this fee. Also, many tourists over the years have complained bitterly about the poor maintenance of foot trails and bridges and the problem of horses not being available on the promised day, a difficulty which was often especially severe around the time of the late summer Peach Festival.[4] And by the late1960s, the frustration of visitors waiting in vain for promised horses had intensified as it became more expensive to buy the extra feed needed to maintain large numbers of pack animals when the limited pastureland of the village had been exhausted (Zaphiris 1968:26 – 28). Also, more of the remaining animals were now being used as U.S. Postal Service "mail vehicles" to pack food and other items to the village store since this provided a steadier year-round income. Thus, few animals then remained to serve the tourist trade.[5]

During my years of visits to Supai (1967 – 1980) those few visitors who came to see "real Indians" as well as the waterfalls were often disillusioned when they found no war bonnets, tipis, or "eager–to-please-the-visitor" dancing natives. They and many of the other tourists also complained about the many overgrazed and often unkempt yards and pastures they passed on the trail. For them, the myth of the native ecologist had been shattered.

The Havasupai, too, had mixed feelings about the tourists in spite of the fact that as early as the mid-60s, tourist dollars began supplying about one half of all the annual income flowing into the tribal economy (Martin 1968:452) and about one third of all direct and indirect personal cash income (Martin 1973a:154 – 155). Supai residents also often had to cope with visitors who stole fruit from trees, infected the creek with hepatitis, endured empty financial promises from photographers and filmmakers and competed with local people for the limited supply of fresh meat that was available on mail delivery days at the village store. However, the main problem with tourism was that the average resident of Supai derived very little direct economic benefit from it during those years (Martin 1973a).

2

Access to the major portion of the tourist dollar was only open to the fortunate few Havasupai males who controlled most of the reservation's small amount of good pasture land, for without good grazing land it was impossible to maintain the necessary saddle and pack animals that the tourist industry demanded.

Also, in spite of repeated attempts through the years by government farmers followed during this time period by older Mormon missionary farm couples sent periodically to Supai to encourage the local people to do more gardening and despite the fact that the average family spent more than 70% of its very meager annual cash income on food, by 1964 when a survey was undertaken (Martin 1973a) only 5 acres of Supai land was in gardens with an additional 3.2 acres in alfalfa. To the outside visitor this merely reinforced the stereotype of the lazy Indian since with the irrigation network present at that time 170 acres of good fertile land could have easily been planted. The lush growth on the few cultivated plots made possible by the long growing season, rich soil, and abundant water increased the typical tourist's impression that the average Havasupai would rather live on welfare handouts than work. (More will be said about this misleading assumption in chapter 8.) Thus, of the total personal income of $63,000[6] earned by Supai residents in the 1963 – 64 fiscal year only $22,450 came directly or indirectly from tourism while almost all of the remaining two thirds came from federal sources (Martin 1973a:154 – 155). [7] Therefore, with the average per capita income of only $350 in cash and $4.78 in kind, it is easy to see why many outside individuals and agencies during the late 60s and early 70s rushed in with various plans and schemes to help these "poverty-stricken" natives out of their misery. However, although everyone, native and non-native alike, agreed there was a serious economic problem at Supai, reaching a consensus about the source of the problem and the solution needed was another matter.

Obviously, by this time, the many years of "saving" attempts by the Federal government to solve any of these problems through assimilation efforts had failed for reasons that will be fully explored in the next few chapters. This will be followed by a discussion of "saving" attempts by those individuals and institutions who believed that the average native was a member of a degenerate race with many moral weaknesses caused either by sinful living or as a direct result of various government "handout" programs. A much different conception of the action "needed" to solve the economic and social problems that plagued the Havasupai Indians was put forward by those individuals and groups who blamed government inaction and the Park Service – backpacker lobby for the poverty to be found at Supai. People like Martin Goodfriend, a California "do-gooder" began publicly attacking the "paradise" image that many summer visitors had about life in the canyon by pointing out the poverty, sickness, and unemployment to be found at Supai which were often intensified during the winter months when the long, at that time partly unpaved, road to the hilltop would be made impassable by snow or rain for weeks at a time and when tourist income was nonexistent (Dedera 1967, 1971). Goodfriend and others[8] tried to convince the Indian people that with improved access to the outside world, a massive tourist complex could be created at Supai that would easily make the tribe the wealthiest in the nation on a per capita basis. Put forward as the easiest way to accomplish this feat would be the construction of an aerial tramway from the canyon rim to the valley floor. The nearby South Rim area of the Grand Canyon National Park was already being over utilized by tourists even during many of the winter months and it was certain that large numbers of these tourists could be lured to the milder winters and spectacular waterfalls of Havasu canyon. All of these visitors could be brought into the canyon below the central part of the village of Supai so that the Havasupai could actually enjoy more privacy than was now possible with the main trail winding past many of their houses. Increased numbers of visitors would mean increased employment and as additional tribal members returned to the reservation to share this new wealth, perhaps additional grade levels could be taught at the local school (or at a new school that could be then be built upon the canyon rim above Supai) to reduce the number of long periods of lonely separation that children and parents had to endure when older students were shipped to boarding schools each winter. And, since at this time food prices at Supai were 140% of the level of retail prices in the nearest outside towns and cities, such a tramway would greatly reduce the main factor creating such a price differential. Also, rapid access to such things as outside medical care would be possible as well as allowing the creation of nearby home site areas on the canyon rim to attract and meet the needs of such individuals as schoolteachers, medical staff, and tribal members who do not have access to such sites in the canyon below.

However, although Havasupai tribal officials initially voted in favor of pursuing this proposal it was not long before they abandoned such support when a totally unexpected opportunity arose for them to fulfill a long-held dream that had seemed impossible, the great expansion of the size of their reservation even though this expansion would require them to forever severely restrict any attempt to greatly expand tourist visitations and accommodations over those few that were already present at Supai.

Has the now successful achievement of this long-held dream also forever blocked any effort to bring economic prosperity and solutions to the many other problems plaguing the downtrodden residents of the reservation? The Tribal Council and the author of this book think not as will be examined in this book's final chapter.

Notes Chapter 1

1. Even the completion of the paving of this road which was greatly delayed did not help much in ending Supai's isolation from the rest of the world since the tribe went on record in opposition to any extension of this road to the village. And, the new east–west Interstate highway across northern Arizona was shifted much farther to the south of the reservation than US 66 thus greatly increasing the distance a tourist was forced to travel off the main highway to reach the hilltop above Supai.
2. Sometimes mutual Indian-White sexual exploitation occurred during these "brotherhood" attempts. A few Indian girls bragged about "making it" with white tourists while one young female tourist seduced several young Havasupai males during our "outdoor classroom" 1973 visit to the reservation (See Appendix B).
3. This number fluctuates greatly with the seasons, being highest during the summer months.
4. In 1977, the only man who got his promised horse on the opening day of the Peach Festival brought a supply of whiskey to his native packer and judging by his actions may have been a liquor smuggler rather than a tourist. All of the other arriving tourists were left stranded at the trailhead that morning.

5. in 1973, the tribal tourist agent told me that in one day he was "lucky to get 12 horses on the trail" whereas in former years he could usually get 60 per day. He added that the number of people willing to pack for tourists had declined from 20 to 6 or 7 and that some of these remaining packers have only three horses. Zaphiris (1968:31) earlier reported that 15 Havasupai males actually disliked packing as a vocational choice.

6. The value of garden produce grown during this year was only estimated to be an additional $955. 00.

7. By 1976 this dependence on federal sources over tourism had increased slightly passed the two-thirds ratio of 1963 – 64 (B. I. A. 1978:46)

8. I, too, was involved in this effort (see chapters 7, 9 and Appendix C) although I now no longer support the idea of creating a tramway to bring large quantities of tourists into the canyon every day to visit the waterfalls. In retrospect, after reading of the account of the extensive environmental damage that occurred due to tremendous overcrowding in the National Park campground during the 1970 Easter Week and seeing the same thing happening today in many of our national parks, I now agree that the Havasupai Tribal Council has recently made the much better decision that the way to economic prosperity is to capitalize on the increasing number of individuals willing to pay a high price to experience a unique wilderness adventure. Thus, I regret having once supported the bringing of massive numbers of tourists by way of tramway into Havasu Canyon. I still have fond memories of my days as a teenager exploring the unspoiled wonders of Glen Canyon that, thanks to the remarkable lasting powers of Kodachrome film, through the years I have been able to share with others in well-received presentations four summers at Lake Powell and more recently in Salt Lake City. I also treasure the memory of two teen age summers working at the lodge in Zion National Park where after work my friends and I could always find our own private "Shangri-Las" along the banks of the Virgin River and in the nearby Emerald Pools side canyon. Now, on most days even during the fall and winter months, it is impossible to enjoy a true wilderness experience anywhere in this tremendously overcrowded park. Thus, my only hope is that the Council might seriously consider the proposal I make in chapter 9 of this book as a way to find a solution to the many serious remaining problems in the village that Martin Goodfriend and many others including myself have observed (now made worse by the serious effect the Coronavirus Pandemic is having on their new economic model) while at the same time preserving a wilderness experience for visitors to their spectacular waterfalls.

9. This chapter is a revised and expanded version of a paper published in 1981 in *Anthro Tech* (Stucki 1981). Unfortunately, the editor of this journal did not let me proofread the article before publication nor let me submit in the next edition of this publication needed corrections for several serious errors she made when preparing my manuscript for publication.

Chapter 2

Despite their "relatively complete isolation" from the outside world in their canyon fortress, the Havasupai people have always had many struggles against both nature and other humans throughout their known history. Thus, on many occasions their homes and fields have been ravaged by floodwaters and shaken by earthquakes while enemy bands[1] periodically raided them until late into the 19th century.

No one knows for sure when the first ancestor of the modern day Havasupai first set foot in Cataract (Havasu) Canyon but in their quest to prove to the Indian Claims Commission that "their" people have lived there "since time immemorial," spokesmen for the tribe using evidence supplied by certain archaeologists argue that there is a "cultural continuum" that exists from the arrival of the first Yuman-speaking Cohonina[2] people in the plateau region south of the Grand Canyon about 600–700 A.D. through the Havasupai historic occupation of the same area (Indian Claims Commission 1974:333, 344 – 345; Hirst 1976:40 – 42; Schwartz 1956:78; 1983:14; Whiting 1958:60)[3]. However, as Manners, et al. (1974:35 – 36) point out, it is impossible to prove either from the historical or archaeological record that the present-day Havasupai Indians are indeed the direct descendants of the first Yuman speaking group to live in Havasu Canyon and the surrounding plateau area. And in spite of tribal legends cited by some modern scholars to prove this continuity (e.g., see Hirst 1976:40, 43; Indian Claims Commission 1974:334), in 1881 Lieut. Colonel Price in his official report stated that the Havasupai then believed "that they had first occupied the country 80 to 100 years (previously), when it was abandoned by the Moquis (Hopi)" (Casanova 1968:272).

Euler (1979:12, 14) too, in a 1979 article based upon his own and his associates (See Euler et al. 1979:1091) extensive archaeological, ethnohistorical, and ethnographic research among the Havasupai states emphatically that the Havasupai are not direct descendants of the earlier Cohonina people but instead are descendants of groups of Pai people coming from the west that arrived in the Grand Canyon area "shortly after 1300 A.D." and that prior to their arrival "it is clear that the entire Grand

Canyon area (had been) uninhabited for at least one hundred fifty years" due to "severe droughts (occurring) year after year." He then goes on to state that:

> ... while (the Cohonina) life way was not too different from that of the later Havasupai, archaeologists have no difficulty in distinguishing the ruins they left behind. The Cohonina were in friendly contact with the Anasazi, or Pueblo Indians, farther to the east and they copied much of the Pueblo culture. They constructed masonry houses, made pottery with designs in imitation of those of the Anasazi, and farmed the bottomlands of Havasu Creek as well as hunted game and gathered edible wild plants.

Euler (1979:12, 14) then adds that climatic change "around the middle of the twelfth century" bringing "year after year" of drought and fewer winter snows that were needed for seed germination, drove these people out of the Grand Canyon region to some unknown destination and that, as mentioned earlier, it was "at least one hundred fifty years" before the Grand Canyon region (including Cataract Canyon) was again inhabited, this time by the direct ancestors of the present day Hualapai (Walapai) and Havasupai.

However, it was Schwartz (1983:13 – 24) who four years later was still a believer that "the Havasupai are probably the direct descendants of ... the Cohonina" who was chosen by the Alonzo Ortiz (volume editor) of the Handbook of North American Indians, Vol. 10 to write the "official" Smithsonian ethnography of the Havasupai. Thus, although he acknowledges that Euler had "another view on Havasupai prehistory" it was his viewpoint that was chosen by the Smithsonian editor.

In Schwartz's version of Havasupai prehistory as presented in a 1956 article (pp. 79-82) the first permanent occupation of Havasu Canyon occurred sometime in the period 900 AD to 1100 AD as a result of the fact that population growth had reached the point where all available farming areas on the plateau were being used thus forcing some families to begin farming in the virgin fields surrounding Cataract (Havasu) Creek using irrigation techniques they may have learned on trading visits to the inhabitants of the Verde Valley. However, McGregor (1951:142) suggested an even more important causal factor than population pressure forced the Cohonina people to descend from the plateau to Cataract Creek when he states that tree-ring records possibly indicate that in hunting, the Cohonina people burned the surface cover of the plateau to drive game thus causing extensive soil erosion which in turn would lower the water table making water sources hard to find.

Still, Schwartz (1956:80) felt that this occupation of Cataract Canyon may have been even in this early period only seasonal because of the difficulties of winter life in the depths of the canyon due to a lack of sufficient sunshine, fuel, and wild plants and game. Also, the high humidity in the canyon caused by the stream and high water table would have further added to the Indian's winter miseries.[4]

And despite the "cultural continuum" that Schwartz saw in the transition from the Cohonina culture to the historic Havasupai one, he also (1956:80 – 81) found evidence that suggested that beginning about 1100 A.D., different groups of "foreign peoples" begin to move into Havasu Canyon from both the south and the east as the population of the plateau land above dropped sharply due to increasing drought conditions and the pressure of raiders who may have commenced this new lifestyle as drought came to their own homelands.

It was shortly after this new influx of refugees, Schwartz (1956:81) believed, canyon population density reached its greatest level, three times greater than the estimated density in historic times. Thus, it is even more certain according to him, that these people even though they had probably sought refuge in the canyon from both human enemies and natural calamities would have been forced during winter months to migrate to the plateau lands above the canyon in search of fuel and wild food

By 1200 A.D. according to Schwartz (1956:81), the Cohonina and their "foreign" friends had abandoned the plateau completely, retreating to the safety of cliff dwellings in the canyon until 1300 A.D. when "there was a sharp decrease in raiding, evidenced by the movement of habitation off the cliffs, back to the talus and probably the valley floor." He (Schwartz 1956:82) then went on to say that three hundred years of peace followed this time as all the "foreign" groups except a few "Cerbat" families left the safety of the canyon, leaving behind the descendants of the Cohonina people who now began the summer and winter moves of the historic Havasupai pattern between canyon and plateau while maintaining trading and visiting contacts with the Hopi people to the east.

However, despite this lack of scholarly consensus about what really happened in Cataract Canyon in prehistoric times and who really can claim that they "got there first", all authors agree that by the time of the first known visit by a Spanish explorer to the canyon in 1776, ancestral Havasupai were already well-established in their canyon home and surrounding areas and were obtaining a large amount of their yearly food supply in the form of maize, beads, and edible "greens" from irrigated farmlands (e.g., see the evidence in Coues 1900: 335 – 357; Galvin 1965:65 – 68)

Early visitors, both white and Indian, had little to fear from the Havasupai if they came in peace even though Garces, the Spanish priest, leading the first white expedition to Cataract Canyon, expressed his initial fears that the Indians there might be the dreaded Apache[5] since they "came so decked with pieces of red cloth." However, these initial fears quickly vanished when he "saw how joyous they were at (his) coming" and he was pleased that "they were excepting willingly the peace proposed by him with the Spaniards and the Jamajabs (Mohave)" (Gavin1965:66). And well into the 19th-century similar friendly receptions were given to such early white explorers as Jacob Hamblin, John D. Lee, and Joseph C. Ives (Manners 1974a:110; Euler 1974:292,295; Ives 1861:108) probably because the Havasupai in their Canyon "fortress" escaped much direct involvement in the hostilities that began in the mid-19th century between other Pai tribes and the invading Anglo-Americans (Euler 1974:293). In fact that in 1863, the Havasupai actually perceived certain Indian neighbors to be a much greater threat to their security than the white man is easily verified from the diary of Jacob Hamblin (Manners et al. 1974:110-111) where he records that although the Havasupai "appeared pleased to see him," not long previously these people had been attacked in their stronghold by a band of Indians from the southeast.[6]

Even white "exploiters" seeking souls for Christ, a place to bring tourists, or mineral wealth were usually offered gifts of food, water, shelter, and guide service (e.g., see James 1911:186-7,277-9). And one poor fellow whom the Havasupai found dying of thirst was even allowed to borrow a horse and was given a blanket and provisions in return for a promise of a gift of a "good army overcoat" when the man returned to the nearby white settlement of Williams (James 1911:187).

However, as Jacob Hamblin learned during his first visit to the Havasupai in 1863, they were always very suspicious when strangers approached until they were identified (Euler 1961:16) and Hamblin was asked that he "not lead anyone into their hiding place,… particularly a stranger, without their consent" (Manners 1974a:86). Also, in 1875, the Weekly Arizona Miner reported that after the visit of several miners to the reservation "the Chief expressed great fear that the whites would come there to mine and demoralize his people, who have never been brought in contact with any wicked influences and his greatest desire is to keep them free from temptation" (Euler 1961:22). And in the aftermath of the Pai wars even though their participation had been indirect and they had not been disturbed by white settlers as late as 1878, the Havasupai feared forced removal from their homeland (Dobyns and Euler 1960:82-83).

Thus the news that the President of the United States by executive order on June 8, 1880 was putting them under federal protection and control must have eased some of their fears although it is certain that they were displeased when two years later, in 1882, they learned that their reservation was being reduced to a mere 518.6 acres although they were still permitted to use much of the surrounding land for grazing and collecting purposes (Dobyns and Euler 1960:85; Horwath and Horwath 1963:2). However, until 1892 when the United States first sent a government farmer to Supai (Gaddis 1892:650) little else was done by the federal government to alter the basic lifestyle of the Havasupai people and as late as 1884 (and probably much later) wild stories were still being widely circulated about the physical dangers of a journey into Cataract Canyon and of the hostile natives that lived there (James 1911:176-179,275).

Still, those few visitors who did manage to brave the hazards of the journey to Supai during this early federal period continued to echo the praise given the "industrious" Havasupai by the first white explorer, Garces, when in 1776 he records that he is "pleased… much to see that at daybreak the husband would go out with his wife and older children to work their fields, taking along the tools they needed such as digging-sticks, hatchets, and grub hoes…" (Galvan 1965:66). Garces also was impressed by their engineering skills in taming Havasu Creek (Galvan 1965:66), a praise repeated by Cushing (1965:63-64) who in describing his early 1880's visit to Cataract Canyon writes:

> The engineering skill and enterprise of this little nation are marvelous. Although their appliances are rude, they are able to construct large dams, and dig or build deep irrigating canals, or durable aqueducts, which often pass through hills, or follow considerable heights along shelves of rock or talus at the bases of the rugged and crooked walls of the canyon. The acequias, which have their fountain-heads in these canals and viaducts, are wonders of intricacy and regularity; yet on uneven ground are laid out in nice recognition of and conformity to unevenness and change of level in the surface they are designed to water. Most wonderful of all, however, are their aerial trails….

And James (1911:259) in a book describing his visits to Supai in the late 19th century states:

> Ah! what clever engineers these Indians of a past generation were! To have seen the difficulties would have been enough to discourage ten generations of school-trained engineers, but to the practical necessities of the Havasupai the natural obstacles of making this a place of ingress and egress were soon overcome.

Further adding to this image of a group of people "who-with-just-a-little-help-could-become-fully-civilized" were such statements as those of Garces who admired the fact that the Havasupai were "decently clothed" and was amazed to see women "who were whiter than one generally sees in other nations" including one whom he states "might be taken for a Spaniard" (Galvin 1965:66). Other writers add to this ethnocentric image by such statements as:

> In perfection of muscular physique, the Havasupai men approach the Caucasian race more nearly than the majority of North American Indians….
> The Havasupai are very merry and somewhat vivacious, most affectionate to children and pets, and very hospitable to strangers… they are of a very peaceable disposition, never quarreling among themselves save with their tongues, and then only to resent a supposed wrong….
> They are patient and industrious in the extreme… they are humorous and

quite witty…. (and) are honest in the use of property to an incredible extent (Cushing 1965:46,48-49,70).

And though they were seen to have a few vices such as an initial shyness towards strangers, occasional cruelness toward animals, excessive talking when angry, and a tendency to lie and ridicule others (e.g., see Cushing 1965:54) these were viewed as minor flaws which together with a certain amount of uncleanliness could be easily corrected as Cushing (1965:54) implies when he states that in contrast to the women and older men who were "remarkably careless of personal cleanliness and appearance… the young man… are noticeably neat in the care of their persons, frequently bathing in the river, and careful of their toilet and dress" (Cushing 1965:54).

Thus, it is little wonder that the "almost civilized" Havasupai Indians more than many of their neighbors began in the late 1800's to attract the first in a long series of white "saviors" to their tiny reservation.

Notes Chapter 2

1. Spier (1928:248) states that the main enemies were the Yavapais and the associated western groups of White Mountain and Tonto Apaches although there were also infrequent hostile contacts with some Paiute and Navajo bands. To this list of hated, warring neighbors James (1903:245) adds the Mohaves although apparently according to Spier's two informants on intertribal relationships, during the years 1840 to 1865, at least some peaceful trade was occurring between the Havasupai and the Mohave, the Navajo, and the Paiutes.
2. Hirst (1976:40) claims that the word Cohonina "stems from the response early researchers received from the Hopi upon uncovering abandoned Cohonina sites" who when asked by the researchers "who made these?" replied the "Co'onin" which "is the Hopi name for the Havasupai."
3. Earlier groups of hunters and gatherers whose cultural remains are referred to by archaeologists as the "Desert Culture" had occupied this area as early as about 2000 B.C. (Hirst 1976:41).
4. However, Whiting (1958:56) states that "the conventional picture of the canyon-dwelling Havasupai farmers being driven back to a hunting-gathering existence during the winter months is a myth that I hope my forthcoming analysis of their ecology will dispel." Instead he felt that the "historic Havasupai practiced a hunting and gathering economy on the

plateau… supplemented by the desultory practice of agriculture in Cataract Canyon and elsewhere."

5. See Coues (1900:457-462) to determine which Indians were designated "Apache" by Garces.

6. They showed Hamblin and his party a narrow pass where they had met these Indians and killed seven of them. Dobyns and Euler (1971:6) state that these Indians were Yavapai although this identification is not certain.

Chapter 3

As Emerick (1954b: 34) correctly points out, the "isolation" of the Havasupai Indians from the surrounding world in aboriginal times has been greatly exaggerated in many popular articles. Thus, by 1776 when Garces first arrived in Supai, the Havasupai had already acquired horses, cattle, and European trade cloth and before the 1880s they had begun growing such Old World plants as peaches, apricots, figs, and alfalfa in addition to such crops as corn, beans, and squash which had much earlier diffused into the area from Mexico (Schwartz 1956:82; Euler 1961:16).

There are at least a dozen trails into the canyon some of which are much shorter than the main trail presently used but, unfortunately, the shortest of these begin from points on the plateau above the canyon which are extremely difficult to reach by motor vehicle (Emerick 1954b:34). And in spite of the many horror stories from early white explorers about the great difficulties and dangers that must be faced when entering or leaving the canyon, as Emerick (1954b:34) states, the experience for the traveler has always probably been "far more fatiguing than frightening." Certainly this was especially true for the Indians themselves who frequently left their canyon home to hunt and gather on the plateau above and to visit and trade with their neighbors, both Indian and white (e.g., see Anonymous 1898:3; Shufeldt 1892:388; Casanova 1968:272–273; Spier 1928:244–248). Thus, change producing cultural and social contact was already occurring long before the start of the first official United States government attempts in the 1890s to "civilize" and assimilate these Indians into the larger American society.

However, until the 1890s the Havasupai were still largely "masters of their own destiny" even though they were rapidly accepting most of the material goods offered to them by the outside world. Thus, when General Crook visited them in 1884, his aide, John Bourke reported that the Indians made a good living by trading deer, mountain sheep, and mountain lion skins to the "Moquis" (Hopi), "Zunis" and "Navajoes" (Casanova 1968:272–273). Other trading partners included the Paiute, the Walapai, the Mohave, the Ute and the "Apaches"[1] with the Havasupai often serving as "middlemen" in the trade of a multitude of desired items from east to west and west to east (Spier

1928:244–245; Shufeldt 1892:388). For example, from the Mohave either directly or indirectly through the Walapai, the Havasupai obtained "shells" and "ears of dwarf corn" in return for such items as "mantas," "leggings," and "pieces of cowhide" while from the Hopi they obtained "loom products," "blankets," "sashes," "silver work," "pottery," "stone and shell beads," "Buffalo skins," "shirts," and "ponies" in return for such items as "roasted mescal," " pinon nuts," "red pigment," "baskets," "horn ladles," "tanned deer, antelope, and mountain sheep skins" and "shirts and leggings" made from these tanned skins some of which had been obtained in their raw form from the nearby Walapai (Spier 1928:244–245; Casanova 1968:273). And from the Navajo, the Havasupai obtained horses, blankets, guns, and ammunition giving in return buckskins as well as such food items as dried corn, beans, and squash (Spier1928:244–245; Casanova 1968:273). Nor were the Havasupai reluctant to begin trading tanned skins to nearby whites, at first to obtain such items as tobacco and matches but later demanding such things as iron tools, clothes and money (Anonymous 1898:3; Casanova 1968:273; Spier 1928:245).

At first much of this trade was probably, as Spier (1928:246) suggests, "incidental to other pursuits" such as ensuring a friendly reception when visiting neighboring groups, and probably was "little more than an exchange of presents and the profits of gambling." However, the Havasupai traders were not above driving hard bargains with the Navajo who often desperately needed food (Spier 1928:246) and Bourke (Casanova 1968:272) records in his diary that the Havasupai were good at making a profit on their animal skins which "always commanded the highest prices" and which were eventually traded by other groups to Indians living as far away as the Rio Grande.[2] Even the early miners arriving in the early decades after the Civil War to exploit the mineral resources of the Havasupai Indians were themselves, in turn, exploited by the Indians who quickly learned how useful such items (often left behind by departing miners) as picks, sledges, shovels, and blasting powder could be used in building and repairing trails and irrigation canals (e.g., see Casanova 1968:273). In fact, so apparently self-sufficient and resourceful were the Havasupai that in 1886 Crook sent a strongly worded letter of protest to the Indian Bureau when he learned that the government was planning to begin issuing "rations" to the Supais (Casanova 1968:258) since he felt that once given supplies, the Indians "will probably expect them again and the result will be vagabondage," a prophecy which many modern outside visitors to the reservation feel has fully come to pass.

And it is not surprising that just as in war activities, those Havasupai males who demonstrated prowess in trading relationships became recognized as "chiefs" by both their fellow tribesmen and outsiders (Spier 1928:246, 249). However, by 1875 the arrival of miners in the canyon was causing some concern to one of the most powerful of these "chiefs" who was reported by some early miners to have "expressed great fear that the whites would come there to mine and demoralize his people, who have never been brought in contact with any wicked influences and his greatest desire is to keep them free from temptation" (Euler 1961:22). And by 1880 the Commissioner of Indian Affairs, the Governor of the territory, and the army general in charge of the area all apparently felt that the Havasupai needed "protection" from the incoming miners by having a reservation established for them (Casanova 1968:256; Euler 1961:22; Hirst 1976:55 – 56). Thus the military requested that all people seeking to enter Cataract Canyon proper have its permission (Euler 1961:22) and June 8, 1880 by executive order of the President of the United States, the Havasupai Indian Reservation was created beginning at a point "2 miles below the lowest falls" north of the village to a point 12 miles south with a width of two and a half miles back on each side of the line between these two points (Casanova 1968:256). However, during the June 1881 visit to the reservation by the official military surveying party, stone boundary monuments were placed which reduced the recommended acreage to be included in the reservation to a mere 518.6 acres, a recommendation that was approved by President Chester A. Arthur on March 31, 1882 (Euler 1961:24; Casanova 1968:256).

In retrospect, a cynical observer might suspect that this reduction in size of the reservation by the surveying party might indicate that instead of protecting the resources of the Indians, the government at this point in time was more interested in protecting the rights of certain prospectors who had petitioned federal officials to have their mining claims in the canyon excluded from such a proposed reserve (Euler

1961:23). However, from the official report of the army's surveying party it is easy to discover the real reason why this reduction occurred when we read (Hirst 1976:57-58):

> From the great difficulties presented by the conformation of the ground, and the scanty water supply obtainable at this season, I necessarily gave up all idea of marking upon the ground the boundaries as set forth in the Executive Order referred to; although my sight of the country was a hurried one, I feel justified in saying that it is probably not possible to connect boundaries on the Mesa with an initial point in the bottom of the canyon.
>
> I therefore consulted with Navajo, Chief of the Yavai Suppai, as to the lands occupied or desired by him, and, in his presence, placed at the northern end of his lands two monuments of stone, one on each side of the stream, marking a line which includes all that he desired in that direction.... Accompanied by his son, I placed, beyond the Southern extremity of the lands used by Indians, in a place already determined upon in consultation with Navajo, a simple monument of stone.... Affected, probably, by a fear of encroachments and finally of removal, Navajo appeared to prefer having the boundaries close upon the lands he actually occupied.

Navajo(e), the Havasupai "Captain" was reported by William Price, the leader of the Army surveying unit sent, to have been:

> ... at first nervous and very suspicious – fearful that an effort would be made to remove them to some other reservation.... There was some hesitation among them in accepting anything, food, and so forth, they being very suspicious that it might be the opening wedge towards their removal from their country. They had evidently been informed that the discovery of mines in their country would necessitate the abandonment of their lands as the whites would take them for their own use. (Hirst 1976:59).

And Navajo later told the visiting ethnologist, Frank Cushing, when asked why he hadn't sought a larger reservation, that "to ask for more would bring trouble" (Casanova 1968:268) and to his own people when asked the same question, he said, that opposition to the wishes of the federal government "would be foolish for the reason that it could cause my children to be exterminated" (Hirst 1976:59).

However, to the credit of the chief surveyor, Carl Palfrey, he did show some concern for the Indians' future well-being when he states in his report that "I placed the southern boundary to include more land than he (Navajo) desired" because it appeared to Palfrey that some white person might attempts to dig wells in the canyon bottom above the point where the springs came out of the ground and thus divert water to "the detriment of the supply used by the Indians." (Hirst 1976:58). And Lt. Col. Price, the leader of the surveying party, assured the Indians that the federal government's intention was to locate and set aside for them all the arable land they had ever cultivated, and to secure for them all the water they had ever used for irrigation, from any encroachment of the whites" (Euler 1961:23). Also, even though the land beyond the reservation now became public property, it was reported by a Havasupai informant that when General Crook visited Cataract Canyon in 1884, he told the Indians that they would be "allowed in the future to use land outside the canyon for the only purpose to which that land can be put, i.e., hunting, the grazing of livestock, and food-gathering" (Hirst 1976:60). That the Indians believed these promises becomes obvious when we read of the extreme trust and friendship General Crook and Navajo had for each other as recorded in the diary kept of Crook's 1884 visit to Cataract Canyon (e.g., see Casanova 1968:268-269,273-274).

Obviously, by this point in time the U.S. army and the Havasupai had forged a mutually beneficial partnership with General Crook, and earlier military leaders, supplying modern repeating rifles and ammunition to the Indians (Casanova 1968:258,270) while in return receiving food, water, and such other aid from the Indians as the help they gave to General Crook in assisting his capture of a "renegade Apache-Mohave" Indian who had sought refuge in Cataract Canyon (Casanova 1968:273-274).

That the full realization by the Havasupai that they would begin losing control over most of their hunting and gathering lands as well as their other agricultural lands such as those at Indian Gardens (in what later became Grand Canyon National Park) must have been slow in coming even though they probably quickly began realizing that the establishment of the reservation had done little to protect them from being continually bothered by miners. (Euler 1961: 25). However, an even greater threat to their financial and social independence came in the 1880s as white cattlemen and tourist promoters begin to invade their former plateau lands and as stringent game laws began to be enforced as part of the government's effort to give greater federal protection to the flora and fauna of this highly scenic area (Euler 1961:26-29).

Both Euler (1961:27-28) and Hirst (1976:60-63) give vivid descriptions of the hostilities that began to erupt at this time between the local ranchers and the Havasupai over grazing rights and access to the scarce but extremely precious small sources of water on the plateau. And nearby papers were full of such comments as the following:

> Several Wallapai Indians[3] have visited the happy hunting grounds in the past few weeks, and have become better Indians than they ever were on earth....
> The Wallapai Indians complain of the quality of the flour served out to them by the government, and say it is full of weevils and has an intensely bitter taste. A plentiful supply of arsenic mixed with it would disguise the bitter taste. We offer this suggestion to the contractor and sincerely hope we will adopt it....
> "Music hath charms to soothe the savage beast..." And it is said that the most effective is the whistle of a well-directed bullet. (Hirst 1976:62)

Thus in spite of a valiant attempt by Lt. Col. G.N. Brayton in the letter he wrote to his superior in 1888 to obtain a much larger reservation for the Havasupai to protect their subsistence base (Hirst 1976:62), economic dependence on the government dole with all its accompanying social ills – which General Crook, as earlier stated, feared would be the fate of these Indians – came more quickly than many had suspected to the residents of Havasu Canyon as the 19th century drew to a close. For as one observer wrote in 1882, only two years after the establishment of the reservation:

> The game is all gone. In 1863 the valleys were filled with antelope and the hills with deer. Rabbits and hares were abundant. Now one may travel for weeks and not see any game save an occasional rabbit. The stock have eaten off the grass so that their harvest fields where [the Indians] used to gather grass seeds are destroyed. (Hirst 1976:63)

The next few decades were hard ones for the Havasupai as they witnessed not only the destruction of their winter subsistence base but also the invasion of new diseases like smallpox, measles, and influenza that Hirst (1976:65) feels were particularly responsible for the increasing death rate of women during childbirth so that by 1906 there were three men at Supai for every two women.

It is thus little wonder that the Havasupai participated in the Ghost Dance movement that came to the nearby Hualapai in the late 1800s (Dobyns & Euler 1967) nor is it surprising that within the next few years outside do-gooders begin arriving at

Supai to "protect," "Christianize," and "civilize" these latest victims of America's "manifest destiny."

Notes Chapter 3

1. As Coues (1900:457-462) points out the term "Apache" is an imprecise term applied in the 19th century to many different groups of Indians.
2. James (1903:245), too, was amazed at the valuable items other Indians were willing to trade to the Havasupai "for a simple buckskin." Thus it is not too surprising that the Havasupai by the time of Crook's 1884 visit had amassed an incredible variety of trade items from other Indians and nearby whites including such items as Navajo blankets, tin cups, "American" hoes, spades, hatchets, as well as kettles, brass and silver ornaments, Iron arrowheads, Winchester rifles, and elaborately decorated "American and Moqui clothing." (Casanova 1968:269-270)
3. It is doubtful that the writer of this comment would have had any kinder feelings toward the Havasupai, their nearby, extremely closely related "cousins."

Chapter 4

"Even before the beginning of this century, the tribe's habits and customs were slowly yielding to the pressure of civilization. The clothes they wore, the food they ate, the language they spoke, their very thoughts were undergoing change. Instead of sitting at their grandfather's knee learning the tribes history and the traditions that had molded the character of the people, their children were now bent over books in the classroom. At the Sunday services they were learning about a new and strange God.

But the loss that stirred the deepest resentment was that of their hunting grounds. In this their gods could do nothing...." (Iliff 1954:196)

Early sporadic attempts to "Christianize" and "civilize" the Havasupai starting with the efforts of Garces in 1776 and the visits of the Mormon explorers, Hamblyn and Lee, probably had little lasting effect upon these people. But by the late 1880s many Havasupai were beginning to sense that their traditional belief system had failed them so they increasingly begin to look elsewhere for "new answers" to the uncertainties that had already begun to engulf them. Thus, when three "Chemehuevi" (Southern Paiute) ghost dance missionaries visited the nearby Hualapai to meet with their chiefs and to invite them to return with them to see a ghost dance to be held at St. George, Utah, two Havasupai joined with eight Hualapai to accept this invitation (Kroeber 1935:234).

Obviously, at least some members of this visiting delegation were impressed since an eye witness to these events reported that when the Hualapai chief, Surrum[1] returned from this visit, within a few days he sent out a message for all the Hualapai to assemble at Grass Springs[2] "some seventy-five miles north-east of Kingman" where "they were going to institute a Ghost dance like the Chemehuevi" (Kroeber 1935:234-235; Dobyns and Euler 1967:18).

Many but not all of the nearby Hualapai attended this first dance as did also the two Havasupai who had accompanied the Hualapai and Paiute to the St. George performance of the dance (Kroeber 1935:235). These visiting Havasupai one of whom was probably the main chief, Navajo, (see Stephen 1936:996) then took the dance to Supai where according to the Indian agent S.M. McCowan in his 1892 Report to the

Commission of Indian Affairs (1892b:651) the "Messiah craze" reached its peak in the year 1890.[3]

As Dobyns and Euler (1967:vii) point out, the rapid acceptance of the Ghost Dance religion by many of the Pai people was most likely due to the fact that this millennial religion like the others of its type was able to offer demoralized and politically impotent people a substitute for political action. For by supernatural means, the dance held out hope to the Indians that "sometime within the next three or four years"[4] "a powerful deity" was to come to the earth "in the form of an Indian" and when he came (Anonymous 1892:66):

> … all Indians who have died in the ages that are gone will be restored to life and perpetual youth. Those who are now old, sick, or lame will also be restored. Simultaneously will reappear the game that has existed in past ages, while the white people and all other races except the American Indian will perish.…

The dance itself was a modified form of the Scalp Dance, a Pai and Paiute war dance, danced with a short shuffling sidestep, by men and women in alternate positions holding hands in the circle around a spirally painted pole from which an enemy scalp decorated with feathers was hung over a piece of buckskin upon which a face had been painted (Kroeber 1935:178,179,199). However, instead of taunting the "scalp" as they had while they danced around the pole in the Scalp Dance, in the Ghost Dance the dancers were told that anyone who could climb the pole to within reach of the eagle tail feathers (which in this dance had replaced the scalp) and hang on until he became unconscious, would see the "Other World" and his dead ancestors (Stephen 1969:996; Iliff 1954:179; Spier 1928:266).

Although nearby whites at first feared that the dance might bring about a new Indian uprising in the area, these concerns faded when it became clear to them that the Pai expected the end of the whites through supernatural means rather than military ones (Spicer 1962:273) and one Hualapai chief told a reporter for the Mohave Miner (Anonymous 1892:66), "We do not intend any violence toward the whites; we want to live peacefully with them until the Messiah comes, and then we cannot keep them from being destroyed if we wish." And, a white visitor to the Havasupai Reservation during the very peak of the movement in 1890,[5] George Wharton James, was even allowed to participate in the Ghost Dance himself[6] after agreeing to put it on a "white shirt" and promising not to "laugh" during the dance or "nip" the women with whom he would be dancing (James 1903:250-252).

Accompanying James on this 1890 visit to Supai were two other white men, the tourist promoter W.W. Bass and the Indian agent S.M. McCowan (James 1911:191,257), the latter of whom gave his impressions of the Ghost Dance in the following excerpt from his 1892 report to the Commissioner of Indian affairs (McCowan 1892b:651):

> I saw them two years ago when the Messiah craze was at its height, and they were dancing day and night, for the coming of their Savior. To make these dances more impressive to the uninitiated, certain members would pretend to receive messages from the Messiah, and, suddenly breaking away from the circling dancers, would rush into the center of the circle, throw themselves upon the ground, writhing, shrieking, moaning until utterly exhausted. Their superstition is wonderfully dense, their every act being guided by signs and symbols.

McCowan who was the superintendent of the Indian school at Fort Mojave had been sent by the government to report on the condition of the Havasupai and "to induce" the Havasupai "chiefs" and heads of families to send their children to the government school at Fort Mohave (James 1903:249-250; 1911:191). However, he quickly met a formidable opponent there, a "Chemehuevi" (probably Southern Paiute) "evangelist" who had been invited by the Havasupai chiefs to teach them the ghost dance songs at this particular celebration of their annual harvest ("Peach") dance.[7] Thus in addition to this visiting "preacher's" song and ritual instruction, James (1903:253-255) records that:

> His harangue on this occasion was an unusually fervent oration.... He explained that the reason that tribe had lost so many of its members last year by the dread "grippe" was because of their levity. They had laughed too much, gone hunting and visiting white men's camps when they ought to have been dancing. They were allowing the white man to laugh them out of the traditions of their forefathers. Then he is especially denounced all friendliness to the whites, and singled out Hotouta, Chickpanagie, Spotted Tail, and one or two of the others

who had been the leaders in thus countenancing the whites, and administered to them severe rebukes. After this, referring to the offer of the whites to give them farming implements, food, etc., if they would send their children to the Indian's school at Mohave, he urged his hearers to listen to no such proposals. He said in effect: "Don't send your children to the school of the white man. If you do they will grow up with the heart of the white man, and the place of the Havasupai will know them no more. Your tribe will be broken up, and then the white man will come and take possession of your canyon home where the stream ever flows and sings to the waving of willows by their side. He will rob you of your corn-fields and of your peach orchards. No longer will the place where the bodies of your ancestors were burned be sacred to you; your hunting-grounds are now all occupied by him, the deer and the antelope have nearly disappeared before his rifle, and he is hungry to possess the few things you still have left. This offer is the secret plot against you. He thinks if he cannot drive you out he will seduce you out, and this school is the offer he makes to you, so that he can get your children into his hands. There he will teach them to make fun of you; to despise your method of living; your houses, your food, your dress, your customs, your dances will all be ridiculed by him and so you will lose the favor of "Those Above," and you yourselves will soon die and your name and tribe be forgotten." In other words, he endeavored to make it perfectly clear to the assembled Havasupais that the school proposition was a white man's scheme – a dodge – to get their children away so that eventually they – the whites – might claim the Havasu Canyon for themselves.

Also present during this confrontation was W.W. Bass, the first of many new white "saviors" who would over the years come to the Havasupai to help them "solve" their temporal[8] as well as spiritual "problems." Lured by the spectacular scenery and the many romantic, mystical accounts written about the Havasupai, such people are often shocked by the realities of daily life at Supai.

However, in sharp contrast to other such individuals who would later attempt to "return" the Havasupai to their "noble savage" past, Mr. Bass was a firm believer that education and assimilation would bring about the economic and spiritual "redemption" of the Havasupai. Thus, after seeing that the Indians were being swayed more by the message of the "Chemehuevi" Indian toward rejecting the offer of the Indian agent[9] he:

> … begin to work with his accustomed energy and directness to interest the Indian department to establish a school and send a teacher and farmer to Havasu Canyon to teach the Havasupais good citizenship and good farming…. and… it was (he) who patiently and persistently worked for what was ultimately

25

attained, -- a teacher, a schoolhouse, and a farmer of their own. (James 1911:191)

For a while the Indians apparently had some doubt as to which path they should follow to obtain "salvation" but it was not long before two neighboring Hualapai ghost dance leaders failed in their spring 1891 attempt to restore life to a dead man (Dobyns and Euler 1967:30-31). And the power of this movement was further diminished when all of the men who "visited the dead who were soon to return" during a dance held that July at Supai, themselves died soon after (Illif 1954:180; Spier 1928:266). Thus as Dobyns and Euler (1967:viii) point out, the bearers of "civilization and Christianity" probably found their task easier among the by now demoralize ghost dancers and it was not long before one tribal member began "to dress up in his finest every Sunday and exhort his tribesmen to hear about Jesus" (Hirst 1976:64) while another told of how once when he had been very sick:

> One day Jesus come. Stand by bed. All white. Dress, everything all white. Shine like sun. He say pretty quick get well. He go way. I get well quick. (Iliff 1954:121)

With the collapse of the Ghost Dance, the government quickly began to instigate at Supai a massive program of directed sociocultural change based upon the "few simple, well-defined, and strongly cherished convictions" which had earlier been clearly set forth by the incoming Commissioner of Indian affairs in his 1889 annual report to Congress as being (Oct. 1, 1889:3-4):

> First, -- The anomalous position heretofore occupied by the Indians in this country can not much longer be maintained. The reservation system belongs to a "vanishing state of things" and must soon cease to exist.
> Second, -- The logic of events demands the absorption of the Indians into our national life, not as Indians, but as American citizens.
> Third, -- As soon as a wise conservatism will warrant it, the relations of the Indians to the government must rest solely upon the full recognition of their individuality. Each Indian must be treated as a man, be allowed a men's rights and privileges, and be held to the performance of a man's obligations. Each Indian is entitled to his proper share of the inherited wealth of the tribe, and to the protection of the courts in his "life, liberty, and pursuit of happiness." He is not entitled to be supported in idleness.

Fourth, -- The Indians must conform to "the white man's ways," peaceably if they will, forcibly if they must. They must adjust themselves to their environment, and conform their mode of living substantially to our civilization. This civilization may not be the best possible, but it is the best the Indians can get. They can not escape it, and must either conform to it or be crushed by it.

Fifth, -- The paramount duty of the hour is to prepare the rising generation of Indians for the new order of things thus forced upon them. A comprehensive system of education modeled after the American public school system, better adapted to the special exigencies of the Indian youth, embracing all persons of school age, compulsory in its demands and uniformly administered, should be developed as rapidly as possible.

Sixth, -- The tribal relations should be broken up, socialism destroyed, and the family and the autonomy of the individual substituted. The allotment of lands in severalty, the establishment of local courts and police, the development of a personal sense of independence, and the universal adoption of the English language are means to this end....

Thus on April 10, 1892[10] (Gaddis 1892:650) the Indians of Cataract Canyon suddenly began to feel the impact of this determined policy of forced assimilation with the arrival of their first "government farmer," one of many throughout the country whom an act of Congress had directed the Indian Affairs office to hire "to incite a desire for farming among the Indians and to teach and direct them in the work..." (Commissioner of Indian Affairs Annual Report 1889:11). That this first farmer at Supai and his wife found this to be a difficult task is clearly revealed in the following report he made to his superior, Superintendent McCowan on June 7, 1892 (Gaddis 1892:650-651):

Sir: having just returned from the Suppai villages, where I have been since April 10, assisting the Indians in preparing their land and planting their crops and repairing their ditches, I hereby make the following statement as report to date. Prior to leaving Williams my instructions were as follows: To purchase necessary tools and provisions and deal them out to the Indians as pay for work as far as possible, thereby encouraging as spirit of industry; repair their ditches, prune their trees, and in general develop a knowledge of agricultural pursuits among them.

I left Williams April 4, and arrived at the reservation April 10. My first work was to plant some corn and sow some alfalfa. We kept the plow going as much as possible and Indian men and women at work grubbing and preparing land until about 100 acres were planted in seeds (part white man's way and part Indian way) and some more prepared for a fall crop. I repaired all their ditches and built some new ones to supply all land under cultivation.

Condition of Indians, -- As to food, I consider these people well supplied and always have been. Mescal grows plentifully all over the country. They have abundance of peaches and many other substitutes within easy reach. As to clothing, I consider them very well supplied. They make buckskin clothing and sell to the Navajoes. They have blankets to sell and buckskins to sell. As to shelter, they have no houses. They live in little wickies or willow huts. It is never very cold and very little rain, so they do not suffer for shelter. Moral condition of these people seems to be good. There seems to be no depravity and very little polygamy.

Condition of land, -- The land is a rich sandy loam. I should judge at one time or times 200 acres have been under cultivation, but only about 15 acres were cultivated last year. The rest had been given up to weeds and willows.

Difficulties, -- I experienced many difficulties in getting them to work for supplies "as instructed." They had been so instructed by unscrupulous whites, that they had come in the position of the idea that when I should come all earthly wants would be fully gratified from an inexhaustible supply which the United States Government had on hand for all Indians, and they expected me to deal out to all their various wants for no recompense on their part. But I have labored to convince them that I wished to be just, to deal by them as fairly as they would by me, exchange work with them and pay them honestly for what they did. As to prices on their work, I will recount. For a day's lazy work they want me to give them from one to three sacks of flour. For bringing a sack of flour from the hill top they want me to give it to them and throw in a can of baking powder and a little sugar and coffee. But I have labored to impress on them as far as possible the equity of values, and think in a measure I have accomplished this.

There are 47 families, about 200, or possibly 250, souls in all. So far I have been unable to get a correct census of them. I am satisfied I have done them real good, although if the work should drop with this fiscal year no permanent good would result from present outlay. They have land enough and water enough so their acreage could be easily increased. All they need, in my judgment, is about two or three small plows and as many sets cheap harness. They are very well supplied with hoes and shovels. I think it would be wise for the Department to furnish them with seed wheat and rye. Also about 100 pounds alfalfa seed. There is plenty of water to run a mill which would grind their meal and flour. They raise good corn. I think this an excellent fruit country. Their trees are in very poor condition for fruit raising, as they are in a thicket growth. I think if some of the more intelligent ones were taken to California and shown the proper way of planting and caring for trees, it would help to advance their ideas very much. They have a desire to raise stock; sheep and goats would do well there. It might be well to give them a small start in these lines.

They detest the name of a school, but an institution under any other name would do well. The goal of their ambition is to write; they are great imitators and will sit for hours and work with a pencil on a written copy. My wife has shown them how to cut and fit dresses; they take wonderful interest in it. I would encourage the building of a schoolhouse on the reservation. I think it could be built out of stone at a very small cost to the Government. They are very much opposed to going away to school on account of having been so prejudiced by unscrupulous men for the purpose of accomplishing other ends.

I am, very respectfully, yours,

John F. Gaddis

Just who the "unscrupulous" whites were whom the farmer apparently believed "almost obliterated" the Indians' "industry" is unclear although in his 1893 report to McCowan he identifies them as being "mining prospectors and others"[11] (Gaddis 1893:402). Some of the same "unscrupulous" people we're also troubling McCowan himself who felt it necessary to strongly defend himself from the "many false reports" that had been sent to the Indian Office suggesting that he had been "stealing" the money the government had given him rather than using it to buy tools, food, and clothing for the "destitute" Havasupai. Thus, as he, sarcastically, states in his June 25, 1892 report (1892a:650) to his superiors after returning from an unauthorized visit to Supai:

> … reports of my stealings from the Suppais has now reached quite respectable proportions. In round numbers it is now $7,000, which is doing fairly well, I think, from a total appropriation of $700. The next report will probably be $70,000, and I will be able to retire.
>
> As I took this trip for the reasons herein stated, and without obtaining previous authority from the office, I enclose vouchers for your approval. I did not have on hand quite enough money to bear all expenses, but am perfectly willing to bear the extra amount myself.

And in a supplemental report dated July 20, 1892 (McCowan 1892b:651), he begins by stating:

> Sir: so little seems to be known of these Indians, and so many false reports have been sent to the Indian Office regarding them, that I desire to make as complete a report as possible, based upon actual and personal knowledge of them, their home, habits, resources, etc. Upon orders from your office I have personally in the past two years, visited them and their wonderful and almost inaccessible canyon home, and my report is based upon what my own eyes perceived….
>
> I have taken particular pains to make my report complete and accurate, so that the Department would have on file a permanent answer to mistaken petitioners, and I will vouch for every statement as being absolutely correct….

To apparently counter charges that the Havasupai were on the verge of starvation, in these two reports he then goes on to state:

> … I visited every camp in the village. Their food consisted of corn (last year's), peaches, mescal, kesi, pine nuts, venison, ripe apricots, and flour…. They have plenty to do them until harvest, and some to sell. Mescal is inexhaustible all around their homes, and is really a very appetizing and strength giving food. They have about twenty apricot trees, the fruit of which is just ripening. Deer and antelope are very abundant….(McCowan 1892a:649-650)

> They are well armed with Winchester rifles, and are great hunters. They are seldom without deer or antelope meat, and their rude shacks are filled with skins. Besides deer, antelope, rabbits, and other small game, nature produces every year, without cultivation, an abundance of juniper berries, piñon nuts, mescal, and tunis roots – all of which, and especially the piñon nuts and mescal, are exceedingly rich and nutritious….

> They have either a splendid variety of peach trees, or the soil and lovely climate impart to the fruit a most delicious flavor. During my visit to them in June I counted 1,295 trees, old and in full bearing. The trees are literally loaded to the earth with fruit. They will not have less than 4,000 bushels of peaches this year. This fruit they will halve and dry in the sun. It is then "cached" in the cañon walls many feet above, and used as wanted. The merchants at Flagstaff and Williams are always eager to buy this dried fruit, and it is a source of very considerable revenue. (McCowan 1892b:652)

He also strongly attacks the "false reports" sent to the Indian Affairs office that "these Indians were destitute of clothing and liable to freeze to death in winter…." stating that:

> I did not see a naked Indian in the camp, man, woman, or child. Every man was well dressed, and I counted fifty pairs of pants hanging in the different wickiups. There were also shirts, vests, coats, dresses, shoes, boots, muslin, calico in abundance, some flannel, and some linen. I counted 200 Navajo blankets of the best make…. I counted 150 deer skins, and they had just taken over a hundred to the Moqui villages to trade…. (McCowan 1892a:649-650)

However, in his May 31, 1893 report to the Indian Affairs office, the government farmer now seems to directly contradict McCowan's June 1892 assessment of the health and well-being of the Havasupai that summer when he states:

> … Industry seems at one time to have been quite a common virtue, that was almost obliterated by the whites (mining prospectors and others), who used every inducement to cultivate idleness, persuading them to believe the

Government should and would make all provisions, etc., without any effort on their part. They were at that time (i.e., before these "unscrupulous" whites came) a self sustaining people, raising grain, making buckskin clothing, etc., which they disposed of to other tribes for blankets, etc. In this isolated but grand canyon nature has well supplied their bodily requirements; mescale, pinon nuts, and ke-cy, grow in abundance.

Having been under the said influence (i.e., of the "unscrupulous" whites) so long, without any Government supervision, they were in almost destitute condition, when I assumed my duties as farmer among them last year, being almost without provisions, seeds, or clothing…. (Gaddis 1893:402)

A likely reason for this discrepancy, as was seen earlier in this chapter in the excerpt from his previous year's report (Gaddis 1892:650-651), was his frustration that many Havasupi did not share his passion for performing the work needed to achieve the economic benefits of a farming way of life, especially troubling to him given the abundance of water and rich soil in the valley which at that time was only being very marginally utilized. In this new report, Gaddis (1893:402) was particularly bothered by the opposition he had faced from "their old chief, Navajo, who uses every effort to prevent the younger ones from carrying up my instructions…." and who Gladdis considered to be "a great detriment to the tribe owing to his dislike for all Government improvements and instructions…." However, he then adds that "with the exception of those influenced by the advice of Chief Navajo… all are willing to have ditches repaired, and peach trees pruned….".

Next in this same report he lists his accomplishments during 1892 and the early part of 1893 stating:

Their farms are in fairly good condition, having increased their acreage over that of last year about 30 acres. The variety of fruit trees and vines which were supplied them by the government were planted, making excellent orchards, most of them growing rapidly…

I have, according to my instructions, built the necessary schoolhouse… with a seating capacity for 50 children. Have received part of the supplies – desks, pens, paper, pencils; have no books or blackboard. I find 40 children of school age; most of them are willing to go to school.

However, his attempt to introduce farm animals, in this case goats, had not gone as well. Thus, he goes on to report:

31

The goats furnished them by the government are doing well, but so far I have been unable to get them to accept them; some are willing to take them but the chief will not allow them to do so.

Generally, Gaddis considered his efforts to be successful giving him "encouragement to continue my duties among them with increasing zeal, hoping for greater improvements this year" (1893). And to better carry on his work, he concludes his May 31, 1893 report by stating:

> I herewith desire to ask special requests, namely: a few small plows; a few cheap harness; for a small sum of money to be appropriated for the necessary repairing of the trail leading to the village; a change of alfalfa seed for Johnson grass seed, or red tap, owing to the inability to make the horses eat it. Should the Government include the Cocamno forest in a National park, it would cut off the Indians' winter range for their horses. A small expenditure of money, $125, would open the Beaver canyon and afford them a fine range and would give them an outlet for about 8 miles, which would be of great value to them....

In retrospect, the modern writer Stephen Hirst (1976:65) feels that it was ludicrous for the U.S. government to try to teach the Havasupai how to farm. However, it is perhaps easier for us to understand why the Indians of Supai tolerated the presence of the government farmer if we read the "sermon" that the head chief Kohat (Navajo), had earlier delivered to the visiting ethnologist Frank Cushing (1965:71) in 1881 when he told him:

> … my people will listen to me when I tell them to smile on the Hai-ko (American), to ask him to eat, and to let his poorest or most tempting possession lie in the place it has been laid in; for has not the Hai-ko given to my children the hard metal and the rich garments you see all around you? ... am I not old enough to remember how my people dug the soil with wooden hoes, or cut the poles of their cabins with stone axes, and skinned the deer with a knife of flint? No; I take the father of the Land of Sunrise (Washington) by the hand, and my father of the Land of the Sunset (General Wilcox) do I grasp by the hand, that we may look upon another with smiling faces.

Thus in contrast to Hirst's implicit assumption that the Havasupai viewed the coming of the government farmer as a ridiculous or possibly threatening event, it is obvious that many of Supai's residents must have welcomed the arrival of the farmer in

1892, although probably more for the improved tools, seeds, and trees he brought than for his agricultural advice.

The Indians also probably valued the free services the farmer provided for them such as the repair of trails and ditches, the plowing of fields, the planting of seeds, and the construction of new irrigation canals. However, it is not certain that they fully understood why their fruit tree should be pruned. Nor were they convinced that they should become herders of goats.

Martin (1966:17), in particular, feels that "Havasupai agricultural practices were more primitive in aboriginal ... times" than such early reports as that of Cushing would lead us to believe. Thus, instead of the degeneration in farming practices which the government farmer, John F. Gaddis, believed had occurred among the Havasupai just prior to his arrival due to the influence of "unscrupulous whites," he (Martin 1966:17-20) presents a convincing argument that most estimates of the early farming capabilities of the Havasupai with their primitive tools were grossly overinflated. Thus, the government farmer's suggestion (1892:651) that the Havasupai in the days before they "lost" their "Industry" under the influence of the "unscrupulous whites" had cultivated "200 acres" in contrast to the approximately 15 acres being cultivated in 1892, is most certainly incorrect since it is doubtful (as Martin points out) that the small number of Indians in the canyon during the late prehistoric period and early historic one could have ever, with their primitive tools, planted 200 acres of gardens in a single year. Thus, it is much more likely that the 200 acres of previously farmed land that the government farmer observed represented the total acreage farmed on a rotating basis through time rather than on an annual basis and in fact it was the government "Industrial Teacher in Charge of Walapai and Havasupai Indians and Day Schools" who in 1900 first "ordered .. discontinued" the traditional Havasupai practice of letting land remain idle for "at least one to three" years after the death of "one of the owners or heirs to the land" (Ewing 1900:203).

This second phase of the government's plan to assimilate the Havasupai into the larger American society begin in March 1895 when the first schoolteacher, R. C. Bauer, and his wife arrived at Supai. And as clearly revealed in the following three annual reports by Bauer to his supervisor, Henry P. Ewing, the Havasupai were not the only one to be changed by this encounter:

REPORT OF SCHOOL AMONG SUPAIS

Supai Agency, Ariz.,
June 30, 1895.

Sir: I herewith submit my first annual report of Supai day school.

Location. – Supai day school is located about 100 miles north of Williams, Ariz., in the box canyon of Cataract River, a tributary of the Colorado River. It is about 15 miles from the school to the Grand Canyon of the Colorado, which is one of the greatest objects of natural scenery in the world.

Condition. – Then: Mrs. Bauer and I were ordered to report to you last March for work among the Yava Supais in this day school. We found that nothing, in an educational way had ever been done for these children. They were decidedly raw material. Their covering consisted of a mixture of grease, mescal juice, and other filth, fearfully and wonderfully combined. A chemist who could have made an analysis of the ingredients would have commanded the admiration of the scientific world. Now: -- The children are in school, well dressed, cleanly, mannerly, learning, and much interested in their studies.

Plan of work. – The work is, of course, primary in its character, and embraces reading, writing, orthography, geography, numbers, vocal music, language, gymnastics, and industrial training. Our aim in all work, whether in the schoolroom, or the playground, or in the industrial classes, is to subordinate all else to the acquisition of the English language by our pupils. We are anxious and striving that they may express themselves in correct English at the earliest possible time.

Sanitary. -- The health of our pupils has been excellent. The climate and scenery are said to be the finest in the world, but we have tried to assist these natural advantages by physical culture.

Influence on the tribe. – Chief Navajo, with the rest of his tribe, was very suspicious of our proposed school, and it took great patience and much argument to convince him and the older people that our purposes were friendly and for the good of the Indians. They seem to have accepted the situation and are kindly disposed at present. Already a disposition to live more cleanly and dress better is noticeable among the older Indians.

Prospects. – During the coming year the Government contemplates improvements here. These, together with what will be provided, will place us in a condition to perform effective work in many ways that were impossible in the preliminary operations.

In conclusion, -- I appreciate the cordial relations existing between this school in Fort Mojave, for which it should, later on, furnish pupils. Mrs. Bauer, who has been my able and valuable assistant, unites with me in pleasant acknowledgment of the many courtesies received since we assumed duties under your supervision.

Yours, very respectfully,

R.C. Bauer, Teacher
(Bauer1895:358)

Report of Teacher In Charge of Yava Supai Indians

Yava Supai Agency,
Via Williams, Ariz., June 30, 1896

Sir: I herewith submit the annual report of this school and agency.

Tribe. – The tribe is allied to the Hualapai Indians and is one of the bands of the Pai Nation, all of whom speak the same language with slight variations of dialect. The Yava Supais compose the Blue Water band and number 253 souls, as per my census this year, which is the first accurate one that has ever been taken of these Indians.

Morals and manners. – Like most savages, these Indians are both little above the brute creation in morals and manners. While they have kindly traits of character, such as hospitality and a certain willingness to oblige, yet they are beastly in their filth, appetites, language, and personal decency. Death by perishing on the desert from thirst is the punishment to women for promiscuous amours. They are negatively, at least, virtuous. Whiskey has never troubled them, as they are too far from white settlements to get it, and they are lovers of their valley home. As to personal character, they are much like white men. Everything depends upon the particular individual as regards his veracity, thrift, and force.

Location. – in the deep box canyon of the Cataract River, 100 miles north of Williams, Ariz., is their home. Three waterfalls that are singularly beautiful drop from 100 to 300 feet over precipices of tufa that are constantly forming. Back of the falls are caves and grottos glistening with the stalactites and stalagmites that adorn their roofs and floors. Crags, cliffs, mountains, and deserts surround us that are fascinatingly horrible in their desolation. The agency has been aptly termed an "oasis in hades."

Boundaries. – The boundaries of this reserve should begin at the southeast corner of the Hualapai reserve, thence east to the southwest corner of the Coconino Forest reserve, thence, thence west along the Colorado River to the northeast corner of the Hualapai reserve, thence south to the point of beginning. The tract described is nearly all deserts and "bad lands," and is worthless but for the little "water holes" on it at which the Indians keep their live stock. The country I have described is today actually occupied by the Yava Supais and is necessary for their support, as they can not keep stock in the canyon, which is only large enough for gardens for the Supais. The boundary question should be settled.

Farming. – Twelve miles of main ditches carry water over the 200 acres that are in cultivation. Their irrigating system is very crude, and the work is all done with a hoe. Mr. Charles Bushnell, a practical farmer, stockman, and mechanic, has had charge of the farming this year and his work has been satisfactory. More land could be placed under cultivation if we had lumber to make flumes. Their peach orchards are quite prolific and number about 1,000 trees.

Building. – Four buildings, not including outhouses are in course of construction. We have been somewhat delayed in the work by changes in the disbursing officers, necessitating the return of building funds to the United States Treasury; but we expect that the Department will soon arrange for a speedy completion of the work, so that we can be comfortably domiciled and prepared to execute better school work.

Mail facilities. – Efforts have been made to establish a mail route to this place, but, so far, without success. We consider ourselves exceedingly fortunate if we get our mail once each month. To go to Williams our Indians are compelled to make a horseback ride of 60 miles over a stony, grassless desert, where there is not one drop of water for man or horse. They do not exactly enjoy the trip.

Education. – Supai day school has been doing the usual work of such institutions. The children, 40 in number, have been compelled to bathe, make and wash their clothing, and attend to personal cleanliness and decency. The technical work of the school has been conducted in a way to teach the pupils the English language. All of our work is made interesting to the pupils and no serious infractions of good discipline have occurred. Good counsel has been our only punishment and it has been sufficient in all cases. The children have learned as much as could be expected under the circumstances, full particulars of which have been properly reported to your office for action.

The industrial instruction has not been so full or systematic as it should have been, owing to the fact that we have had but little time to spare from the labor now going on. We have had a garden in which new varieties of vegetables and the culture have been shown. Nothing so impresses an Indian as example. Especially is this true in regard to time of planting.

Missionary work. – No church organization has ever had a representative here. Mrs. Bauer has taken a deep interest in the welfare of the Indians, and has distributed supplies to the sick which she received from her friends in the Women's National Indian Association. Thoroughly nonsectarian philanthropists, those noble ladies deserve just praise for their efforts to ameliorate the condition of the Indian.

Sanitary. – We have had an epidemic of "grippe" and pneumonia that went through the tribe, but owing to the medicines furnished by the Government and the ladies of the Women's National Indian Association no case was fatal.

Effect on the tribe. – The whole tribe are much pleased with their school. The parents often visit us and are delighted with the singing and English-speaking exercises of the school. Regular habits, well-directed industry, a civilized home with its multitude of acts and duties performed, care for their sick, enforced cleanliness of children, exacted obedience, decency, and courtesy from all, and morality and justice on the part of employees, can have but one result in an Indian community – an elevation of moral tone in that community. While no revolution has occurred, we can see a change for the better, because we know the former conditions

Conclusion. – Although we have labored under some trying difficulties, our work has been delightful, for we know that we have accomplished permanent good for our boys and girls. Our relations with the Government officials we have met have been very pleasant. The year 1896 will be one of valuable experiences and pleasant memories.

Realizing the trying situations under which you labor, and thanking you for your kindly consideration and courtesy, Mrs. Bauer unites with me in cordial good wishes.

Yours, very respectfully,
R.C. Bauer, Teacher in Charge
(Bauer 1896:111-112)

Report of Teacher Among Yava Supais.

Supai, Ariz., June 30, 1897.

Sir: I herewith submit my annual report of Supai Agency and school for your consideration.

Tribe. – The tribe of Yava Supais have a legend of the Noachian deluge. Their ark was a raft and their Mount Ararat was the San Francisco mountains, near Flagstaff, Ariz., 150 miles southeast of this agency.

They have always occupied the wildest and most inaccessible parts of the terrific gorge of the Grand Canyon of the Colorado in Arizona described by Hon. William O. O'Neill with vivid force as "The Ditch of Ditches!" This tribe, numbering less than 300 souls, has always visited condign punishment on the cannibal Apaches and hostile Navajos who disturbed them in their Canyon fastnesses, 8,000 feet down in the earth, compared to which the famous lava beds of the Modocs are insignificant. Claiming to be the progenitors of the Apaches, their assertions, substantiated by archaeological remains, philological certain ties, and anthropological similarities, permit the deduction that their legends of tribal strife and subsequent emigrations from the parent tribe (Yava Supais), which occurred periodically for countless generations, are founded on incontrovertible facts. To this day the feuds of past generations, embittered by bloodshed, rankle deep in the hearts of the Yava Supais, and are doubtless the principal reasons why they never joined the Apaches in the murder of white men. They are, however, pure and unadulterated Apaches, and fear no living man, although they will yield immaterial points as a matter of good policy when not enraged.

They are the most industrious Indians I have ever known, being good irrigation farmers and horticulturalists, and as a matter of fact the most progressive agricultural community in northern Arizona. They are expert horseman and hunters, and from the farm and chase procure, without

Government assistance, their food and raiment. At $100 per capita, a reasonable amount for support, this means in cold figures a savings to the United States Government of about $30,000 per annum. To one accustomed to the vagabonds of the ration system it is a great relief to turn to these sturdy, self-reliant mountaineers who simply ask to be let alone, and note the contrast between the "root hog or die" system and the system that overthrew the powerful Roman Empire – the ration system.

Discipline and results. – When we first reported here for duty we found a filthy, obscene tribe of savages. Their personal habits were shockingly indecent in close proximity to the school and our quarters. Their language was interspersed with choice selections of profanity and vulgarity derived from the vile characters they had met among their civilized (?) brethren.

They knew no law. The children were wild, insubordinate, dirty, naked, and described by one of their leading citizens as "All same jack rabbit!" These extremes of perverseness were fondly considered by the idolizing parents as evidences of independence and nobility of character. With no police force, no guardhouse, and no precedent of law or order, the task of organizing a school and controlling the adults was enough to make a man of cast iron flinch. But we are organized, although the organization is not so perfect as could be desired, or the discipline equal to that of West Point. However, indecent habits, vulgarity, and profanity are rarely indulged in or tolerated near the school or quarters. Gambling, which was once very annoying, is confined to the camps. Drunkenness does not occur, and no serious breaches of the peace have disturbed our 120-degrees-in-the-shade tranquility. Since civilized men consider police and prisons essential to good government, and whereas we are without these desiderata, we claim to be an economically governed and law-abiding community.

Game law. – The legislature of this Territory enacted a law at its last session making it a crime, punishable by fine and imprisonment, for anyone to kill deer for the next five years. Our Indians killed about 300 last winter, and look upon the parks and forests of northern Arizona as their lawful "meat barrel." This law will deprive them of their meat. The skins they have always tanned and traded to the Moquis and Navajoes for blankets. Thus by one act their meat and blankets have been taken away from them. The problem is: "Where are they to get their meat and blankets for five years?" The solution will probably be that they will go without. I devotedly hope that the "Jackson Hole" trouble will not be repeated with these Indians as victims.

Buildings. – Our buildings are still in course of construction and not completed, owing to lack of funds to pay for irregular labor. The additional farmer has acted in the capacity of farmer, blacksmith, carpenter, stone mason, and master of transportation. He has performed his duties in an eminently satisfactory manner, but there are limitations to the amount of work any one man can perform. The incomplete condition of the schoolhouse has been a serious hindrance to schoolwork. Our quarters have been very uncomfortable for the employees, but we have tried to be cheerful and at times gay waiting for the "good time coming bye and bye." These building should all be completed as speedily as funds will permit.

Farming and stock. – The farming has been under the immediate supervision of Mr. Charles Bushnell, one of the most competent men I have met in the service. There are about 300 acres under cultivation, all of which is irrigated by flooding small patches of ground inclosed by elevated borders. The value of their crops – corn, beans, pumpkins, sunflowers, melons, and peaches – approximates $30,000 per annum, as previously noted. The prospects are exceedingly right now for a large crop this year.

The Indians have little "water holes," some of them 40 or 50 miles distant, at which they have kept their horses from time immemorial. These springs will not sustain many head of stock, but white men are gradually encroaching upon the springs, and unless protection is afforded it will not be long before the Indians will have neither springs nor livestock. Last winter these Indians build about 12 miles of good log fence, stake and rider, from the cliffs of the Grand Canyon to Cataract Canyon, hoping to save these springs, which are as much their property as any land ever claimed by any of the aboriginal inhabitants of the United States. The large stock territory and the intense farming, together with much other important work, has demanded hard and unceasing labor from the farmer, who should be allowed another horse, instead of the vicious, dangerous brute now owned by Uncle Samuel, who has been aptly christened "The veteran bucker of Arizona."

Educational. – Our training has progressed steadily on the usual lines of such institutions as Supai school. We have not made the advancement that might be expected for the time we have been at work, for the reason that we have never had a schoolroom to use until two months since. Now, with 60 bright children in attendance, the classwork is being done in a more satisfactory manner. Ninety-five per cent of the school population is enrolled, and the remaining 5 percent could be had if we could care for them.

Owing to lack up guardhouse or force of any kind, it requires eternal vigilance to keep the attendance up to the proper figure. After much thought on this matter I am persuaded that means should be devised to take those children whose attendance is very irregular from day schools to nonreservation boarding schools, by force, if necessary. The annoyance of a regular attendance at day schools would not then exist. There is something radically wrong with the home influences surroundings such children. They should be taken where a constant supervision of them can be maintained and discipline applied. These are the pupils who are likely to be the future insubordinates and nonprogressives on the Indian reservations unless dealt with in a scientific manner. The restraint of the reformatory, such as the boarding schools should be ought to be applied when the delinquents are known. The sooner the Indian learns to obey and respect law and order, the sooner he will become fit for citizenship.

We have constantly borne in mind the fact that the future advancement of the pupil depends upon his English vocabulary; that what he uses daily is of more importance to him as a future citizen than what he knows and tries to conceal or is incapable of expressing. Each employee is expected to converse with the pupils as much as possible each day in the industrial classes and on the playground. We strive to impress upon the pupils that intelligent Indians can be good citizens; that the ideal should be a potential power rather than an impossible change of color to a pseudo white man.

Missionary work. – The religious training has been limited to teaching the children hymns, the Lord's prayer, commonly conceded ethics, and right living. It has been a sort of Sunday school, and has been much enjoyed by the pupils. As yet no clergyman has devoted his attention to the spiritual needs of these people. The Woman's National Indian Association has helped Mrs. Bauer generously, but no one has pledged a missionary support. The field is not large, but the opportunities are great.

Conclusion. – The year has been a trying one, but results with school and tribe are gratifying. All the men and 60 per cent of the women dress in civilized garb. The school is happy, large and alive. We are not a pauper community, and have no desire for rations. All we ask is a good school and intelligent, honorable, and industrious employees, and the problem of civilization, citizenship, and survival will be solved by the Yava Supais themselves. The employees have worked in perfect harmony. No jar, no dissension, no unkind word or thought has marred our efforts as factors in the scheme of civilization here being developed.

Appreciating the many courtesies extended to us all and the deep interest you have taken in us and our work, the other employees unite with me in cordial good wishes for your future welfare.

Yours, very respectfully,
R.C. Bauer,
Teacher in Charge, Yava Supais.[12]
(Bauer 1897:104-106)

Thus although Bauer and his wife were initially shocked by the "filthy," "undisciplined" children they encountered, in sharp contrast to the earlier government farmer, notice that Bauer states that the Havasupai are "the most industrious Indians I have ever known, being good irrigation farmers and horticulturalists ... (and) expert horseman and hunters ...." Also, he places the blame for their adoption of "choice selections of profanity and vulgarity" on the "vile characters they had met among their civilized (?) brethren" (probably miners but possibly also ranchers, tourists, or town residents in nearby Williams). And as further proof of his growing empathy for the

Havasupai people in their battle to maintain at least some semblance of control over their own economic destiny, notice that he states that their grazing and hunting rights and water holes needed protection through a major enlargement of the reservation and an overturning of a recently passed territorial law "making it a crime … for anyone to kill deer for the next five years" in the Grand Canyon area. Otherwise, Bauer fears that these "self-reliant mountaineers who simply asked to be let alone" will become yet another group of "vagabonds of the ration system."

Evidently, Bauer's superior, Henry F. Ewing also shared Bauer's growing concern for the Havasupai people since when in November 1896 Ewing learned that the government was considering removing the Havasupai to La Paz, he wrote an angry letter to the Indian Commissioner stating that "they asked nothing except to be allowed to live in this cañon; they love the spot as no white man ever loved his native country, and so sure as the sun shines they will never be peacefully removed from it, … and should force be used, then every man and boy, who could carry a rifle must first be killed" (Hirst 1976:65).

However, although the Havasupai were not removed by force from their canyon home, the Indian Commissioner was apparently less sympathetic to the appeal by Bauer for the protection of the Indians' right to hunt deer in the Grand Canyon Forest Reserve which had been established in 1893 (Hirst 1976:67). Thus in his July 30, 1898 report to the Commissioner of Indian Affairs, Ewing writes concerning the Havasupai that, "formerly they took a vacation of two months each year and went deer hunting on the great mesas north of the San Francisco Mountains, but now the game law forbids this and they get little venison" (Ewing 1898:122). However, the Supervisor of the Forest Reserve was apparently not convinced that the Havasupai were really obeying the game law as shown by his letter to the Indian Commissioner in November of that same year in which he complained that:

> Indians boast and threaten to kill the deer and antelope so long as the "Government does not supply them with cow meat." The Grand Cañon of the Colorado River is becoming so renowned for its wonderful and extensive natural gorge scenery and for its open clean pine woods, that it should be preserved for the everlasting pleasure and instruction of our intelligent citizens as well as those

of foreign countries. Henceforth, I deem it just and necessary to keep the wild and unappreciable Indians from off the Reserve…. (Hirst 1976:66)

Thus the Office of Indian affairs wrote to Ewing, that December, advising him that "In fact it would be best to forbid their entering this reserve for any purpose; and should you learn of any of them being therein it would be well to cause their return to the reservations, even though they may not be detected in the act of hunting" (Hirst 1976:66). And Flora Gregg Iliff (1954:104) recounting her experiences as a schoolteacher and temporary superintendent at Supai in the year 1901 states that she:

> … learned, too, that the superintendent must cooperate with the officials of the Grand Canyon Forest Reserve, who controlled the plateau region surrounding the small Havasupai Reservation. There were many infringements of the law by the Indians, who claimed the reserve as their age-old hunting ground, and the officials made occasional trips to the school to request an investigation.

and later adds (Iliff 1954:196-197):

> The restrictions on their hunting range were brought home to me forcibly the day a forest ranger stopped at my office and said, "I'd like to see the one in charge down here."
> "I am in charge," I told him.
> He regarded me coldly, then made his accusation: "You permit the Indians to kill deer out of season. It's against the law."
> Someone had told. A picture flashed through my mind, one that I had acquired only a day or so previously. In the late afternoon, I was following the trail through the village when laughter and shouting broke the silence. At a home a short distance off the trail, Chickapanyegi, hot and tired, with headband askew, stood by his horse, unlashing from his saddle the carcass of a small deer. My first thought was of the violated game law. I said to him, "You know this is the closed season. Why did you kill that deer?"
> He wiped the sweat from his face on his sleeve before he replied, "Indians, deer, here first. White man no here. Now white man make law. We got no meat. My family hungry."
> "Eat your meat, now that you have it, but don't break the law again. I can't protect you. You will be taken away from your wife and children and sent to jail."
> The crowd had grown while we talked, but they were silent, knowing well enough what was wrong and wanting to see what would be done about it.
> They and the deer were here first; a close relationship existed between them. They killed only for food, and the deer spirit understood that. If one of them killed wastefully, the spirit that protected the deer would punish him with sickness and death.

I explain to the forest ranger the Indians' idea as to his ancient relationship to the deer and reminded him that the white man killed for a sport, taking the legal limit and leaving to spoil the meat he could not carry away, while the Indian killed game for food and this was a sacred privilege. The ranger was as helpless as I. We both were obligated to demand respect for the law, regardless of our sympathy, but I wanted him to understand their idealistic attitude. The time would come when these Indians would need a friend at court.

"My sympathy is with the Indians too," he admitted," but that will not keep them out of jail if they break the law." So Vesnor and Lanoman (Supai's two Indian "Policemen") went through the village, warning every man of the penalty of breaking the game laws.

To partially compensate for the now "forbidden" deer meat, the government in 1898 supplied "a few plows, hoes, shovels and some barbed fence wire" to the Indians and encouraged them "to adopt more civilized ways of farming" so that they could "raise more to the acre after plowing and put it in larger crops than formerly" (Ewing 1898:122). And Ewing (1898:122) indicates in his official report to the Commissioner of Indian Affairs that the Havasupai "are not slow to fall in line" and that:

> Owing to the isolation of the Supai Indians they have not been corrupted and demoralized with the vices of civilization like the Hualapais, whose cousins they are. ... If no other tribes were more trouble to the Government than the Supais the administration of Indian affairs would not be the great burden that it now is.

Bauer left Supai on April 1, 1898 after he was promoted to the position of "supervisor of Indian schools" and was replaced by the cook, Miss Ferry, "who for some time then performed the duties of teacher, housekeeper, and cook" until in May a new teacher and housekeeper arrived at Supai (Ewing 1898:123). However things did not go as well at Supai for the Indians during the stay of this new teacher. Thus, on August 18, 1899 Ewing (Ewing 1899:156) trying to sound as optimistic as possible reported to the Commissioner of Indian Affairs that:

> Of the Yavasupais, or Supais as they are usually called, little need to be said. They have plodded along in the even trend of their uneventful existence, providing their own subsistence without aid from the Government, except in the case of the disastrous floods last summer, when their crops were nearly all washed away by a flood. It then became necessary to aid them to tied over until a new crop could be raised. This was done and 25,000 pounds of flour and 4,000

pounds of beans were issued to them. This year's census shows a decrease of 25 in the tribe, or a total of 247.

And in the year 1900, Ewing, despite the massive amount of government food that had been given to the Havasupai two years before, curiously begin his August 1 Report to the Commissioner of Indian Affairs stating that (Ewing 1900:202):

> Living, as they do, in the bottom of a canyon, isolated from the outside world by great, perpendicular barriers of rock, the Havasupai Indians are perhaps nearer their original state than any other tribe in the Southwest. Their methods of gaining a living have thrown them but little within the influence of whites in the adjoining settlements.
> The Havasupai are entirely self-supporting, providing an abundant subsistence from agriculture. Three hundred and fifty acres of fairly productive land, with the finest stream of pure spring water in Arizona for irrigating, renders the cultivation of corn, pumpkins, beans, melons and peaches an easy problem, even for the untutored mind of a savage. In store houses built of stones and mud, securely hidden in the great cracks and clefts in the canyon wall, the Havasupai are reputed to have stored away enough provisions to tide them over three unproductive years. But there is no such thing as an unproductive year at Supai. True, a flood may come and wash away their crops, but whatever may be the rain or snowfall on the mesas above or in the canyon, the flow of water is practically always the same.

Then in contradiction to that which he has just written in the above paragraphs he continues by stating that (Ewing 1900: 203):

> In former years it had been the custom among this tribe to leave their homes for several months in the fall and winter to hunt on the mesas. The setting aside of the forest reserves and preventing their killing game in the great Coconino forest has reduced them entirely to a vegetable diet. To make up for this loss to their food supply it became necessary to put forth renewed efforts to induce the Indians to cultivate every available foot of land in the canyon. One of their religious customs compelled them to abandon a farm for at least one to three years upon the death of one of the owners or heirs to the land. This custom having the tendency to leave a large part of the land vacant each year, I ordered it discontinued. Now all available lend is under crops.
> By making a survey of the land in the canyon it was discovered that two tracks of land that has never been cultivated could, at no great cost, be put under irrigation. The Indians constructed a ditch under the direction of the farmer, following the survey, and succeeded in adding 8 acres to the arable tract. A ditch that will reclaim 25 acres more is under course of construction, but will require some blasting to get water on the land.

An irrigating system for the school grounds, by means of a gasoline engine and pump, has been authorized, and is under construction. It is expected that this plant, when completed, will allow the cultivation of sufficient land to provide all the hay necessary for the Government stock in the canyon, and as hay costs $50 per ton delivered, this is no small item.

An additional farmer is employed to teach the Havasupai improved methods, but as there is no appropriation from which plows or other agricultural implements can be purchased, the teaching of improved methods of agriculture is rather more in name than in fact at Supai.

Finally, although he is pleased that, "The Havasupai not being thrown much in contact with the whites have not acquired so many of the vices of civilization as their Walapai cousins," he is greatly displeased with their progress relative to the Walapai in becoming "educated." Thus in discussing the progress of the educational program at Supai, he concludes his report by stating that (Ewing 1900:203):

The Havasupai School is taught in a stone building erected by the employees, at little cost to the Government. It is well-equipped, but other buildings are greatly needed. A room for preparing and serving the noonday luncheon and another for use as a laundry and sewing room are greatly needed.

The attendance at this school and the enrollment has been all that could be asked. The enrollment has been 70, with an average attendance of 65. The cost of maintaining the school has been $4623.47, or $66.05 each pupil. The capacity of the schoolhouse is 46[13].

Of the progress made in the educational department of the school, I regret to say that I can not speak so highly as of the Walapai schools. Few of the pupils even those who have been in school four years, are as far advanced as Walapai pupils of the same age who have been in school but one session. It seems advisable that under the present conditions and circumstances more attention should be given to industrial training among this tribe, and the pupils of suitable age and advancement could be put at school in the Truxton Canyon Boarding School, provided dormitory room is added to the projected buildings.

I have the honor to be, most respectfully, your obedient servant.

Henry F. Ewing.
Industrial Teacher in Charge of Walapai
and Havasupai Indians and Day Schools

And a short time later, the U.S. Superintendent of Indian Schools, Estelle Reel (1900:417,421) also expressed her concern about the "failure" of the educational and other programs at Supai after a visit she made to the canyon in 1900 as part of a series of personal inspections of Indian schools throughout the United States. Thus, in her

August 20, 1900 report to the Commissioner of Indian Affairs, she states concerning the Havasupai (p.421):

> These Indians, about 250 in number, are located in an almost inaccessible canyon, to reach which requires most arduous and difficult climbing. I reached Supai, after traveling 76 miles by wagon and another 8 miles on horseback, on a burro, and on foot, it being impossible to ride over a portion of the trail.
>
> The Havasupai live along a stream called Blue Water, and have about 350 acres of land, a very small portion of which is under cultivation. I saw about twenty gardens, all in poor condition, as the Indians have no idea of irrigation. They plant their wheat in handfuls in little holes and their corn in the same way. These Indians farm as they did hundreds of years ago and live in as primitive a condition as then. Their houses are built of willows, and many superstitions still remain, such as refusing to cultivate the land of deceased Indians for three years.
>
> The land in this canyon is quite fertile and can easily be watered from the streams. The Indians now have many fruit trees loaded with fruit, but as the trees have not been pruned the fruit is small and of poor quality. A considerable quantity of wheat can be raised if the Indians are made to irrigate at the proper time. Old Manakaga, chief of the Hava Supais, stated to me that he would try to cultivate a better crop next year, and specifically requested that plowshares be allowed them.
>
> The Government school building is good, and about 65 children were attending this day school, which has been in session several years. Literary training in an almost inaccessible canyon, where the children do not come in contact with white people, and who, after leaving the schoolroom, have no further occasion to speak the English language, is of little value. The Havasupais, who are cousins to the Hualapais and speak their language, frequently visit them at Hackberry. The agent, who has lived among them many years and has their confidence, can, I believe, induce the parents of these children to allow them to be placed in the Hackberry school and board among their cousins, and I recommend that he be instructed to bring as many of the children as can be accommodated this year from Supai Canyon and place them in the Hackberry school when completed.

Thus, this independent observer in this report cast considerable doubt on the accuracy of the "success" stories sent by previous government farmers and teachers from Supai to Washington and she concluded that the children of Supai must be removed from their canyon home to ensure the success of the government's English language training efforts. Her strong belief was that this removal would help overcome "one of the greatest obstacles to be found in the elevation of the Indian race" which in her mind was (Reel 1900:435):

> ... the difficulty of overcoming the prejudices of the mothers of the tribe. The men, from constant contact with the white people have their ideas broadened and absorb many of the ways of civilization, but the women, remaining in the camps, cling with tenacity to their old-time superstitions. The homes of the camp Indians are to be reached mostly through our school girls, who are to be the future wives and mothers of the race, and on their advancement will depend largely the future condition of the Indian. All history has proven that as the mother is so is the home, and that a race will not rise above the home standard.

However, the first removal of some of the students from the overcrowded school at Supai to an outside boarding school did not occur until December 1901 when the "Truxton Canyon Training School for the Walapai" was opened (Iliff 1954:199—200,211). At that time, according to Flora Gregg Iliff, who in 1901 as a young schoolteacher had accepted a temporary assignment at Supai, twenty children went to the Truxton school from Supai. "partly to relieve the congestion in the Havasupai school, but also, the children wanted the industrial training we now could offer with our new equipment."

By now the Havasupai were beginning to feel the full impact of the government's assimilation and control program and while they seldom openly opposed it, at times they did decide to engage in a "game" of "brinkmanship" with the local government agent. Thus, when Miss Flora Greg in June 1901 was asked to be the "temporary superintendent" at Supai in addition to performing her teaching duties there, she (Iliff 1954:91) records:

> ...I (did not) admit my doubt as to my ability to handle situations that might arise, although I had been told that, on one occasion, the Havasupai men had terrorized the man in charge with knives and guns until he reversed his previous decision. How, I wondered, could I hope to control grown men – the chief, for instance, or the medicine men?

And she (Iliff 1954:91) adds:

> ... my interview with the departing Havasupai superintendent was scarcely more heartening. He told me that he was not coming back to the reservation. "I'll

<u>never</u> bring my family into that hole!" he stated with emphasis. The details he told of the hardship, deprivation, isolation and actual danger to life in the canyon were disillusioning....[14]

However, despite these warnings, Miss Gregg accepted the temporary position at Supai, drawn to Supai by the very same "mystery and enchantment" that has through the years attracted so many white "saviors" there; for when discussing why she had first come to Northern Arizona. She vividly recounts her moment of "conversion" in the following story (Iliff 1954:3-5):

> "These Indians are almost completely out of touch with the civilized world," the lecturer explained. "Their village on the floor of the gorge can be reached by either of two trails, both of them steep and both of them dangerous."
>
> I gripped my purse and listened intently.
>
> "The canyon in which they live is so inaccessible that it is difficult to find teachers to work in such isolation. The Havasupai ... the People of the Blue Water – need you."
>
> I sat very straight in my chair. Would I go? I was practically there!
>
> It was 1900 and I was young and unwilling to weigh consequences. Adventure? Danger? Life was waiting to be lived!
>
> The lecturer at the Teachers' Institute where I was supposed to be increasing my ability to teach in the city schools in Oklahoma Territory, must have caught the excitement in my face.
>
> "It's a land of mystery and enchantment where red-angled walls of the canyon hold between them a rollicking stream of sparkling blue water," she continued. "The Indians living there have an intriguing, primitive culture, rich in the lore of their ancestors. This tribe believes that their gods speak to them through rustling trees, flying clouds and running water. Even today, as through passed ages, the mythic Bear, Deer, and Coyote talk with them and influence all their activities."
>
> The few Indians I had seen had appeared uncommunicative, stoical and unsocial. Yet under their stern behavior must be hidden this secret religion. Suddenly I wanted to learn at first hand what the Indians of the Colorado River country believed, and how their belief affected their lives.
>
> Such an experience would not mean merely learning to speak a strange tribal language. No! I would be living with people who conversed with unseen forces – wrapped in the mystic wonders of another age. Nobody told me that the Indians in this locality were not far from the days of scalping at the drop of a tomahawk, or that floods, more destructive than earthquakes, could trap a tenderfoot. Or that the trail down was so steep in places that not even a mule, trained in mountain climbing, could stand on its feet.
>
> But it wouldn't have mattered. Born of pioneers who pushed ever westward in search of space and freedom, the lure of the untried, made more

exciting by the thought of life in an Indian village on the floor of an isolated canyon, was a challenge I could not lightly cast aside. Add to that appeal to help a bewildered people find its place in the social and business world encroaching upon it from all sides, and there was no alternative.

The rest of Teachers' Institute was a total loss to me. The picture of a brown-skinned people whose hopes, whose very existence, depended on the stream of blue water, pushed all thought of any other future away. I wanted to board the first train and start down either of those trails to the canyon floor.

In October 1900, after passing a preliminary Civil Service test instead of obtaining an offer to teach at Supai she was instead given an offer to teach in the nearby Hackberry Day School for the Walapai tribe (Iliff 1954:3-5). Seeing that this position "might be the springboard to [her] goal" she accepted the offer reasoning that:

These were not the People of the Blue Water the lecturer had told us about; that disappointment had to be accepted. But the Walapai were related by blood to the People of the Blue Water; the reservations of both tribes were in northern Arizona. This position might be the springboard to my goal, might even prepare me better for work with the Havasupai.

Her wait to achieve her goal proved to be extremely short. Nevertheless, as with many other "saviors" to the Havasupai before and after her, this desire "to serve" them did not last long; thus, less than five months after she first came to Supai, Miss Gregg left the Canyon never to return again (Iliff 1954:199-200,209). However, from her brief stay there, she, in a book published in 1954, wrote a remarkably perceptive eyewitness account of the events that were occurring at Supai in the beginning years of the 20th Century. Hence, we learn from her narration that by 1901, in addition to her almost overwhelming duties as a teacher of 72 children, she was expected to "issue" drugs to sick Indians and to "settle the Indians' disputes" (Iliff 1954:104,138-139). And since no missionary was present at Supai, she and the other school employees felt it their duty to hold a Sunday Church service for the children (Iliff 1954:121,196).

To aid her in accomplishing these tasks were two local Indians who were hired by the government as "policemen" whose official duties were, here as on other reservations, "to suppress traffic with Indians in intoxicating liquors, to put down other forms of lawlessness, and to preserve order generally…" (Iliff 1954:100;R.C.I.A. 1889:27). However, at Supai one of these men had been given an additional

assignment as discovered by Iliff (Miss Gregg) in the following excerpt from her account
of her first school day at Supai (Iliff 1954:105-106):

> I had rung the warning bell, and it was time for school, but no children had
> appeared. Then the bushes parted violently and dozens of little Indians burst.
> through on the run. Behind them, maneuvering his well-trained pony with all the
> skill of a cattleman rounding up strays, rode Vesnor (one of the policemen). The
> older pupils followed more leisurely; Vesnor did not drive those who came of their
> own volition. Nevertheless, this method of bringing children to school seemed
> wholly unnecessary, if not cruel.
> "Why do you drive them?" I protested. "They should come to school
> without that."
> "I no bring, swim in creek all day. I got no time to fool," came his indignant
> answer.
> Vesnor's method of maintaining an average attendance of seventy-one
> out of an enrollment of seventy-two doubtless had been instituted by a former
> teacher, and must have grown out of necessity. I decided not to change it until I
> became better acquainted with conditions governing school attendance.

Miss Gregg, in general, developed a great empathy for the Havasupai, shielding
several "breakers" of the game and anti-polygamy laws from federal officials and
praising such aspects of their culture as their childrearing practices (Iliff 1954:138-
139,143-145,196-197). However, although she states that "The Intelligence used by the
parents in training their children would set a worthy example for any race," she was not
against the removal of some of these children from their home environment to relieve
the serious overcrowding that existed at the Supai school and to give the children better
"industrial training" (Iliff 1954:117,143,211). Thus, in her 1901 report to her superiors,
Miss Greg pleads (Iliff 1954:117; Gregg 1901:528):

> I trust that either 20 of the largest boys and girls will be transferred to the
> Truxton Canyon Training School when it opens September 1, or a kindergarten
> department will be added to this school, as it is impossible for one teacher to
> instruct 71 pupils in a credible manner.

This suggestion apparently alarmed the parents of the children since, when "at
the request of the Supai Indians, [the Arizona Indian Service Supervisor, Mr. Holland]
met with them in Council" that year about this as well as important land and water
concerns. The Indians ended the meeting "with the request that they be given some
increased school facilities in the cañon so that their children will not have to be sent to

away…" (Hirst 1976:68). However, Holland in his official report to the Secretary of the Interior concerning this meeting, apparently did not have much sympathy for the Indians' school request for he states (Hirst 1976:68):

> Death is doing a great deal toward solving the alleged troubles of the Supais, and my idea is that the decimation of their number by that cause should be further increased by getting as many as possible out to school. After being at Truxton and Phoenix for a while it is not probable that many of them will want to go back to their little hole in the ground where they seem to suffer from malaria or too much inter-marrying or both. They are generally weak-looking.

Thus, in December 1901, the event long feared by many Havasupai parents finally occurred win 20 of their older children were sent out of the canyon to attend the new Truxton boarding school (Iliff 1954:211).

And to further add to the Indians' old fear about being displaced from their canyon home, while Miss Gregg was in Supai, Ewing wrote to her that "an Eastern firm had been granted authority to harness Mooney Falls to manufacture electrical power for distribution to cities in Arizona and neighboring states" (Iliff 1954:191). Thus, although Iliff states that she protested this planned development repeatedly to Ewing who had been able that year to block one individual who "…even went so far as to locate a homestead within the reservation claiming all the water power and water" (Hirst 1976:67), it was not long before:

> …Engineers, surveyors and workman swarmed into the canyon where so few white men had ever ventured. Miners had once worked the ledges on the walls for silver, but never had the Indians' authority over the Blue Water or its canyon been questioned. These white men who were now tinkering with the old Mooney Falls did not consult the Indians. They were authorized to complete the project, they explained to me, and, intent upon this, they kept pretty much to themselves. We sensed an intimation of things to come….
> The Indians realized now that, before they were through, these white people would fill the canyon. After the machinery was installed, men would remain to attend the plant; their families would come. To whom then would the canyon belong, and who would be forced to go? Who always went when the Indian had land that the white man coveted? (Iliff 1954:191-192).

And though "The white men had plenty of cash with which to allay the Havasupai's fears" by buying "alfalfa from them for their horses, paying five dollars for the load a woman could carry suspended from a strap across her forehead" and despite the fact that they "gave a silver dollar to those who posed for a picture":

> … this proved little compensation for the Indians, who could only stand by and watch as heavy machinery rumbled in along the widened Lee Canyon trail, and old Mooney began to lose her wild timbered beauty….
>
> The Indians fears these invaders as they have never feared the Yavapai or the Apache. They could meet the latter and deal with them as they deserved, but these white men – working like ants, building roads, making permanent improvements – had taken possession without need of battle. Mr. Ewing wrote that the contract had been negotiated in Washington; he was powerless to interfere. And in increasing numbers the white men continued to come….
>
> …[Even the most influential Havasupai "chief" in 1901] Manakadja, was as helpless as any of us…(Iliff 1954:192-193).

However, just as the Havasupai had about given up all hope of maintaining any semblance of control over their canyon home, Iliff (1954:193-194) goes on by recounting the following "miracle":

> … so again the security of the People of the Blue Water rested in the laps of their gods.
>
> And the gods spoke – through a storm cloud – deciding the issue with one swift blow. Work was progressing toward completion when a flood roared down the canyon, wiping out the widened, costly trail, demolishing the equipment that had disfigured Mooney Falls, and causing the firm such financial loss that the project was abandoned. The white men rode out, one afternoon, over the hastily repaired trail, leaving the canyon to the people to whom it rightfully belonged.
>
> The power of the gods was manifest once more, renewing courage and inspiring the whole village with fresh vitality. The people worked in homes and gardens, their former cheerfulness restored by this assurance that the gods who led them to the canyon and taught them the skills by which they had survived, were still able to defend them.

However, this euphoria was rather short lived, especially as the government in the following years increased its pressure on the Havasupai to force them to cease their "roaming" of the plateau lands above the canyon during which the government suspected many "violations" of the game laws had occurred. Thus, during this period of trial for the Indians "one old man expressed the sentiments of all when he cried bitterly, 'We are no longer men, but are little children (who) must ask when we go out or come in' " (Iliff 1954:198). Also, an attempt in 1901 by the privately sponsored "Indian Rights

Association" to help the Havasupai obtain either individual allotments or a larger reservation and their lost hunting rights was dismissed by Holland who said in his official report to the Secretary of the Interior, "My information is that when the Indians had undisputed possession of these lands, about the only use they made of them was for hunting purposes, grazing a lot of worthless ponies and a very few cattle...." (Hirst 1976:67,68). Thus, it is not too surprising that when Assistant Indian Commissioner A.C. Tonner forwarded Holland's report to the Secretary of the Interior, he added the following comments (Hirst 1976:68-69):

> In view of the facts, as reported by Mr. Holland, it would seem to be unadvisable to attempt to secure a part of the said forest reserve and the withdrawal of public lands contiguous thereto for these Indians in order to give them allotments in severalty or to disturb them in their present manner of living. Nor is it deemed necessary to use any of the fund – Support and Civilization of the Apache and other Indians in Arizona and New Mexico – in the purchase of agricultural tools, etc. as they seem to be getting along quite satisfactorily in their primitive way, and it might cause them to expect other gratuities from the Government should tools be issued to them.

However, on this last suggestion he was apparently overruled since Iliff (1954:118) reports that in the fall of 1901 a large shipment of gardening tools arrived for the Havasupai in response to her earlier plea in her August 6, 1901 report to the Commissioner of Indian Affairs in which she stated (Iliff 1954:117; Gregg 1901:528):

> The most discouraging featurette present to the Havasupai is the fact that many of them have no farming implements. The farmer often loans them plows and hoes, which are always promptly returned. When unable to borrow implements, they laboriously loose in the soil with sticks. If farming implements were furnished them, they could easily cultivate all the land to which they have access. Much labor and time would thus be saved, and what is still more important, their surplus products thus gained could be marketed, which would enable them to provide themselves with warm clothing for the winter months.

She had further supported this plea by stressing in the following excerpts from her report, the "worthiness" of the Havasupai to receive this aid (Iliff 1954:116,117: Gregg 1901:528):

> The Havasupai is entirely self-supporting. He depends on the products of his farm for his livelihood. He is proud of his gardens and his orchards, but prouder still of the fact that he labors. Living on the banks of a clear, sparkling

stream, he is never troubled by crop failure. He utilizes the water of the stream for irrigating purposes and an abundant crop is assured him. The almost perpendicular walls of the canyon, which he has made his home, are lined with storehouses which in the autumn he fills with corn, beans, and other products of his labor....

All of the Indians of this tribe dress in part in citizens' clothes, and most of them are quite willing to adopt the ways of the white man. They depend very little on the professed abilities of the medicine man. If one of the tribe is sick they come to us repeatedly for medicine, and even though the case is a hopeless one, insist on having medicine for the patient until he dies or recovers....

Work in the laundry and sewing room is ably conducted. Both boys and girls are detailed to assist in cooking the noon day lunch, and under the supervision of the cook, do excellent work....

However, the "gods of nature" did not deal kindly with Miss Gregg and the Havasupai that year for that very same summer, a massive flood once again swept through the canyon terrorizing the young schoolteacher and completely destroying many of the Indians' houses, gardens, and orchards[15] (Iliff 1954:185-188). The Indians, as they had so many times following previous floods, "patiently repaired their houses, dried out the furnishings, rebuilt fences, replanted gardens and orchards" (Iliff 1954:189). However, Miss Gregg's experience with the flood and the rockfalls that followed it was probably the most significant factor in her decision to leave the canyon that November, never to return again (Iliff 1954:199) .

1901 was also a bad year for Ewing who in the following excerpt from his July 30, 1901 report to the Commissioner of Indian Affairs had made an especially strong plea for the return of ancestral lands and hunting rights to the Havasupai (Ewing 1901:527):

... In former years (the Havasupai Indian) spent a few months each fall on the high mesas surrounding his canyon home, where he hunted deer, antelope, and mountain sheep. This region, bounded on the north by the Grand Canyon, on the east by the San Francisco Peaks, and by Bill Williams Mountains and Mount Floyd on the south, and Pine Springs on the west, was recognized by all neighboring tribes as the hunting grounds of the Havasupai, and he defended it against the Apache and the Navaho, and made them respect his rights. But now that this region had been set aside as a forest reserve, the superintendent of the reserve has even forbidden the Havasupai to cross or be on his once undisputed territory, and to kill any game thereon would mean instant arrest and imprisonment. As the little 4 by 10 mile reservation which he is now allowed to call his own is entirely within the Grand Canyon Forest Reserve, the justice of forbidding his passageway across the forest reserve is not apparent. The Havasupai asks nothing of the white man nor the Government, except to be allowed the peaceable possession of that which is rightfully his own.

By that time Ewing was apparently not only being attacked by miners, ranchers, and the Grand Canyon Forest Reserve officials for his strong defensive of Havasupai land, water, and hunting rights but he was also apparently being attacked by his own immediate supervisors in the government's Indian education program for the "failure" of the English language training program at Supai. Thus, in his defense, in that same July report he states concerning the Havasupai (Ewing 1901:527-528):

> … This tribe, a branch of the Walapai, speaking the same language and following the same customs and having the same religious beliefs, has led a different existence from the Walapai since the advent of the white man. Living as he does in an inaccessible canyon, being entirely self-supporting from his own efforts at agriculture and the chase, he has come but little in contact with the whites, and as a result has never felt the effects of the terrible blighting influences that at one time dragged his Walapai cousin to the lowest depth of degradation and vice. But while he has escaped the baneful effects of a Western civilization he has also missed its advantages, for the Havasupai is to-day almost in the same condition of savagery and superstition that he was thirty years ago. He has not learned to speak English nor to adopt a white man's ways; he is still a primitive savage….
>
> The Havasupai day school has a capacity of 46, an enrollment of 72, and average attendance of 71. The school has not made the progress that could be desired, owing to the overcrowded condition of the buildings and a lack of sufficient instructors. The lack of progress has in no way been the fault of the employees, for the force has been efficient, earnest, and energetic, and have worked together in perfect harmony. The fact, however, that one teacher is required to instruct 72 pupils is in itself alone responsible for the unfavorable results. Unless a new schoolhouse is provided and an additional instructor the enrollment should be decreased one-half….

However, this defense and the backing of such people as Miss Gregg were not sufficient to prevent his "enemies" from having him "removed" from his government position sometime during November of that same year. Thus Iliff (1954:210) states:

> I never learned the exact charges against him. He had bitter enemies – cattlemen and ranchers he had forced off the Indians' land and others who accused him of being arrogant, rejoicing to see how the mighty had fallen. He

also had staunch friends. No jury would convict him, but he died a broken and disillusioned man.

The year 1902 brought additional pressure on the Havasupai to give up their old way of life as Ewing's duties were then added to the already heavy burdens of Dr. J. S. Perkins, the medical doctor for the Hualapai tribe and the staff and students of the new Truxton boarding school (Iliff 1954:210). Heavy emphasis was now placed on forcing the Havasupai to give up their old habits and customs which Perkins strongly felt hindered their progress towards the "civilized" state. Thus in his 1902 report (Perkins 1902:163) to the Commissioner of Indian affairs he stated that:

> The Havasupai Number 233. They live in Cataract Canyon, a spur of the Grand Canyon of Colorado. They have about 300 acres of fertile land with an abundance of running water for irrigation. Fruit, corn, alfalfa, and garden vegetables grow excellently and without much effort. They live from the products of the farm and garden and game from the mesas for about nine months in the year, then they resort to mescal. If they could be persuaded to see the folly of owning so many ponies, and give more time and attention to their farms, they would never want for food. Their funeral customs are another drawback. When an Indian dies his property is all destroyed, his camp burned, fruit trees cut down, and land turned out to grow up in brush, and his family goes to one of the neighbors to live. This ought not to be, and must be stopped. They are now supplied with farming utensils and seeds, which were badly needed. Their health is not good. They suffer from tuberculosis and malarial poison.

And although he lavished great praise upon the "industrial" teacher and his wife at Supai for their "excellent" instructional program for the boys and girls there, he admitted that "the literary work has not been satisfactory, owing to the fact that the school had no teacher a large part of the time" (Perkins 1902:164). However, as increasing numbers of young Supais were forced to attend the Truxton boarding school to "remedy" this "deficiency," even Iliff (1954:213) was forced to admit that:

> By changing to a boarding school we had unwittingly increased our problems. The warm fall days added to them. The children always resented confinement; they wanted to mount their ponies and gallop up the mountains or across the mesas to secret places they knew, where nature was lavish and completely wild.... Confined to quarters, the children grew moody; and a moody Indian means trouble....

Modern summer visitors to the "wilderness paradise" of the Havasupai Indians usually fail to experience the feeling of confinement, isolation, and depression that forces nearly every long-term resident there to seek a periodic escape from the "bondage" of the canyon. However, Iliff during her brief stay there in the year 1901 learned the "true" secret behind the annual winter migration of the Indians of Supai from their canyon home to the plateau above as revealed in this very perceptive message from her 1954 book (Iliff 1954:200-201):

> As jealously as the Havasupai guarded their canyon and as passionately as they loved it, the tang of autumn in the air turned their thoughts to a winter home on the mesa, and started them packing their possessions with a happy abandon. All summer they had planned for this – harvesting, preserving their food, and setting aside a portion to take with them....
>
> The Indians used various arguments to prove the necessity for the migration. They claimed that there was not enough wood in the gorge for their cooking fires and to warm their houses. Yet they had wood to sell. They needed the wild seeds, fruits and roots that grew on the top, they insisted. But, when I saw their childish delight as they made their departure, ponies loaded with cumbersome bundles, I knew that they were motivated by the very human desire for change, to get outside, where they could look about, with the full sweep of the vaulted sky above, with endless miles in which to wander.
>
> Not an Indian who was physically able to ride but longed for this trip to the mesa. Only our policemen and the few persons needed to care for the sick and the aged stayed on through the winter....

Thus, it is not altogether surprising that most long-term government employees stationed at Supai also, then as well as now, have always sought periodic escape from the canyon for as one told Miss Greg (Iliff 1954:93-95):

> ... it's fun to get out of that dreary old canyon and have supper and breakfast up here where you can see more than just a scrap of the sky....
>
> I'd like to start walking and not stop until I reached Los Angeles... I want to see a train. I want to wear a dinner dress, dine by candlelight, and see people laugh and have fun. Those walls down there hold one like a grave.

And Miss Gregg herself expressed the following feelings after escaping from a nearby canyon on the Hualapai reservation (Iliff 1954:224):

> ... surprisingly, we were out of our canyon. So long as I live I shall never forget the exaltation of that moment. Each of us felt it. No enclosing walls to shut out the sky and distant views! Even Ben [the Indian boy accompanying their

group] felt the same joyous reaction. We laughed, sang and shouted listening to the echo from the distant cliffs, our exuberance unbounded. I realized now how our schoolchildren felt when they gazed with dreamy eyes at the far heights looming above our canyon rim. This was their playground. Here in the harmony of the sun and wind and space they were in tune with their surroundings.

Initially, government officials bowed to wish of the school-age children at Supai (and of their parents) to participate in the annual winter outing. Thus Iliff (1954:200) records concerning the Supai school in the year 1901:

> Even though it was depressingly hot, the employees as well as the Indians were obliged to work harder through the summer, so that this winter outing might take place. I had taught at Truxton until school was dismissed for the summer vacation, and had quite naturally expected to be free from such duties during July and August. But no; here I must hold school through the summer and fall so that the Havasupai children's vacation might come in the winter. Nothing could be permitted to interfere with this jaunt to the outside.

However, beginning that fall, the export of large numbers of Havasupai youngsters to distant boarding schools did interfere with this annual "jaunt" since all such schools observed the traditional American school year. And the shocker of such change came early to the twenty children who like Miss Gregg left the isolation of the canyon that first year (1901) to attend the Truxton Canyon School (Iliff 1954:211) where she recollects (Iliff 1954:213):

> By changing to a boarding school we had unwittingly increased our problems. The warm fall days added to them. The children always resented confinement; they wanted to mount their ponies and gallop up the mountains or across the mesas to secret places they knew, where nature was lavish and completely wild. High in the mountains were meadows with bubbling streams, thickets in which the crested quail gathered at nightfall, and rocky heights sheltering wild burros to be lassoed. Confined to quarters, the children grew moody; and a moody Indian means trouble….

Many of the young girls, in particular, had trouble adjusting to the new environment of the boarding school and they and some of the boys begin experimenting with the extremely dangerous, hallucinogenic, omnipresent Jimson Weed (Datura) that the girls knew that tribal medicine men used "to induce the hallucinations through which the shamanistic spirit is acquired" her (Iliff 1954:215-218). Disease also began to spread among the confined children, beginning with outbreaks of pneumonia, chickenpox, and smallpox in 1902 and culminating in the killing influenza and measles epidemic of 1904 (Iliff 1954:229-230,259; Hrdlicka 1908:179). Thus, it is not altogether unexpected that the following violent confrontation occurred "not long after"[16] Miss Gregg's departure from Supai (Marshall 1907):

> The summer vacation was over, and the forty Indian boys and girls who had been enjoying it in their native canyon home had returned to the government boarding school, 150 miles distant.
>
> Or, rather, all but one had returned. Joseph Panya, a young fellow about 18 years old, had given many excuses for remaining at home, and when the other pupils had left he had lingered in the hope that he would be permitted to stay. But the agent was determined that the boy should return to school, as, otherwise, the time he had already spent there would be wasted.
>
> "If he can not find a horse to ride he can walk. One thing is certain, if he does not start early tomorrow morning I shall have one of the policemen take him." These were the words of the agent, Mr. Stanton[17], to the friends of Joseph when they complained that he had no horse on which to make the trip; a most absurd excuse, for there was not an Indian in the tribe but had so many ponies he was "horse poor." The agent's word ended the interview, for he went about his business, and the Indians, after discussing the matter in their own tongue, left the room.
>
> The next morning, when the two Indian policemen came to make their daily report, they said that Joseph Panya and his cousin, Tuluweesee, who had gone along to bring back Joseph's horse, had left long before sunrise, and were probably well on their way to the top of the mesa. Mr. Stanton heaved a sigh of relief when he heard this news, for he dreaded to compel a boy to leave the canyon to attend school, as the Indians resented such coercion and were apt to cause trouble.
>
> All thought of the matter was dismissed, and the work of the day was progressing as usual, when the weird cry that announces a death to an Indian community startled us. Another and another voice took it up, until it seemed that the whole canyon was bewailing the dead. In a minute the muffled noises of horses galloping in the heavy sand could be heard, and suddenly around a curve in the trail a long line of excited Indians, gesticulating and yelling, came into view.
>
> We could not imagine the cause of their excitement, and were still more surprised when they alighted at the agency and gathered around the mystified agent. As each one seemed to be anxious to tell the interpreter what to say, it was some time before anything could be made out of the babel of voices. Finally, Tuluweesee, whom we thought well on his way with Joseph, spoke through the interpreter. He said that he and Joseph Panya had reached the top of the mesa, and that he had galloped ahead some distance, thinking that Joseph was close behind, but upon looking round he found that he was alone. He hastily turned

and, retracing his steps, found Joseph and his pony lying dead, with an empty rifle beside them.

Interruptions of this narrative were frequent, and the threatening looks of Indians plainly showed that they blamed the agent for the boy's death. This fact was borne out by the interpreter saying: "All Indians plenty mad. I think you no have money, may-be-so they kill all white people. What you think?" Mr. Stanton was from the southern mountain regions and did not always stop to think. The sudden turn of affairs and the demand for money made him so angry that the interpreter had hardly finished the last word before his revolver was out of his pocket. He aimed at the most threatening one of the group and told them all in very emphatic words to "Get out, or there would be more dead Indians to howl over."

A few hesitated for a moment, but, having seen specimens of Mr. Stanton's marksmanship, and knowing him to be a man of his word, they decided it was best to obey. The interpreter was told to tell the policemen to report immediately, and while we were waiting for them to arrive we held a council, consisting of the white people of the village – three men and two women in all – to consider what was best to do should the Indians attempt to carry out their threats. What could we do? That was a question, indeed. The perpendicular walls of the canyon rose 3000 feet above us, and there were but two ways by which to reach their tops, and if the Indians really meant to kill us it was not likely that these would be left unguarded. One Indian perched upon the heights above could start an avalanche that would sweep the trail clear of any travelers who chanced to be upon it, and would bury all evidences of the crime as well. The nearest town was seventy-five miles away, and but one solitary house stood between us and it. The nearest telegraph station was more than half as far, in could be reached only by a trail that was next to impassable. We could hardly spare one of our three men to carry a message there, and, if we did, there still remained the difficulty of getting him out of the canyon.

There seemed but one thing to do – to send one of the Indian policemen to the station with a message to the government asking aid and to keep the other near us to inform us of affairs in the village. Our minds being thus made up, we informed the two policemen of our plans so far as they concerned them. We were sure of Vesnor, the older of the two men; he had never failed us in emergencies; therefore Mr. Stanton told him that he would be expected to keep watch of all that went on in the village and report to him. Lenoman[18] was told that it would be his work to take the message asking for aid. Vesnor approved of our plans and promised to keep us will informed, but Lenoman grew sullen. Presently he said: "Me no take message. Me stay here. All Indians plenty mad. May-be-so me all the same."

Again Mr. Stanton's temper rose, and when Lenoman went out of the office he was dressed in the primitive fashion of his tribe, for his blue uniform had been taken from him.

The situation was now worse than ever. We dared not risk sending one of our own number, and if we sent Vesnor we would be deprived of our only reliable source of information of what was taking place in the village.

Vesnor had remained after Lenoman had been dismissed, and it was from him that we got a suggestion of what to do. He had sat for some time without speaking, while we considered various plans. All at once he spoke: May-be-so Joseph no kill himself. Indian no like go dead. May-be-so some other Indian he get mad, kill Joseph. One, two, may-be-so three Indians all the same think, I no sabe." Vesnor was discreet, and, with all our questioning, we could get no more definite information. It finally dawned upon us, however, what was meant – Tuluweesee, for some reason, had killed Joseph; perhaps they had quarreled, or he may have known that the boy's parents had given him a good sum of money. At any rate, this offered a way out of the difficulty, and Vesnor was sent for Tuluweesee.

Meanwhile, Lenoman's return to the village, disgraced and stripped not only of his clothes, but of his authority, had still further increased the popular wrath, and more than once that blood-curdling cry, which it is impossible for a white person to imitate, came to our ears, and we knew that something must be done soon to secure aid, or our cause was hopeless. Therefore, when Tuluweesee appeared, escorted by Vesnor, Mr. S. boldly accused him of murdering the boy and robbing him. Curiously enough, this last statement was re-inforced by the dead boy's sister who came in at that minute wildly excited and crying that all Joseph's money was gone.

This strengthened our case considerably and Mr. Stanton told Tuluweesee there was but one thing for him to do to show that he was not guilty, and that was to take a letter to the telegraph office and return with evidence that he had delivered it. He was told that otherwise it was only a matter of time until he would be taken to Yuma and hanged, for no matter if we were killed the government would find it out sooner or later and visit him and his tribe with dire punishment. Yuma, the Arizona Sing Sing, had an awful significance to these Indians, as several of their number had been taking there for various offenses, and had never returned. Vague tales of the horrors of the place had reached the canyon from time to time, and had made Yuma a name to conjure with.

Vesnor, who acted as our interpreter, evidently translated our words in a way that he knew would terrify Tuluweesee, for he soon decided that he would go. We did not allow him to return to the village for fear that he would be persuaded to change his mind, nor did we allow the news of his departure to get abroad until he was well on his way.

Toward evening Mr. Stanton told Vesnor to go to the village and tell the Indians that Tuluweesee had gone, and that the first Indian who came in sight of the agency while he was gone would be shot. We knew when the message had been given, for a howl of rage echoed up and down the canyon. We felt relieved, however, to think that a message telling the outside world of our plight was on its way. But could we keep off the savages three days? We did not dare to hope for aid sooner than that. Three days! Could we stand the strain that long? What if Tuluweesee should not deliver our message, but take the opportunity to escape instead? Our anxiety was increased when Vesnor returned and told us that his life, too, was in danger, and he would not dare to be seen in the village again.

He would now have to rely on stealth to find out what took place in the Indian council.

Night came on, and with it came new terrors. Never before had we realized our complete isolation. The Indians gathered as near to the agency as they could without being seen, and danced and yelled and shot off their guns the whole night long. Sometimes we heard the willows along the creek bank move, or thought we saw a shadowy form creeping stealthily toward us, and then our rifles rang out, for it would not do to let them think they could surprise us. Thus the long, sleepless night passed, and morning came. Through the day we felt somewhat safer, and took our turn at watching and sleeping. The Indians seemed to do only the latter, for not a sound came from the village the whole day. This did not reassure us, however, as we feared it was only a calm before the storm.

As it grew dark, Vesnor quietly made his way to the village. He was gone for some time, and when he returned we saw by his face that he had brought bad news. We were not mistaken, for slipping up close to the tepee where the council was in progress, he had heard it decided to attack us just before daybreak, when they thought we would most likely be worn out and off guard.

Upon learning this, we decided that during the first part of the night two would watch while the remainder slept, and at three o'clock we would all get up and get ready to meet an attack. Our house was made of stone and we intended to make it cost the Indians something to take our lives.

The hours passed slowly, but at last 3 o'clock came, and we posted ourselves, leaving only the dog outside to warn us of the approach of our enemies. The minutes dragged by like hours, and while we waited hardly a word was spoken.

Suddenly the dog began to bark vociferously; we cautiously opened the door and listened. Far down the canyon we could distinguish the sound of horses' hoofs as they pounded the sand. It sounded nearer and nearer; then, suddenly it stopped; and we thought we heard voices. We waited some time and still we could hear them, though apparently no nearer than at first. Finally, Vesnor said that he would make his way in the direction from which they came, and see if he could learn anything. He was gone but a short time, though it seemed hours. "Indians plenty mad," he said. "They havem big talk. All Indians say to other Indian, 'You go first.' Other Indian say, 'No, I no go first, you go.' I think may-be-so they plenty scare."

We could only hope that this question of precedence would remain undecided until morning, but we did not relax our vigilance until the sunlight commenced to creep slowly down the walls of the canyon.

We now began to feel reassured, though we dreaded to think of having to pass another night before we could hope for aid.

The day passed without incident, except that a small party of Indians were seen approaching the agency during the morning. We placed ourselves where we were sure we could be seen and waited to see what they would do. As they still approached, we determined to take no chances, and leveled our guns and fired. The bullets struck the ground in front of them. Instantly they turned and disappeared in the bush, and we saw no more Indians all day.

As night was coming on and we were preparing for another vigil, our attention was attracted by the dog barking and running up the canyon. Our hearts sank within us, as we thought that the Indians had outwitted us after all and had gained a position on the canyon wall in our rear.

We seized our guns and waited breathlessly. The canyon in our neighborhood was exceedingly narrow and the high walls rising to a height of almost four hundred feet only a few rods from our house made the darkness almost impenetrable. We heard footsteps and lifted our guns and pointed them in the direction from which the sound came. Suddenly, from somewhere in the darkness a voice cried out in good English, "Hello, there! Don't shoot! We've come to help you."

Notes chapter 4

1. Also spelled Surahm, Serum, Sherum, or Cherum by various other writers.
2. Grass Springs was a particularly appropriate spot to hold this first dance which among other things emphasized the return of dead ancestors since it was the site of the most ancient Hualapai cremation areas (Manners 1974b:174).
3. Mooney in his famous study, The Ghost Dance Religion (1973:813) was misled into believing that the dance did not reach the Havasupai until 1891 and this mistake, in turn, has been perpetuated by many modern writers on the subject (e.g., see Hirst 1976:64; Spicer 1962:273; Dobyns and Euler 1967:26). 1891 was the mistaken date supplied to Mooney by a white trader who submitted to Mooney a "revision" of a "very meager and confused" story from a Hopi informant which Alexander Stephen had earlier included in a letter written to Mooney (Mooney 1973:813). However, Stephen, himself, in his journal (1969:996) records that this Hopi informant and three others had witnessed the ghost dance being performed at Supai in the year 1890 (not 1891). Unfortunately, Mooney's mistake also led Dobyns and Euler (1967:27) to discount the testimony of one elderly Havasupai woman who was an eyewitness to the introduction of the Ghost Dance to Supai and who told them that the dance had been transmitted to her tribe directly from the Southern Paiute.

4. In one of the earliest accounts of the dance among the Hualapai the time of this event was to be within "two moons" (see Dobyns and Euler (1967:48) quoting an 1889 newspaper account).

5. Both Spier (1928:266) and Whiting (n.d.131) mistakenly put the time of this event at about 1900 but it occurred during James's first visit to the Havasupai (see James 1903:248) which was listed as "over a dozen years ago" in his April 1901 article (James 1901:75). Also present at this event is the Indian agent S.M. McCowan (James 1911:191) whose account of the Ghost Dance was published in 1892 (McCowan 1892b:651) and later in 1899 (Dobyns and Euler 1967:27-28). However, in contrast to Dobyns and Euler (1967:27) who on the basis of only the 1899 version of the story mistakenly guess that this event occurred "circa 1895," McCowan clearly states in his 1892 account that this first visit to the Havasupai took place "when the Messiah craze was at its height" two years earlier (i.e., in 1890).

6. Many white Mormons had earlier participated in the Paiute dances.

7. Judging from James's description of the event this must have been perhaps the first or at least one of the first times the ghost dance songs had been sung at Supai since he (1903:252) records that at this "Peach Dance: "The "evangelist" sang over a strain of a new song. A dozen or so of the new leaders took it up, and as soon as they were fairly familiar with it, the others joined in." It also appears from his description (James 1903:250-255) that some of the Indians of Supai especially those that had been friendly to the "Whiteman" were prior to the dance not yet fully aware that the "Chemehuevi" song leader was bringing a new "gospel" to their annual harvest celebration and they did not apparently anticipate that soon after the dance began that he would begin attacking them for their friendliness to the "Whiteman." Even James himself having never seen one before seemed to be unaware that this was not a "normal" annual peach dance, which probably also helps explain why most modern scholars have not realized that this event being described took place in the late summer or early fall of 1890 not in "1895" or "1900" as some have incorrectly guessed. (See also Notes three and five for this chapter.)

8. Bass "was active in behalf of aid for the Havasupai Indians, helping to get a school start of there, obtaining medicine for them during an epidemic of measles, and even going as far as Washington to request congressional action. He carried mail between Havasu and Grand Canyon for a time, and often employed Havasupai Indians at his camp." (Hughes 1967:73).

9. James (1911:191) states that "though the Havasupai rejected this offer, it was Mr. Bass's kind efforts in their behalf that had secured it" (i.e., the offer that the Indians had now rejected) thus implying that Mr. Bass had somehow at least in part been responsible for the offer.

10. He was hired on February 1, 1892 (McCowan 1892b:652).

11. Possibly James or Bass or some of the tourists, Bass was now bringing to the Canyon. (See note 6, chapter 5).

12. Hirst (1976:66) mistakenly attributes quotations taken from this report to Bauer's supervisor, Henry P. Ewing who put his name on this report when he submitted it to Washington indicating his approval of the report not the authorship of the report. Hirst (1976:65) makes a similar mistake about the authorship of Bauer's 1896 report which he states was co-authored by Ewing and Bauer.

13. The school was apparently designed for a maximum of 46 students. Thus, it was very overcrowded and perhaps helps explain why the students there were lagging far behind their Hualapai "cousins."

14. Her supervisor, Mr. Ewing, had earlier told her that this man has been granted a leave of absence from Supai and would be away "for only one month" (Iliff 1954:90).

15. This flood apparently occurred prior to the one that later destroyed the Mooney Falls hydroelectric project. (See Iliff 1954 chapters 21 and 22)

16. This event probably occurred in the fall of 1903. (See Iliff 1954:198; Marshall 1903:13-17; Collins 1955)

17. For some reason, either deliberately or accidentally, Marshall changed the agent's name from Shelton to Stanton. (In his diary he also spells Shelton's replacement's name "Flores" (Marshall 1903: 17) rather than the correct "Floren"(Floren 1905)).

18. Both Iliff (1954:100) and James (1903:263) spell this name "Lanoman."

Chapter 5

Troubles continued to multiply for the Havasupai in the years that followed the departure of Mr. Ewing and Miss Greg from their positions of authority over the Havasupai. Thus in 1905, the Havasupai superintendent, Albert W. Floren (1905:163) records that:

> Owing to frequent destructive floods during the last 15 months and the visitation of measles in the most virulent form, the general conditions of the Havasupai is (sic) not what one would wish to see…

But then trying to sound as positive about the situation as possible then adds (pp. 163-164):

> Through it all, however, they have done the best they could, making use of every available resource with a fortitude certainly commendable. Up to the present there has been but little suffering from want of food….
>
> The Havasupai Indians have a system of farming in a measure peculiar to this canyon, and while much can be done to lead them away from their slovenly methods of farming, I find that two or three hundred years of experience with wind and flood has taught them many things the white man has to learn as well, even though he is obliged to learn them from an Indian. For example, there is not a 15-year-old schoolboy in the village, if one were to undertake to build and anchor any sort of water-wheel contrivance in Cataract Creek, but would say, "crazy, no good," and yet agents, coming into the canyon for a few hours, grasp the whole situation so entirely that turbine wheels and electrical plants, are recommended with the utmost confidence as to their practicability. Either contrivance would have been floating about in the gulf of California more than once during the last [12] months.
>
> The health of these Indians has been good the past year. The decrease in population of about 37 in the last 15 months is almost wholly due to the above-mentioned scourge of measles. A few very old Indians also have died. There have been but few births.
>
> The morals of the Havasupai Indians, I think, will compare favorably with any tribe in the United States, or for that matter with most white communities. Not a drop of liquor, so far as we know, has been drank (sic) on the reservation. Not a complaint of theft, and only one or two frivolous broils or fights. They pay their debts with scrupulous exactness. We lay their excellent habits to their seclusion and remoteness from the influences of the white man. I am told they have no "cuss" words in the Havasupai language. The Havasupai have always been self-supporting.

And by June 30, 1906, the population of Supai declined by another 8 individuals to what was to become the record historic low of 166[1], a precipitous drop from the year 1903 when the population numbered 237 (Harrison 1906:179; Spier 1928:99). However, on July 1, 1906, a physician was sent to live in Supai and perhaps either through his work or merely the fact that many of the least disease resistant genotypes had died, the population decline ceased (Henderson 1928:17; Spier 1928:99,209; Martin 1966:22; Harrison 1906:178). Still, by the year 1919, the population had only increased to 177 (Spier 1928:98) and by 1928, to only 186 (Henderson 1928:6) probably in part due to continuing outbreaks of measles, whooping cough, tuberculosis, and syphilis coupled with a serious shortage of women of childbearing age[2] (Henderson 1928;17; Spier 1928:99,209).

However, by 1906, the economic health of the surviving Supais did seem to be improving though the doctor-agent (he called himself Superintendent and Physician) stationed at Supai complained that in the canyon, "Not all available land is utilized, and the cultivated area produces only about one-third as large a crop as the land is capable of producing" (Harrison 1906:178-179). But he was quite pleased with the Indians' economic "progress" in the raising of livestock stating (Harrison 1906:179):

> The Havasupai Indians are good workers, and are eagerly sought after by surrounding ranchmen; but their love for their canyon home prevents their remaining away very long at a time.
> These Indians have a nice start of horses and derive quite a little income from their sale.
> One young man was employed by a ranchman near the reservation for a period of two years, and when he returned he bought a small number of cattle, which he very carefully cares for and which are increasing rapidly. He recently bought 30 head of cattle to increase his herd. This has all been done by his own effort, and his personal effort and success are sure to be silent but effective instructions for this little band of Indians.

And though this doctor-agent lamented that there "never has been any missionary work done among this tribe" and that the records in his office "show that school was in session but a part of the school term of last year" he then adds that, "The children seemed bright and active mentally and physically and seem anxious for school" (Harrison 1906:179).

But it was a major event that occurred in 1908 that seem to be the best omen of a coming period of revitalization of the Havasupai economy for when the Coconino National Forest and the Grand Canyon National Monument were created out of the old Grand Cañon Forest Reserve, the Indians were granted "free permits" to "graze… cattle" on over 100,000 acres of the newly created national forest (Hirst 1976:74).

However, in the predawn hours of January 2, 1910[3] when luckily only five families of Indians remained in Cataract Canyon,[4] the "gods of nature" again in their "anger" struck Supai filling the canyon "from wall to wall,"[5] destroying the government school building and agency house as well as every home in the Indian village (Anonymous 1910:17; Hirst 1976:75). Also, much of the topsoil from the valley's farms was washed away and "about twenty" horses and "one feeble, blind" lady were killed (Hirst 1976:75).

There had been heavy snow storms that winter on the plateau and by early January, one Havasupai states that just before the flood, the snow was "about 4 feet deep" up there, but that "then it got warm and it rained all the time for five days" melting the snow so that "there was water all over" (Emerick 1954a:75). This Indian then met some Hualapais who told him and his companion that:

> … a flood washed away everything in Supai. All the hogans. All the crops and some horses and people. The next day we went back to Pine Springs and I told Anjelik (his wife) what I heard those Walapais say and we were scared for all those relatives down here. We saw some Supais on the Walapai Trail and they didn't have no bedding. They didn't have nothing. They told us a whole lot of water came down through the canyon early in the morning and it washed everything away. That water all came at one time and it was as deep as way up on the sides of the canyon. They said some people heard that water when it was coming and they hollered and people ran out of their hogans and just ran up on the cliffs and the water came through and washed away all the hogans and trees and horses and everybody's stuff. It all went down the river over those falls. They said maybe some people went down the river too.
>
> We came down here to see it and we were scared for all those people down here. There wasn't any trail and we just went over rocks and we saw where the school-house used to be, there is just some stones. The white people didn't

have any clothes and the buildings were all gone. The agent was Mr. Coe and he only had his underwear and one shoe and the lady had his nightshirt. They didn't have nothing else. Nobody had nothing left. No houses and no crops. They told us an old blind lady just stayed in her hogan when the water came and she went over the falls. Some fellows saw her hanging in a tree down there and she was dead.

Nobody had nothing to eat. Some people found some sacks of flour from where the government had them in a building that got washed away. Some of those sacks of flour got caught in some trees and brush and that's all there was to eat. All those horses and colts that got drowned got rotten and the meat wasn't good to eat.

Everybody stayed up by those ruins near the Apache Trail and they were afraid maybe there'll be more flood. After a while everybody had a meeting up there by that place and that white man, Bass,[6] wrote on a piece of paper what he saw about the flood and all the stuff gone – the horses and hogans and corn. He sent that paper to the government and he said we wanted some groceries and some tools and some bedding. After maybe two months all that stuff came down here. Every man got one shovel and a pick and a hoe and a plow and a pitchfork and a rake and some bedding. Everybody got two sacks of flour and five bags of coffee and some sugar and beans and salt.

Everybody was afraid to come down off those high places. They were scared maybe more water might come down here and maybe they'll be drowned and lose all their stuff. Me and Anjelik and my mother and Hanna (his stepfather) stayed up on a high place over a year. Hannah was old and he couldn't do much and I helped him. (Emerick 1954a:75-77).

Thus, according to this eyewitness, it was the "do-gooding" tourist promoter, Bass, who "saved the day" for the Havasupai rather than the government agent and his wife who fled from the canyon just as they were preparing to turn over their duties to a new incoming superintendent and his family (Anonymous 1910:17). The new agent also, after assessing the situation, decided that "there was nothing left of Supai for him to superintend" and thus "took his family back to the Truxton Canon (sic) school to remain for the present" (Anonymous 1910:17). However, by April of that year the government decided to rebuild the school and housing for the schoolteachers but this time downstream in a much wider part of the canyon. Fifty dollars was pay to the "owner" of a five acre parcel of land in this section of Supai and a large tent was put up on it to serve as a schoolhouse until the new permanent building could be completed (Hirst 1976:75-76; Wampler 1959:82). Most of the building activity on the new schoolhouse and other government buildings in this area of the canyon was completed by 1912 and all of these buildings were reported as still being used in 1959 although not in all cases for their original purpose (Wampler 1959:82).

Also, beginning shortly after the flood, according to Mark Hanna, an eyewitness to the event (Emerick 1954a:82-84,86), the government initially supplied the materials for the construction of five houses at Supai and the loan of a government wagon to bring the materials from Seligman to the Hilltop but the Indians who wanted the houses, themselves brought the construction materials from Seligman to Supai and helped each other with some assistance from the schoolteacher to "put them up." [7] Other house materials were later brought in (but all before the year 1919 according to Hoover (Hirst 1976:76)) to bring the total of this "new style" Indian house in the canyon to 18 according to an official government report (Henderson 1928:10) although the much later writer Hirst (1976:76) claims without documentation that the maximum number of these houses had only been 15, a number which is certainly wrong since in 1953 Emerick (1954a:59) discovered that 17 of these pre-1919 houses were still being used. However, the Indians for many years used these houses only for storage purposes and refused to live in them, claiming that they were "too hot in summer and too cold in winter" (Hirst 1976:76) although a government official writing in 1928 thought that this claim was only a "plausible (excuse) for continuing to live the primitive Indian life" (Henderson 1928:11). And, Iliff (1954:29-30) states concerning an earlier reluctance by the nearby Hualapais to occupy similar but somewhat smaller government housing:

> The government had erected flimsy board shacks at an expense of fifty dollars each, and the people had tried to live in them but the buildings were cold and drafty, and no Walapai would have boards under his feet when he might have instead the feel of good familiar earth. However, there was more than that against the cheap little one-room houses.[8] When death occurred in one of them, the government officials refused to allow it to be burned, according to the Walapai custom. So the Indians would have nothing to do with them.

Similar funeral customs appear also to have been a factor in the initial reluctance of the Havasupai to occupy this newly constructed government housing[9] but whatever the "real" reason or reasons, by 1928, three of the houses were being used as dwellings

(Henderson 1928:10-11) and by 1940-41 when Whiting (n.d.:34) did his field study at Supai, he writes:

> Most of the frame houses… are now occupied by younger people. The prestige factor of living white-style, together with a better understanding and a willingness to operate kitchen stoves, are factors in this change.

However, this slow acceptance of the "civilized" style house as seen at Supai was certainly not due as Henderson in 1928 (p.11) and others even to this day[10] have suggested to an "irrational" desire on the part of the Indians to maintain their "traditional" cultural lifestyle. Thus even by the time Garces contacted them in 1776 he reports that they had already eagerly imported horses, cows, and pieces of red "Spanish" cloth into their "traditional" cultural lifestyle (Galvin 1965:65-66) and as was earlier discussed in Chapter 3, in the 19th century the Havasupai eagerly traded their skins and food for almost any material item the outside world had to offer. Nor was the strength of "tradition" stronger in their belief system for as we saw in chapter 4, many of the Indians were in the late 1800's beginning to sense that their traditional religion had failed them so they often looked elsewhere for "new answers" to cope with their rapidly changing world. Thus, we must look more closely to explain the sometimes seemingly "irrational" way many of the residents of Supai appear to disregard and often openly oppose the "progressive" advice given to them by government personnel, missionaries, and various other "do-gooders" such as Mr. Bass.

Certainly, more puzzling to most observers than the Havasupai rejection of the flimsy, often "too hot or cold" Government housing supplied them after the 1910 flood, is their apparent opposition to almost all efforts to get them to "rationalize" and modernize their agricultural pursuits. Thus, the many repeated attempts by government agents and farmers, school teachers, and in more recent years by older Mormon missionary couples to get the Indians to modernize and increase their agricultural production have met with little success on a long-term basis and in fact by the mid 60's, the Indians were producing less of their own needed food than at any time in their recorded history. Thus, in a survey conducted in 1963–64 there were only 5 acres of gardens planted at Supai within the average plot size of merely .15 acres and these gardens produced only 2% of the food consumed that year by the Havasupai even though they were spending over 70% of their meager $350 yearly per capita incomes on food[11] (Martin 1966:67;1973a:154,156).

Most of the time those involved in these various efforts to rationalize and modernize Supai farming efforts place the blame for the failure of such programs on the laziness of the Indians caused by such factors as "sinful" living habits and the many government "handout" programs. Thus, on numerous occasions during my visits to the reservation in the 1960's and 70's, I heard very negative comments from tourists, missionaries, and certain government officials about the "lazy," "undependable" Indians at Supai who through "their lack of industry" had allowed their fields, yards, homes, trails, irrigation canals, and public buildings to "decay."

However, all such critical observers of the "obvious" social and economic deterioration that they saw occurring at Supai by the 1960's and 70's, failed to realize that any perceived lack of individual or group initiative on this and other Indian reservations can largely be blamed on many years of government attempts to "solve the Indian problem" (See Chapter 8). Thus, as we saw in the last chapter, beginning in the 1890's government agents on the reservation quickly and relentlessly undercut the authority of such a strong native leaders as Navajo who, as earlier stated, had ironically in 1881 expressed to the visiting ethnologist Cushing (1965:71) his feelings of gratitude for the coming of the whiteman who had brought metal tools and "rich garments" to make his people's life easier and more enriched.

This feeling of gratitude was, however, mixed with the awful fear that if his tiny tribe requested too large a reservation or if it sheltered refugees fleeing from the other reservations, these acts might be "offensive to the Americans" which might "endanger his own people, leading ultimately, perhaps, to their removal… (Cushing 1965:60). Thus, when an Apache, who did not want to be removed to the San Carlos reservation sought refuge among the Havasupai, Navajo although he "felt for him" said he:

> … could give him the choice of but two alternatives, -- return to San Carlos or death. The Apache, hoping Ko-hot (Navajo) would relent, replied that die he might, but return to San Carlos he never would. Ko-hot arose, then and there, without one more word, and struck him dead[12] (Cushing 1965:61)

However, as was mentioned previously in chapter 4, even this extreme act of demonstrated loyalty to the American government did not later prevent the first government farmer sent to Supai from accusing Navajo from doing everything he could to block "all government improvements" and to "prevent the younger ones from carrying out [the farmer's] instructions." And with the death of Navajo in 1898 (Iliff 1954:153; Hirst 1976:64) many of his leadership powers over community affairs passed not into the hands of his successor, Manakaja, but instead into those of government farmers, teachers, agents, and outside white "do-gooders" such as Mr. Bass. Still, this rule by outsiders has never been fully accepted by many Havasupai who through the years have either actively or passively opposed various "community improvement" programs, thus leading to a situation in Supai where most individuals now try to maximize their own or their extended family's control over reservation resources often to the detriment of other individuals or families or to the community as a whole.

However, not all of this desire to pursue one's own or family self-interest over what is best for the community as a whole is due to white influence since even before the coming of the government agents, farmers, and teachers to Supai, there had been competition for parcels of irrigable land which when described in 1881 were "carefully protected by hedges of wattled willows or fences of cotton-wood poles"[13] (Cushing 1965:34). Thus, when describing the unequal land distribution that existed between families in the year 1901, Iliff (1954:116) states:

> Regardless of how the land had been distributed when the People of the Blue Water settled in the canyon, through inheritance some individuals had acquired more land than they could till, and it was loaned or rented to friends or relatives. There were a few whose plots were no larger than the floor of a room...

Fruit trees, too, from the earliest recorded times were privately owned, sometimes independently of the land upon which they grew (Spier 1928:233; Martin 1966:72) and again the distribution of these trees among the various families has always been unequal. And even the sharing of food had "traditionally" apparently long been largely the result of personal rather than community wide decisions and usually only involved close relatives and friends so that hunger and theft of crops was not unknown as early as the 1880's (Emerick 1954a:A-4,5).

Ironically, the continual crusade by various government agents to eliminate the "waste" associated with the aboriginal Havasupai funeral customs which is described in the government report already quoted in chapter 4, that "when an Indian dies his property is all destroyed, his camp burned, fruit trees cut down, and land turned out to grow up in brush, and his family goes to one of the neighbors to live..." (Perkins 1902:163), removed the most powerful indigenous control over this attempt by each extended family to maximize its resource holdings at the expense of its neighbors[14].

However, even if these scarce resources would have been more equally distributed among the various extended families ("camps")[15] it is still doubtful that the early utopian dream of government planners to create a self-sufficient agricultural community at Supai would have succeeded given the alternative economic options that have through the years been available to the Havasupai to replace their earlier lifestyle which as Whiting (n.d.:77-78) correctly points out was basically a non-agricultural way of life with an "agricultural supplement." Thus, we often today make the same ethnocentric mistake as did those early government officials in assuming that people given the option a becoming "successful" farmers will automatically choose this way of life because of the "increased leisure time" and "security" it will bring them, not realizing that all modern studies (e.g., see Lee 1969:74) of so-called "primitive" hunting and gathering people have revealed that there is often more leisure time and more security associated with the hunting-gathering economy than with an agricultural way of life.

Certainly, this was the case at Supai since we do not need to search far in the literature to discover the many reasons why the Indians living there through the years have not made a greater commitment to agricultural production. Thus, in Mark Hanna's autobiography (Emerick 1954a:9) we discover that even in the 19th century there were years with crop failures so severe that the people were forced to consume even their seed corn and seek refuge among their Hopi friends. And even though it was true that there were years when "everybody had a lot to eat" (Emerick 1954a:A46), this often misled various short-term observers to mistakenly write such things as:

> ...(Supai) with its abundance of food and carefree atmosphere formed a strange contrast to the Wallapai community, where hunger nibbled at the edges, and poverty and sickness stalked within. Contentment, even happiness permeated the village. Secure in their homes, crop failures unknown, store houses filled, the People of the Blue Water very naturally remained loyal to their gods, who, from the Days of Old, had watched over the Havasupai families and provided for their welfare (Iliff 1954:145).

In reality, these years of plenty were often followed by years of massive shortages of cultivated crops due to floods, spoilage[16], late frosts[17], or in earlier years, enemy raids. Nor was recovering from such shortages always as easy as was the belief of the writers of those early government reports that we examined earlier in chapter 4. For as Emerick(1954a:18, A-78) states "most" fruit trees were destroyed in the 1910 flood which also "completely washed away" most Havasupai farms "leaving only gravel in their wake (Hirst 1976:75). And after the massive floods of the late 19th and early 20th centuries lowered the riverbed in relation to the neighboring fields, the farmers of Supai were required to greatly increase their labor to bring waters again to their fields through the construction of an elaborate irrigation system in contrast to the building of simple dams which had earlier effectively controlled the diversion of water from the stream (Martin 1966:16-17).

Also, even in "good" years, Supai farmers must constantly wage battles against numerous bugs and rodents that attack the corn, beans, squash, and melon plants in the stored harvest (Emerick 1954a:17-20; Martin 1966: 75-76; Iliff 1954:114) and flocks of birds that attempt to "harvest" peaches and other fruit (Emerick 1954a:19-20; Whiting n.d.:64). Squash bugs in particular were dreaded since the wilt they carry can some years completely destroy the melon or squash crop (Martin 1966:76). And by the 1960's, the invasion of Bermuda grass into Supai fields has greatly multiplied the labor needed to farm in the canyon (Martin 1966:73; 1973a:157). Also, damage or theft of crops by other residents of Supai, at times, has in the past been reported, usually motivated by hunger or the desire for revenge (e.g., see Emerick 1954a:A-4-5; Iliff

1954:124-129). And finally, perhaps due to such things as changes in soil fertility, weather patterns, etc., acknowledging that crop failures sometimes occur for purely unknown reasons, as one Supai farmer fatalistically commented that some years "stuff (just) didn't grow good" (Emerick 1954a:A-180).

To these "acts of nature" we can also add several important social, economic, and political factors which have especially during the reservation period discouraged many Supai residents from investing large amounts of time and labor in agricultural pursuits. Thus, the reservation system here as well on many other Indian reservations while protecting the Indians' remaining prime farmland from falling into non-Indian hands has at the same time almost completely insulated the individual land "owners" from the ordinary economic and political pressures that in other areas of prime farmland have tended to shift land ownership into the hands of those who are able to maximize production from the land.[18] Thus freed from the pressures of property taxation, the "owner" of the piece of Supai property is usually free to exploit the land he or she "owns" as little as she or he wishes without the fear of losing control over it even when, as was the case of eight individuals in 1964, he or she no longer lived on the reservation (Martin 1966:58). And by the mid-sixties even though lip service in casual conversations was still being given to the notion that ownership or control of land should rest on use as it had in the old days, "the Tribal Council, in response to pressure from the land owners,… asked for the deletion of the clause in the Constitution and bylaws that provides that land unused for two or more years may be reassigned to needy individuals" (Martin 1966:58-59). Therefore, ambitious Havasupai, often have not (as they would have been able to do in the non-reservation world) been able to take advantage of the economic neglect, mistakes, or misfortunes of others to expand or consolidate their land holdings at Supai. And such individuals even if they have fathers (or other relatives) with sizable holdings that they have a chance of someday inheriting, often through their inpatient, ambitious plans and actions alienate such family heads thus leading to power struggles which the ambitious son usually loses (especially if his father is still relatively young) leaving him without an inheritance. Instead, less ambitious, "more manageable" sons usually eventually inherit the land of their fathers (or other relatives) and continue the marginal land use patterns established by their ancestors (Martin 1966:123-128). This "laziness and lack of personal initiative" on the part of the son selected as heir thus ensures that the father even after his physical powers wane will still have some control over the land use patterns and the flow of resources in his camp (Martin 1966:48). Thus, those individuals who are more "ambitious" usually turn to sources of income outside of the camps controlled by their fathers. And even those less ambitious sons who remain behind often have little incentive to labor diligently for their fathers, growing corn and other crops, since all produce grown usually must join the camp's common pool of resources and it has been estimated that by the mid-60s, the value of food produced at Supai per hour of invested labor was as low as 16 cents (Martin 1973:158)!

To reduce labor costs and increase yields would not only require that individual land "owners" combine their scattered, small holdings of land[19] and agree to share labor and rewards but would also necessitate a massive outlay of money and much additional labor to regrade the land, improve the irrigation system, and purchase needed farm machinery and chemicals (Martin 1973a:160; F.N. 1980). Not even if such a "cooperative" farm could be created despite the present tendency at Supai to maximize individual and family self-interests at the expense of others, it is not certain that such an experiment would succeed any better than those attempted in many Communist countries where small private plots rather than the larger collective farms often continued to supply the bulk of the locally available food. Thus, without the religious zeal of such individuals as those who participated in the early kibbutzim experiments in Israel, such a venture at Supai like most similar attempts throughout the world would probably result in production losses rather than gains.

Not surprisingly then, as other income producing opportunities increased on and off the reservation, the amount of farmland in crop production declined from its high point under extreme B.I.A. pressure in the mid-1930s of about 60 to 70 acres to only 8.2 acres in 1964 (Martin 1966:20,64). Thus, in addition to performing much off-reservation work for ranchers, miners, etc., many Havasupai Canyon residents began to find other employment opportunities right at Supai doing such things as supplying wood and food to the miners, building trails and buildings for the government, repairing flood damage, and providing services for the school and agency. However, by far more important than any of the above was the increasing demand through the years by miners, government officials, and tourists for packing services which could only be supplied by those camps "owning" enough canyon land to at least marginally support strings of pack animals. And packing has always been viewed by most Havasupai as being superior to other forms of labor since it perpetuates many of the same features that made the old hunting and gathering way of life so easy, dependable, and satisfying such as:

1. Horses, in contrast to most other livestock, require minimal care, especially the varieties that through many years of natural selection have become well adapted to the heat and meager food and water resources of the Grand Canyon area.[20]

2. Packing requires minimal physical exertion except for brief periods when the cargo is loaded or unloaded and is certainly easier work with less worry than farming.

3. The troublesome Bermuda grass that has invaded the fields of the Supais that is a curse to those who tried to farm, for packers is instead a blessing in the form of a permanent carefree wild pasture which their horses can exploit.[21]

4. Packing gives the packer greater mobility, variety, and adventure in his life than working all day in a small field[22] (although as we shall later see, packing on the same trail day after day can become somewhat boring).

5. Packing allows the Indian an easy way to exploit the energy resources of the dry upper canyons and plateaus since he can bring in fat animals from these marginal areas, overwork and underfeed them while packing, and then return them to these dryer areas to recuperate (Martin 1973a: 156).

6. Packing allows the Havasupai male a chance to identify more fully with the romantic folk hero of the old West – the cowboy. Thus, it is no surprise that "western dress" is the accepted standard of male attire at Supai nor is

it puzzling that the major feature of the annual peach dance festival is today a western-style rodeo.

7. Packing also gives the Indian a sense of independence and control over his own destiny since at Supai, packers through the years have strongly maintained their freedom to choose when they will accept or reject a packing request, a practice which has often frustrated both that tourist manager at Supai and many stranded tourists at the hilltop.[23]

Thus, because of the prestige associated with packing and the control of the land-base that makes this way of life possible, the family head who packs usually also is able to maintain strong control over the labor and income of all those subservient to him in his camp. And, the son wishing to remain in line to someday take his father's place as a landowner and packer is required to share his income and labor with the entire household unless he is allowed by his father to pack at which point:

> … the earnings are his (the son's) contribution to the household purse is just that – a contribution. Thus to allow a son to pack with the family horses reduces the household's purse and creates another purse within the household. When this occurs, it marks the beginning of the decline of the household head… Hence, vigorous family heads seek to control their own pack strings (Martin 1973a:158).

Hence, especially ambitious sons are usually forced to look elsewhere for ways to excel, especially if they reach maturity while their fathers are still relatively young and in good health. And even younger sons who are usually willing while still young to help their fathers, mothers, and sisters with the preparation of the family garden and do some weeding:

> Later, as they mature… begin to resent their father's domination of the horses and their own economic dependence. They come to want economic independence, their own income and resources, while their wives grow to want their own households (Martin 1973a:158).

And, since packing is a less strenuous way to exploit the land than farming at Supai, the household head by packing rather than farming is able to maintain his control over the household and its physical and human resources for a much longer period of time than if he exploited the land for its agricultural potential. Thus, at times, even an ambitious younger son often looks elsewhere for employment either on or off the reservation as he grows impatient for his father to weaken and/or die especially if he fears that he will lose his inevitable struggle at that time for power over the camp's resources with his brother(s). And even if he should win this battle, he will invariably choose to exploit the camp's land for its packing rather than food producing potential so that he too can maximize the duration of his control over the camp's limited land base and other resources. Thus it is not altogether surprising that by 1964 Supai residents devoted almost 40% of what little acreage they planted that year (8.2 acres) to the growing of alfalfa for their horses[24] rather than human food despite the fact that that year the Indians of Supai spent over 70% of their meager cash income on food (Martin 1973a:154). And when we also learn that "a field of alfalfa persists for about five years and, once in, requires only watering and cutting so that the costs in time, labor, and cash... is at a minimum" (Martin 1966:42) for a crop that yields "four or five cuttings a year" (Emerick 1954a:19), we can again realize that most Havasupai were indeed making rational choices in their land use patterns despite numerous statements to the contrary through the years by many frustrated government officials and in more recent times, tourists, and Mormon farm couples.

Corn stalks too were left standing in the fields to be ravished by the hungry horses (although much is wasted this way since the animals tread many stalks into the ground) (Martin 1966:78) as were also many of the surviving young fruit trees[25] which had been given to the members of the tribe by the Mormon Church. And even ears of corn in the 1960s were sometimes fed to the half-starved horses (Martin 1966:77). However, as Martin (1973a:160) further points out in his excellent article on the organization of land and labor at Supai, even if all the many highly visible unemployed males residing in the canyon who have access neither to the packing trade nor to the few permanent government positions could be induced to work in gardens instead of "idling away" their days, given the present social and political structure in the canyon, this would have raised average personal income levels there less than 5%.[26] Thus,

Martin (1973a:160) concludes his analysis of land use patterns at Supai in 1964 by saying:

> ... to fully use Havasupai agricultural land and labor would require large amounts of capital, the use of heavy machinery, and a radical transformation in ... family organization and land tenure. Given that the Havasupai can eat only so much fresh corn, beans, and squash and that to switch to other crops and more complicated modes of preservation would require more labor, the anticipated gains seem rather low in the light of the monetary and social costs. More important, since the Havasupai had neither the financial means nor the organizational and technical resources to make these changes, a fuller use of their land and labor was simply out of the question. This situation will not change until the expansion of tourism and/or wage labor either alter(s) the role of land in the family and political organization or creates a market for agricultural produce.

Furthermore, attempts by the various Government superintendents assigned to Supai through the years to rationalize land use and maximize agricultural production there, have always been viewed by many Havasupai "landowners" as part of a long-term scheme to seize control of their lands and ultimately dispossess them, a fear which seemed to be further supported when in 1939 under the Indian Reorganization Act, a tribal council was formed at Supai with constitutionally granted power to reassign land "ownership" and to seize land for public purposes (Martin 1966:27,158). And as it became increasingly obvious to the landholders that by its nature the Council tended to be dominated by "younger, more articulate men skilled in English and having a superior knowledge of the outside world" (Martin 1966:28) (or in other words, often those individuals who controlled very little, if any, of the reservation's lands), their fears intensified especially when in 1963 the B.I.A. tried unsuccessfully to manipulate the Council to seize some "unused" land for the creation of a new overflow campground for tourists (Martin 1966:158-165). Therefore even though several landholders had unemployed sons who would have benefited from the wage labor that the project would have provided, their support for it was not enough to overcome the opposition of the majority of the landholders who feared that if they allowed this seizure to take place, they, too, at some future date might lose their lands to a similar "development project" and thus lose the last source of "independence" left to them (Martin 1966:27-28). Hence, as Martin (1966:28) points out:

... whenever the B.I.A. makes a strong effort to manipulate land through the Council, the landholders react by denying the validity of the Council's jurisdiction and, by extension, the rights of the community, since the Council is the paramount community level institution....

The reaction to B.I.A. control of the Council and the Council's constitutionally defined control of land has thus been to emphasize individual and/or family rights in land....

It is, therefore, highly ironic that many observers have mistakenly felt that the stubborn refusal of Havasupai landholders to endorse and support community wide economic development projects is the direct result of the Indians' "irrational" desire to cling to the "slothful" patterns of their ancestors[27] when in reality the development of their present extreme emphasis on individual and/or family rights over what is best for the community as a whole only mirrors that found in today's modern American society. Certainly, one does not have to search far in nearby non-reservation rural and urban areas to find similar violent "irrational" protests by individuals and groups whose control over property is being threatened by such proposed public projects as highway construction or urban "renewal."

Notes Chapter 5

1. Spier (1928:99) apparently has some doubts about the accuracy of this number but I found no reason to suspect that this number is less accurate than others given in these early government reports. Indeed, the decline in the population at Supai due to disease may have been much higher than the official government figures indicated since a fairly reliable eyewitness, Mark Hanna, in his autobiography states that in one three-week period sometime between the 1903 census and that of 1905 "over a hundred people died" (Emerick 1954a:58). But as Emerick points out in a footnote concerning the statement, "Mark may will have been counting among the dead, those people in the canyon who would not appear in the Havasupai census such as Walapais and those whose fathers were Walapai."

2. In 1906 there were 100 males in the Supai population but only 66 females (Harrison 1906:178) and although by 1919 the ratio had changed to 98 males and 79 females, there were more females than males in the oldest age group and about equal numbers of males and females below the age of 20 and above the age of 45 so that Spier (1928:209) estimated that "between the ages of twenty and forty-five... there are twice as many men

as women." He also suggests that this possibly might be due to "loss in childbirth." (That such loss occurred is documented by Smithson (1959:126) but other factors may have also at times selectively eliminated females from the population during the 1875-1930 period. For example, it has been stated that one or more of the early 1900 epidemics "killed most of the girls and young women" (Association of American Indian Affairs, Inc. n.d.:5) or perhaps fewer young women than men returned to Supai from boarding schools.

3. Some authors even as recently as 1979 (e.g., see Euler 1979:65) have mistakenly written that this flood occurred in 1911 even though an eyewitness account of this flood was published on January 15, 1910 (Anonymous 1910:17). (See also Hirst 1976:75-76 for further verification that this event occurred in 1910.)

4. The rest were on their winter outing or in boarding school.

5. Emerick (1954a:A-76) estimates that the flood crested at 30 to 40 feet above the normal level of the creek.

6. This indicates that it may have indeed been Bass who had been responsible for at least some of the "many false reports" that had been sent to the Indian Office concerning A.M. McCowan in the early 1890's (see chapter note 11 in chapter 4). And Bass obviously was still actively involved in Havasupai affairs as least as late as the year 1910.

7. Although the government was supplying these construction materials in anticipation that the Havasupai wished to obtain them to create family home replacements, it appears that the natives valued them more to be able to build useful storage units.

8. The houses at Supai had two rooms according to Henderson (1928:10) but in commenting on these same houses later in 1948, Breed (1948:662) states that "some have two rooms, but most have one large room...." Thus, either Henderson was mistaken or perhaps some families had "remodeled" their houses to create one larger room out of two smaller ones.

9. Thus, many years after the construction of these houses, even though the burning of a dead person's house had been suppressed by heavy government pressure, on at least one recorded occasion the dead person's friends and relatives felt obliged to "tear down" the house in which the death had occurred even though at the time of her death, this house was not even owned by her (Emerick 1954a:173). And the apparent mystery of why at least some Havasupai had labored so long and hard to secure and construct these houses (Emerick 1954a:82-84,86) to serve "merely" as storage facilities rather than living quarters is no mystery to anyone who spends some time in the campground by Havasu Falls where extreme measures must be taken to prevent ravenous squirrels from destroying one's backpack in their "greedy" search for food. Thus, although as late as 1928 only three of these dwellings were being used as

living quarters (Henderson 1928:10-11), all the rest were providing greatly needed, relatively secure, storage space for the early 20th century Havasupai, something which would have been sorely missed if the house had had to be destroyed because of someone's death.

10. During my visits to Supai, I often heard from certain government personnel and the Mormon farmers and their wives how the traditions of the Indians' "forefathers" were continually hindering economic and social "progress" on the reservation.

11. According to Martin, a small amount of this "food" money was money spent on other "consumables" such as kerosene for lanterns but "food" money did not include that spent on "other necessities" (clothing, etc.).

12. A similar event occurred in western North Carolina where a man named Tsali was hunted down and executed by fellow Cherokees in the hope that this act of demonstrating loyalty to the American government would prevent their removal from their homes in North Carolina (King 1979:174-178).

13. During my 1973 visit to the reservation when the BYU Farmer invited me to visit the house in which he was staying, I had to climb through two barbwire fences to reach it since no surrounding landowner was willing to give up even the foot or two of the land needed to create a path to this particular house.

14. This struggle to maximize individual and family self-interests at the expense of others has at times become quite violent. Thus Martin (1966:131) states that: "the home of one man was burned by his cousins and his patrilateral uncle, and he was literally chased from the canyon under the threat of death. Years later, in 1963, the same fate befell his married son when he returned and attempted to claim his family's share of the contested land."

15. "Camps" (land holding and resource sharing units) have at times included people other than those related by birth or "marriage." These are such individuals as close friends or trading partners who have chosen to pool their labor, land, welfare checks, wages and/or other sources of income with all members of the camp.

16. Mark Hanna (Emerick 1954a:A-184) records that once when he returned to Supai, "There was a lot rain when we came back here and there was some flood and some dried peaches got spoiled and Mack Putesoy got fifteen sacks of corn spoiled."

17. Mark Hanna (Emerick 1954a:A-187) records that one year: "When it was April there was some flowers on all those peach trees and then it got cold again and there was some snow down here and no fruit came on any trees that year. We only had some figs."

18. Most Americans today can trace their ancestry back to individuals who lost farmland in this or other countries for various economic and political reasons.

84

19. Even though land here at Supai usually passes from father to son, due to demographic reasons as well as white influence in the last 100 years, much land has been transmitted through women and from men to secondary male kinsmen, leading to estates consisting of scattered, small patches of land (Martin 1973a:160; Emerick 1954a:67-73). Thus in 1964, the approximately 200 acres of irrigable land in the canyon was divided into about 130 tracts controlled by 34 "land using units" (camps) (Martin 1966:67).

20. Emerick (1954a:46) records that: "A few goats and sheep have been owned by several individuals for short times, but never with any success. The animals always run off or die. A number of families also have cattle, but they are little more than an investment for surplus capital for they are only occasionally eaten and, in fact, cause a considerable amount of trouble to their owners. They are easily lost and do not survive low water seasons as well as horses do."
    However, as Mark Hanna recounts (Emerick 1954a:A-33), not even all outside horses brought to the Supai area do well there as witnessed by the trouble he had with a Navajo horse he once obtained which had so much trouble finding food and water as well as walking on rocky ground that it died.

21. Martin (1973a:157) records that throughout the growing season Bermuda grass with it deep resilient roots thrives in the moist, sunny fields of Supai.

22. In the larger American society such occupations as truck driver or flight attendant probably offer similar lures too many.

23. An example of this frustration occurred while I was at the hilltop in 1980 on the day that the annual peach dance festival was beginning. The mood of the many visitors there was extremely angry as they waited in vain all morning for the packers and their horses that had been promised them by the tourist manager. And to make matters worse when one packer and his horse did finally arrive, he came not to transport a visitor or the visitor's camp gear but instead take a large supply of alcoholic beverages to the village despite the large sign at the trailhead warning visitors: "This is a land of Peace. Please leave liquor and Firearms: they do not belong here."

24. Whiting (n.d.:75) wrote that during his 1940-41 field visit, there was even at that early date "a considerable portion of the irrigated farm land… devoted to alfalfa." And by 1964, there were 34 land using units (i.e., camps) in the canyon and 33 of these had in production 41 kitchen gardens totaling 5 acres while 12 of the 34 had planted 3.2 acres of alfalfa in 16 different plots (Martin 1966:67).

25. The resident Mormon farm couple in 1980 told me that many of the trees had earlier died of neglect (usually a lack of watering and proper planting and pruning) before their root systems were established enough to tap the high-water table of the valley.

26. Martin (1973a:160) estimated that in 1964 the total amount of produce produced in Supai was only $955. However, even if all the idle men present in the village that year could have been induced to labor in the village's gardens, this would have, at most, under the existing physical and social conditions there, only added about $3,000 worth of produce to the total personal income of the tribe that year.

27. In reality, the heavy government pressure to end the funeral custom of "When an Indian dies his property is all destroyed, his camp burned, fruit trees cut down, and land turned out to grow up in brush, and his family goes to one of the neighbors to live" (Perkins 1902:163) and the property left vacant for "at least one to three years" (Ewing 1900:203), probably hastened the development of this present extreme emphasis on individual and/or family rights over what is best for the community as a whole.

Chapter 6

...desires for such things as guns, "civilized" foods, and "cowboy" style clothing became insatiable "needs" that increasingly destroyed the last vestiges of economic self-mastery the Havasupai retained from their aboriginal past... (Whiting n.d.: 114)

Inevitably, as the strongest land "owning" family heads sought to strengthen their hold over their fields more and more "dispossessed" Havasupai males either became very dependent on members of this new "aristocracy" or turned instead increasingly to the government or outsiders for employment, protection, and material and emotional support. And as was earlier "prophesied" by General Crook (Casanova 1968:258), even before the beginning of the 20th century, gifts of food, clothing, and tools given to the Havasupai to entice them to attend school and to adopt "modern" living habits and farming techniques had already increased the dependence of almost all of the Indians on the government. Thus, Mark Hanna in his autobiography relates that in the 1890s because of the plentiful supply of corned beef and rice that the school gave him every day at noon, his mother reduced his night meal to a bowl of cornmeal so that she would not have to labor as hard finding food for the family (Emerick 1954a: A 24). And in times of crisis such as the years when major floods destroyed their crops, most Havasupai began to rely more and more on shipments of government food and clothing to relieve their suffering (e.g., see Emerick 1954a: A 77; Ewing 1899:156) and less and less on aid from the traditionally most important trading partners, the Hopi and the Hualapai.

The symbiotic relationship between the Havasupai and these two nearby neighbors although oftentimes a very close and essential one, had never been a perfect one since the same heavy rains that often brought disastrous floods to the Havasupai did not always bring increased quantities of wild game and plants to the Hualapai or a greater corn harvest to the Hopi while drought on the high plateau not only reduced the food supply for the Hualapai and Hopi but also for the Havasupai especially during the winter months when they relied very heavily on the plateau's wild food supplies for both themselves and their horses. Nor could the small acreage being farmed in the canyon yield the large supplies of food needed not only by themselves but also by their neighbors during times of drought. Thus the incoming Americans by providing government disaster relief to all three groups from sources often distant and unaffected by northern Arizona weather conditions, quickly destroyed the economic dependence these trading partners had formerly had for each other during times of crisis, while even in ordinary years, the Indians became accustomed to receiving such things as free housing materials, agricultural tools, healthcare, and Christmas presents (e.g., see Iliff 1954:118, 249; Emerick 1954a: A 41 – 42). And, as always happens in such cases, desires for such things as guns, "civilized" foods, and "cowboy" style clothing became insatiable "needs" that increasingly destroyed the last vestiges of economic self-mastery the Havasupai retained from their aboriginal past, leading Whiting (n.d.: 114) after his field visit to them in 1940 – 41 to state:

> It is apparent that the Havasupai are not today an independent social unit. To be sure they never were completely independent. The links with the Walapai for example, were very close and trade relations with the Hopi were certainly essential to the maintenance of [the] Havasupai economy. [but] Today … The group has become virtually parasitic upon white civilization, and in particular upon the Indian Service. Most of the administration of the tribe, and a considerable share of their cash income, is derived from this branch of the United States government….

However, the aid provided by the government, both as outright gifts and as income producing employment, never has been enough to meet the modern "needs" of the "relatively deprived" Havasupai, so many of the canyon's adults have often in the 20th century sought employment on nearby white ranches, at the main tourist complex on the south rim of Grand Canyon National Park, and at many other Arizona locations (see Mark Hanna's autobiography (Emerick 1954a: appendix)). But such outside contact always carried an element of risk, thus Mark Hanna in his autobiography (Emerick 1954a: A 154-55) tells how one of his friends, Frank Wilder, was "murdered" by one of the local policemen in nearby Seligman:

> We went in there to Seligman and we got some groceries and Frank Wilder wanted to stay around that place for a while and I didn't want to stay there. He

was sore about that. When we were going back we saw some car on the road and there were some Mexicans there and Frank said, "I'm going to stop and see if they got some trouble." They didn't have no gas in that car and Frank gave them some. He didn't give them a lot and they said "You come back there to Seligman with us or maybe we'll run out of gas again and we'll be stuck." I told Frank, "Don't go back there with those fellows. It's going to be dark and we got to go back there where we're camping." He said, "I'm going back there with those fellows." And we went back there with them. When we were coming into the town I saw a car with some police in it and it was behind us. I told Frank Wilder, "if you stop for that gas those police are going to make us get some trouble."

When he stopped that car in that gas station, those police got out and came over by us and he said, "Are you drunk?" And we told him, "No we're not drunk." We didn't have nothing to drink, but he said, "I think you're drunk." Then he took the rifle out of that car. It was broke and we didn't have no bullets but he took it out of there. Then he told me to get out of that car and he got in there and he drove that car away and Frank Wilder was [s]till in there.

Mark waited all night in vain for his friend to return and was finally told by a white man the next day that, "The policeman shot him last night because he was drunk and … had a gun and … tried to run off." (Emerick 1954a:A155). This statement upset Mark who after having retreated in fear to the hilltop got together with some of his Havasupai and Hualapai friends and for a while they talked about "getting" the guilty policeman possibly with the aid of a lawyer. But even though a white doctor from Kingman who examined Wilder's body found no trace of alcohol, the local townspeople in a meeting declared the policeman innocent of any wrongdoing and Mark and his friends finally decided that the matter was "all over" (Emerick 1954a: A155-157).

Also, Mark's own brother-in-law died in the Flagstaff jail after having been kept in a cell where he was forced to sleep on a wet floor for four nights (Emerick 1954a: A 88 – 89). The dead man had been accused of cattle theft after he had butchered an unbranded calf that some Supais (including Mark) said belonged to the dead man although a nearby white rancher had insisted that the slaughtered animal was his (Emerick 1954a: A 88;Hirst 1976:122).

Mark and some of his Supai friends and relatives set out to reclaim the body when they learned it had been buried in Flagstaff but their initial anger and frustration greatly increased when after digging up the "rotten" coffin[1] that the citizens of Flagstaff had used for the body, they saw that the dead man, "... didn't have no clothes on and some white man had put red paint on his face and they put some chicken feathers in his hair." (Emerick 1954a: A 89).

A trusted white friend gave Mark and his friends a big box for the body and let them use his buckboard to transport the dead man back to the hilltop from where it was packed down to a burial spot near the "first falls" (Emerick 1954a: A 89 – 90) where according to another informant (Hirst 1976:123) it was also first learned that the dead man had been castrated. Inflamed by the death of their fellow tribesman and the humiliating way his body had been treated, many Supais threatened to kill the two white ranchers believed to be most responsible for these repugnant deeds, but again these proved to be "idle" threats made by an obviously intimidated people who were according to Mark "just talking " (Emerick 1954a: A 90).

However, although often afraid now when traveling to unfamiliar locations and when dealing with unfamiliar white men, Mark and many of his fellow Supais continued to seek work not only on the nearby mines, ranches, and farms doing such things as digging for gold, cutting wood, breaking horses, planting crops, and building fences and water tanks but also in such distant locations as Phoenix where they became "chiefs" in an Indian show and in Parker where they helped construct an internment camp for Japanese Americans during World War II (Emerick 1954a: A 61–62, 66–69, 95–97, 101, 134–136, 139–144, 189–191). Still, when rumors swept through the labor force working on the Japanese internment camp that the American government was beginning to kill some of the Japanese being held there, Mark fearing for his own safety quit his job and returned to Supai later stating that:

> I didn't like to work down there no more and I was thinking maybe they'll kill some of these Indians too and I thought maybe I'll get killed down there so I told those fellows, "I'm going to quit." I told them, "I don't want to get killed." (Emerick 1954a: A191).

Thus for Mark and many other Supais like him, Supai often became a place of refuge to retreat to whenever things "went wrong" in the outside world, a behavioral pattern repeated to this very day not only by discouraged or fearful Havasupai but also by many members of other tribes which still provide such reservation "sanctuaries." In fact, the presence of such nearby refuges is often considered to be one of the most significant factors undermining the effectiveness of the government's attempts since the 1950s to solve the Indian "unemployment problem" by relocating large numbers of Indians to urban centers.[2] And it is a mistake to believe that it is only Indians that feel a need for places of refuge from the outside world as witnessed by such events as the creation of the modern state of Israel or the migration of hundreds of thousands of Mormon converts and expatriates for over a century now to the state of Utah. Nor does it take very long for this type of mentality to develop as witnessed by the reluctance of large numbers of Japanese American internees to leave their newly created "refuge centers" when the government tried to quickly close them down near the end of World War II (Spicer 1952).

Notes Chapter 6

1. According to another informant the "coffin "was just "some old carton " (Hirst 1976:122). This informant also states that this event occurred just before the snow melted in the year 1914.
2. In discussing this post-World War II official attempt to "assimilate "American Indians into the mainstream of American society Olson and Wilson (1984:153) state:

> Native Americans in the cities … encountered serious economic problems. Accustomed to free medical care, low rent, low utility bills, and limited transportation costs, they were inundated with bills and debts. Limited to low-paying, unskilled, and often seasonal jobs they were vulnerable to layoffs; they rarely had the financial resources to meet their obligations. During the early 1950s only three thousand of the thirty-five thousand relocated Native Americans found jobs in "permanent" industries, and even those jobs were closely related to Korean War production…. Of the more than thirty-five thousand people relocated between 1952 and 1960, about 30 percent returned to the reservation.

Many scholars suspect that the actual return rate was much higher than this conservative estimate since the BIA did not keep long-term records on the individuals and families being relocated to the cities. Hirst (2006: 190) states that among the Havasupai "A few … chose to try resettlement but nearly everyone -- disillusioned and lost -- returned to Arizona if not to the Havasupai reservation itself." Also, in tribes such as the Navajo many tribal members began a pattern of frequent moves back and forth between city and reservation, returning to the reservation when discouraged, lonely, or unemployed, a pattern that continues to this very day as witnessed by me during the 18 months (2013-2015) I spent as the unpaid director of an "employment resource center" on the Navajo reservation near Window Rock, Arizona.

Chapter 7

Although small numbers of adventuresome tourists had through the years visited Supai the difficulty of getting there was far from easy as was described in a May 1948 National Geographic article (Breed 1948).To get there involved a 35 mile drive on a dirt road from Grand Canyon village, the last 2 miles of which "required careful driving to negotiate a twisting rocky wash" (p, 655). This was then followed by a 14-mile trail that in the first mile and a half dropped "a dizzy 1000 feet by means of 29 switchbacks down a steep talus slope to the floor of the canyon" (p. 656). This was a new trail "built by hand by the Indians" to replace an older trail "still clearly visible on the opposite wall of the canyon [that] had been used as a wagon road by early miners" (p. 656). However, it was possible for the visitor to avoid having to drive to the Topocoba hilltop in his or her own vehicle on Tuesdays or Fridays by arranging for a ride on the mail bus and continuing into the canyon on the mail horses. On other days individuals driving to the hilltop in their own vehicles could arrange in advance for a Havasupai guide with riding and pack horses to meet them at the hilltop.

Not only did the US Postal Service benefit adventuresome tourists but also the permanent residents of the canyon since "it [was] much cheaper to mail provisions to Supai than to hire a private packhorse" (p. 662). Jack Breed, the author of this article, "was amused to see the assortment of letters, packages from mail order houses, boxes of groceries, and picture magazines that arrived on these occasions…" (p.662). Also, there were many requests coming from "ardent philatelists" who sought a return letter bearing the Supai, Arizona postmark "one of the few remaining post offices in United States accessible only by horse or muleback" (p.662).

Another observation by this author is also important in documenting the continuing importance of farming in the lives of these people in 1948. Thus Breed (1948:671) states:

> Every morning the Havasupai men and women were busy in their fields, often with several babies propped up nearby as an interested audience. Today, as in the past, they are outstanding farmers. They thoroughly irrigate and plant the 175 acres of arable bottom lands in corn, beans, and squash, their staple

crops. Delicious peaches, apricots, melons, and figs are grown also in the neat orchards below their farmlands.

At present the Havasupai maintain two dams for irrigation purposes, one above the village and the second in the dwelling area. The main irrigation ditches are one or two feet deep and perhaps 3 feet wide.... Smaller connecting ditches divert water to the fields, which are laid out in a simple pattern to facilitate irrigation to all sections.

A few important aspects of their pre-European contact way of life seemed to be continuing such as producing their highly prized tanned deer hides (Breed 1948:671). Also, many of the older generation still commonly lived in "the aboriginal mud and brush hogans similar to those of the Navajo" (Breed 1948:662) and:

To relieve that tired, run down feeling, the "Blue-green Water People" strip to breech-cloths and parboil themselves in the sweat lodge....

The lodge consists of a pit covered by tarpaulins or blankets stretched over a willow framework. Rocks are heated ... and carried inside. Bathers sprinkle water on the rocks to produce steam. Temperatures sometimes reach 150°.

Between 10-minute periods of steaming, bathers loll outside, letting sand dry on their bodies. The process is repeated four times: then the Indians leap into Havasu Creek for a cool dip and return to their fields to work with new vigor (Breed 1948:672).

On this visit after leaving Bridal Veil (Havasu) Falls, Breed (1948:659), on his way to Mooney Falls, walks through "a heavy grove of willows and cottonwoods where the buildings of a small mining camp still remain." This area between the two falls that had originally been used by the Havasupai for cremation burials "early in the 1930s" was part of a patented mining claim originally owned by a prospector named W.J. Johnson (Hirst 2006:191). The cabins Breed encountered built by Johnson and the next owner of the claim E.F. Schoeny by the Second World War although probably originally constructed to house miners were now being rented out to visitors coming to see the waterfalls as mine production fell to very low levels. However, visitation to the reservation probably essentially ceased while demand for lead "soared" during the war years and the mine was reopened for full production and "about eight or ten Havasupai" were hired as laborers (Hirst 2006:191).

The war ended and so did the demand for lead and the mine closed down. It was not long before the visitors returned so the Havasupai arranged with the mine owner, Schoeny, to rent out the cabins to these visiting outsiders giving the mine owner a share of the rental fees (Hirst 2006:191). Then according to Hirst (2006:191) "During the 1950s the National Park Service begin quiet negotiations with Schoeny to buy the claim and add it to the park, without alerting the Havasupai." Achieving a settlement with him, they then after adding it to the park "fenced off the 62 acre area and destroyed the cabins there (Hirst 2006:191) and in 1962 "made it into a public campground" (Hirst 2006:192).

Other crucial Government actions immediately after the end of the war that would forever shatter the idyllic portrayal of life in Supai as described by Breed in 1948 began two years earlier with the passage of the Indian Claims Commission Act in 1946 that "was designed to settle all further Indian land claims and complaints against the United States government by encouraging every Indian tribe to file a claim … for lands unjustly expropriated by actions of the United States government" (Hirst 2006:179). The suits submitted would then be adjudicated and each tribe would receive a financial settlement for its lost lands but as (Hirst 2006:179) points out: "The act made no provision for returning any land." Apparently, somewhat reluctantly, the Havasupai tribe filed such a claim just prior to the 1951 deadline (Hirst 2006:180).

And even more important event occurred just after the election of President Eisenhower in 1952 when in 1953 the 83rd Congress of the United States "adopted House Concurrent Resolution 108 setting forth the policy of terminating "as fast as possible" the special relationship existing between American Indians and the federal government (Brophy and Aberle 1966:vii).

For the Havasupai, after earlier attempts to encourage families to relocate to the Colorado River reservation where the government "had once thought of forcing them to live and take up life as farmers" had failed, the Bureau of Indian Affairs in 1956 began its formal program of encouraging young members of the tribe to leave their reservation and be resettled in Major American cities (Hirst 1976:226). However, Hirst (2006: 190), commenting on this new assimilation attempt, states that among the Havasupai "A few

... chose to try resettlement but nearly everyone -- disillusioned and lost -- returned to Arizona if not to the Havasupai reservation itself."

Meanwhile in 1955, a new would-be savior, Martin Goodfriend began his many years of involvement with the tribe challenging what he felt was the commonly held but very destructive equation of Supai with Shangri-la (Dedera 1971):

> ... a paradise of red rock, an oasis of turquoise waters. Removed from the clutter and clatter of civilization. Simple pleasures. Pure environment. And the friendly natives even looked a bit Tibetan.
>
> We whites – tourist, medic, photographer, ranger, anthropologist, auditor, reporter, bureaucrat, missionary, politician – were in ethnocentric agreement. The Havasupai *had it made*.

Arriving for the first time at the reservation in 1955, Goodfriend observed (Dedera 1971) that:

> Supai's homes were not quaint. They were hovels of cardboard with leaky roofs and dirt floors. No heat. No plumbing. No privacy.
>
> The school was boarded shut, It being more economical for the government to take the Supai children at age six and ship them off to boarding schools 350 miles away. Parents were lucky to get one brief communication a year.
>
> Food prices at Supai were double those of Beverly Hills.
>
> The richest Havasupai breadwinner had an income of $1500 a year. So scarce were jobs, wages for the entire tribe of 220 Indians totaled just $833 per month.
>
> Cataract Creek was Supai's bath, laundry, sewer and drinking water supply.
>
> Supai had no road, no clinic, no electricity. Out of government indifference, the one telephone was dead more often than not.
>
> When a government doctor. made his monthly trek to Supai, one-fourth of the village's population would be lined up, sick. When the doctor was gone, women bore babies in the snow, as they struggled up the trail toward the nearest hospital, 129 miles away. Infant mortality was triple the national average.
>
> The historic Supai farms lay fallow, with not 50 of 500 arable acres in production. The fences burned to heat huts in winter.
>
> With forage sparse in the narrow canyon, pack horses were being worked until they dropped. The modest tourist industry was grossly mismanaged.
>
> Frequently the village store, sole source of food, was stocked with as few as six items: soft drinks, coffee, dried beans, salt, potatoes, flour. The villagers were slowly starving.
>
> This was America in 1955 and Goodfriend was horrified.

At this point he "vowed to agitate for a better life for the Havasupai Indians" and by January 1971 he had "hiked in and out of the canyon 30 times" staying there on some visits for as long as three weeks. And when not in the canyon he had spent much of his time writing letters, making speeches, and meeting with government officials and politicians. However, until the mid 60s his efforts were met with little success and were denounced by some members of wilderness groups "for attempting to import civilization into *their* Grand Canyon". And despite having by this time gained a powerful ally in Washington, Senator Paul Fannon as well as Howard Stricklin, then Superintendent of Grand Canyon National Park and sympathetic workers in the nearby U.S. Forest Service, "as late as 1967 never had an area director of the BIA or Public Health Service visited Supai" and that year the BIA area director in Phoenix "cautioned his chief" "We could do great harm to these people by forcing change on them" (Dedera 1971). To this criticism Goodfriend responded by saying:

> "That's too goddamn bad for your precious wilderness," [he] snapped in rare anger. "A new house might deface nature, but a cardboard house defaces humans. A hunger pain in the stomach of an Indian child is no less than one in my grandchild."
> "Some more efficient way must be found to transport the things that Supai needs. A tramway? A road?" (Dedera 1971).

Not waiting for government officials to solve the many problems he saw at Supai, he began taking actions on his own (Dedera 1971). These included such things as persuading his home city, Santa Monica, to raise $5,000 for materials to construct a Community Center using volunteer labor supplied by Supai men. And to provide for the regular and cheaper delivery of fresh meat, vegetables, and baked goods to the reservation, he discovered that it would be cheaper, easier, and more reliable to mail these items to the village using parcel post stamps than making individual arrangements with packers. Goodfriend then successfully lobbied in Washington for thrice-weekly mail mule service. He also in 1968 found a much cheaper supplier for the village's butane fuel supply (e.g., For the same amount of butane for which they had paid $1,323, another dealer was willing to sell for $371) and he went all the way to Phoenix and St. George, Utah to sign up competitive food wholesalers.

However, he, alone, was able to do little to solve two of the most vexing problems facing the Havasupai in1955: the closing of the local school in the village that year and the need to create a better and faster way to transport humans and goods in and out of the canyon.

Examining first the school problem, the last qualified teacher there, Roland Herzog, strongly felt the school should be closed as did also the reservation school principal (Meador and Roessel, Jr.1962:29). At that time only between eight and 12 students were still attending the local school and the Phoenix Area Director honoring this shutdown proposal justified his decision by saying that:

> …Supai children were unable to obtain the kind of experiences necessary in order to obtain an adequate education in such an isolated spot as Supai … [adding that] … an additional factor [was] that the moral situation was extremely bad at Supai (Meador and Roessel, Jr.1962:29).

With the 1955 closure of the local school now even the youngest school-age children would be sent away to the far-off Fort Apache Boarding school. And as Hirst (2006:192) vividly describes this "Time of Despair:"

> By 1960 the Havasupai had reached a low point in their history. Their children were torn from their families during the most dependent post-infancy years and cast into a boarding school for incorrigibles, as Fort Apache was in those years. The bureau allowed other reservations their own day-schooling and only problem children were shipped off to Fort Apache – problem children and Havasupai children. The tiny Havasupai children had their money and clothing stolen, and they found no one to protect them except the older Havasupai children. They learned to be hard and crafty; few of them had the time or opportunity to learn to be Havasupai. They were constantly in and out of trouble, involved in drinking violations, fighting, and theft. The pressure fell most unrelentingly on boys, and the number of them who graduated from high school during those years can literally be counted on one hand. Girls, comparatively more sheltered, withstood the experience somewhat better, but even many of them dropped out through pregnancy or simple school violations.

And data collected by the U.S. Public Health Service demonstrated in a 1957 table listing the percent of Havasupai Indians "6 years of age and over who read English and who speak English" (Meador and Roessel, Jr. 1962:14) that shifting the education of the Supai young children from the closed Canyon school to the far-off Fort Apache Boarding School was a failed educational "improvement" experiment. Thus, although the percentage of those who could speak English had increased from 27% of those 45 or older to 94% of those between ages 18 and 44, it had dropped to 82% among those ages 6 to 17. And although the percentage of those who could read English had increased from 11% of those 45 or older to 81% of those between ages 18 and 44, it had dropped to 68% among those ages 6 to 17.

This decline in achieving the necessary communication skills for successful life in modern day America greatly strengthened the argument by Havasupai leaders that a better educational solution must be found then forcing their children to be sent to the problematic far-off Fort Apache Boarding School. Thus six years after the local school shutdown, hoping to reverse this societal and educational breakdown, tribal leaders wrote a letter to the Area Director of the Bureau of Indian affairs requesting that the school be reopened for children ages 10 years of age and under, followed by a June 27, 1961 Tribal Council meeting with Bureau Officials during which they further justified this request by telling the officials:

> The Havasupai Council would like the school re-opened in the Canyon for the younger children. The parents and the Council realize that the older children must leave to get good schooling, but the children from six through 10 should be able to go to school and live at home. When the younger children have to go to boarding school, they get extremely homesick; they become discipline problems when they return home; they can't write their parents and the schools are too far away for their parents to visit them; the Government should provide to school in the canyon for the 30 or so children who would attend it; The government has a responsibility which it should meet (Meador and Roessel, Jr.1962:21).

The bureau representatives present at this meeting remained unconvinced that the five reasons given for closing the school (i.e., Poor attendance, Difficulty in securing and keeping the teacher, Poor teaching situation, High cost of schooling, Bad moral conditions) would not also plague a reopened school adding that:

> We then commented that the attitude of the parents directly involved had generally been favorable towards boarding schools; they had sent their children to boarding school with minimum protest; but after normal homesickness the

children had been happy and had made fine progress; and that generally the parents most concerned were pleased with the present arrangements (Meador and Roessel, Jr.1962:22).

And after hearing from one concerned parent that he would be willing to send his sons away to a boarding school but not his daughter, the bureau officials ended their remarks by saying:

> We proposed the Tribe send their children to another school for another year in which time we would have a meeting to discuss the situation... (Meador and Roessel, Jr.1962:23).

And to attempt to achieve an "acceptable compromise solution" to solve one of the major concerns of tribal parents, during the summer of 1961 the Bureau of Indian affairs explored the possibility of sending Supai children to the public school in Grand Canyon where the children would not be as far from home as they would be if they continued to attend the Fort Apache school (Meador and Roessel, Jr.1962:30). However, since this possibility would require the construction of a dormitory near the school for the children, it would require the National Park Service to be willing to provide the necessary land on which a dormitory could be built. But, unfortunately, such a request was denied thus ending this attempt.

They, however, did make the suggestion that they were willing to try to see if a small dormitory might be constructed near the public school at Peach Springs, or near some other public school near Supai to make it easier for parents to visit or live near their children (Meador and Roessel, Jr.1962:22).

However, not waiting for a proposed meeting a year later to again consider this possible solution, the Havasupai Tribal Council on January 15, 1962, wrote a letter to the Indian Education Center at Arizona State University and asked for a school survey stating:

> We want to survey to determine if there is a need for a school in Supai, the kind of a school, how to get such a school, and anything else that will help our education here at Supai. We already have information about the number of children etc., which we can provide (Meador and Roessel, Jr.1962:23).

A positive response to this letter came back quickly and on March 1, 1962 a survey team from the University met with BIA officials to discuss the Havasupai School situation. At this meeting, Frederick Haverland, the Phoenix Area Director, "declared that there was no interest at that time in having a a school at Supai as most of the parents desired to send their children to school elsewhere" adding that "the moral situation was extremely bad at Supai" (Meador and Roessel, Jr.1962:29).

Not being satisfied with this negative justification for not reopening the Havasupai school, the survey team next examined the Bureau files on the Havasupai Tribe where they were "unable to find documented support" for the reasons given by Haverland (Meador and Roessel, Jr.1962:30). Then, turning to field work, the survey team held conversations with the Superintendent of the Truxton Sub-agency who told them that "lawlessness and drinking were not as severe among the Havasupai as they were among the Hualapai" and with the U. S. Public Health Service Director at Peach Springs who said "that in his estimation the drinking problem was less acute among the Havasupai than with the Hualapai" (Meador and Roessel, Jr.1962:32). And Dr. Kehle at Peach Springs told the survey team that venereal diseases were less prevalent with the Havasupai than with the Hualapai (Meador and Roessel, Jr.1962:34). Further, in a meeting with the Havasupai's themselves, one tribal member stated that:

> … if the accusations and allegations concerning the moral degeneracy of the Havasupai people were true, was it not the function and role of education to improve a community? Was it not the function and role of education to help with community problems and aid in the solution of these problems? … If these allegations are true … how could they be corrected if all outside influences directed at improvement were denied the Havasupai people? ... This man further indicated that the school could serve as a community center and could include adult classes and be designed to meet the needs of the Havasupai people…. He seemed to feel that the very fact of denying the Havasupai a school the government was compounding the problems instead of working toward a solution of these problems (Meador and Roessel, Jr.1962:32,33).

Turning now to the question of whether or not as was suggested by two Bureau of Indian Affairs officials that it was the grandparents who wanted the children to live at home while attending school at Supai – not the parents, a supposition strongly rejected by tribal leaders, a three-man survey team from Arizona State University went to Supai to answer this apparent contradiction (Meador and Roessel, Jr.1962:41). There after interviewing all the parents, every one of them said that they wanted to have a school at Supai and there was no indication that they were feeling pressure from grandparents to give this answer to the survey team (Meador and Roessel, Jr.1962:46,47). And all of the parents "responded that they would send their younger children to the school at Supai If it were re-opened" (Meador and Roessel, Jr.1962:47). However, all also agreed that older students would need to be sent elsewhere even though there was no uniformity in the answers given by parents as to which grade such an outmigration should occur with answers ranging from fourth grade to ninth-grade with the grade level most frequently mentioned as being the highest grade that should be taught at Supai being the sixth grade (Meador and Roessel, Jr.1962:44,47)

In the final chapter entitled "Conclusions and Recommendations" of the survey team's May 1962 published report (Meador and Roessel, Jr.1962:49-53) addresses itself to the five major objections to reopening the school at Supai listing both the objections and its response to these objections on page 53:

1. The parents do not want their children to attend school at Supai. They want them to go to school off the reservation.
    The Survey Team talked to virtually all the parents of the children who would be eligible for the school at Supai. None of them indicated that they would not send their eligible children to that school. As a matter of fact, most of them indicated a strong wish that their younger children would not have to be sent away to school.
2. A qualified teacher could not be found who would take the position.
    The Survey Team knows of several qualified teachers who would like to teach at Havasupai.
3. The number of children who would attend the school would be too few to justify having a school there.
    The Survey Team feels you would have at least enough students for one teacher. One-teacher schools are not considered ideal, but the alternative to not having a school at Supai is farther from the ideal.
4. The moral climate is undesirable[1].
    The Survey Team believes the immorality of the Havasupai has been exaggerated. As a matter of public policy we do not separate children from their parents unless their home environment is extremely unwholesome. In the opinion of the Survey Team the home environment among the Havasupai does not even approach this point of unwholesomeness.
5. The cost of a school at Supai would be prohibitive.

The construction, maintenance, and operation of the school at Supai would all be high. The Survey Team is of the opinion that the additional cost would be justified because it would provide a better all-round educational program for the students and society.

And, although the possibility of establishing a public school at Supai as part of a Arizona school district was explored, such attempts were abandoned since the survey team concluded that because of prohibitive cost to nearby non-reservation taxpayers "…there is no reason to believe that this would will take place until the Havasupai are more powerful politically than they seem to be at the present time" (Meador and Roessel, Jr.1962:52). Thus, in its concluding statement the Survey Team recommended the re-opening of the Bureau of Indian Affairs school at Supai as being:

> "the only one that seems within the realm of possibility for the next few years … the only alternative which could be achieved without creating ill will in the process and thereby put the school off to a bad start … the only alternative which would put this school under the direction of men who have a great deal of experience in comparable circumstances." (Meador and Roessel, Jr.1962:52).

Undoubtedly, at least in part to the work of this Survey Team, the fight by the tribe to reopen their school succeeded two years later in 1964. However, "with only two grades, the children were still forced to leave the canyon by eight or nine years of age to attend school at Fort Apache" (Hirst 2006:194). Still, this partial victory was enhanced in 1967 with the arrival of Steve and Lois Hirst to operate a Head Start program (Hirst 2006:276). And in the 1960s, as will be discussed more fully in the next chapter, a new alternative to the Fort Apache school was provided for Supai's older students by the "Indian Placement Program" of The Church of Jesus Christ of Latter-day Saints (More commonly known as the "Mormon" Church[2]).

However as will be seen in chapter 9, the reopening of the school at Supai did not end the problem of providing a successful educational experience for every Havasupai child.

Notes Chapter 7

1. Hirst in a section of his book (2006:192,193) titled "A time of despair" States that "by 1960 the Havasupai had reached a low point in their

history…. [where] … Drinking and fighting became rampant in the little canyon village…. The late summer Peach Festival had become an occasion for drunkenness and violence. Suicide, an act almost unknown among the Havasupai began to occur…. Occasions arose when individuals would stage an armed standoff with a rifle during an alcoholic bout or would run through town threatening to use a knife on anyone they encountered. Gas and glue sniffing became widespread among young people, and their despairing parents ceased offering them any direction." This he felt was the result of their children being "… torn from their families during their most dependent post-infancy years and cast into a boarding school for incorrigibles, as Fort Apache was in those years…. The tiny Havasupai children had their money and clothing stolen … they learned to be hard and crafty … they were constantly in and out of trouble, involved in drinking violations, fighting, and theft." Martin (1966:183-187) on the other hand in describing the reasons for the great increase in drunkenness and extreme violence occurring in Supai in 1964 gives as the major new factors "the "introduction and increasing availability of alcohol … the demise of chiefly authority, and the ineffectual B.I.A. police and court…." Thus "during 1964, fairly serious incidents occurred about once every five weeks. These incidents usually begin with a drinking bout and ended in, at best, a fist fight and minor injuries and, at the worst, shooting and assaults and assault and battery with axes, knives, etc."

2. The current Church Prophet strongly wants to have all members and outsiders stop calling the church, "the Mormon Church" but instead always refer to it as "The Church of Jesus Christ of Latter-day Saints."

Chapter 8

Although the extremely scenic waterfalls had attracted adventuresome tourists since the promotional efforts of Bass in the 1890s and several feature articles in the National Geographic magazine[1] in the decades after, the real upturn in tourist visitation occurred followed such publications as the July, 1963 special issue of Arizona Highways that devoted most of its content including cover and many other full color internal images to a "Havasu Adventure" (Griffith 1963:9-39; Chemi 1963:40-43). Being an avid lover of wilderness adventures (especially hikes to waterfalls) since my early youth, after obtaining a copy of this issue, I was completely obsessed by the overwhelming desire to find a way to view and swim beneath the spectacular waterfalls of Havasu Creek. However, it was not until the fall of 1967, as I was about to begin my field research for my Ph.D. degree in Ajo, Arizona, I was able to fulfill this desire by taking my wife and two-year-old daughter on a wilderness vacation trip. And though my research in Arizona had focused on the problems that Native Americans were having living in a copper mining town, on this first trip I had no intention of looking at the problems that the Havasupai were experiencing in their canyon home.

That fall we were the typical hiking tourists that had arranged to have our backpacks carried down to our campsite by one of the Havasupai packers. And in common with most tourists our interaction with the local residents was minimal as we greatly enjoyed life in the campsite and in the nearby pool beneath Havasu Falls. I even completed the fearful climb down to the base of Mooney Falls although both Karen and little Linda stayed behind at the top of the falls. The weather was perfect during this first visit and the only major imperfections in this paradise were an occasional bite of a horsefly and the omnipresent campground squirrels that chewed through my backpack to get at our food.

This would be the first of the six visits I would make to this reservation in the years between 1967 and 1980. Little did I realize on my first visit to Supai that three years later in the summer of 1970 I, too, would join the ranks of the many would-be "saviors" of the Havasupai.

However by now, the many articles with their vivid images of the spectacular falls had created a massive influx of new visitors to the reservation, which immense increase in visitation while providing increased revenue for the tribe, at times such as the Easter Week in 1970 (Rukkila 1970) brought also severe environmental damage to the National Park Service campground. That week over 2000 individuals had passed through the village on their way to the campground overwhelming its capacity "…camping above Havasu, below Mooney and some in the mines and caves along the canyon walls." (Rukkila 1970:9,11). In an attempt to deal with the crowds coming to Supai, estimated to have been 16,000 in 1969[2] by the Park service, the government had "provided a ranger station, new outhouses, chlorinated drinking water, picnic tables, charcoal grates And campground rules such as no wood gathering and pack your garbage out." (Rukkila 1970:8,9). However, during Easter week 1970 no Park Ranger had been present at the campground to enforce such rules. Then, as now, due to continuing underfunding of the Park Service, the Park Ranger assigned to Supai, arrived there a few days after the crowds had departed having been kept busy Easter Weekend at Grand Canyon National Park his other assigned location. (Rukkila 1970:9).

Commenting on the environmental damage left after the crowds had departed the campground, the Ranger said, "Unfortunately, Havasu gets a lots of people who don't have any concern for tomorrow and for the people who come later." (Rukkila 1970:11). Especially troubling to the Park Service was that many backpackers bring in "everything but the kitchen sink" but faced with the much more difficult hike up to the rim leave much of it behind in the campground. After finding that trash pits did not prove sanitary or sufficient to contain the one-way flow of disposables, the Park Service's new policy was "if you can't burn it, pack it out" but "the cans and trash in the bushes and behind rocks indicated what many footsore backpackers [thought] about that policy." (Rukkila 1970:11).

In addition to the trash problem, the Ranger in assessing the environmental damage occurring that spring in the campground told the Arizona reporter (Rukkila 1970:11):

Prickly pear cactus entries suffer most from vandalism, [he] said as he pointed to some trampled cactus and a young barrel that had been chopped open. You can see a definite grab line on the trees where people have pulled down branches for firewood.

Wood gathering and wood fires are prohibited in the campground. Sitting around the campfire is a camping tradition though, and the canyon foliage is still being stripped for firewood especially when the ranger isn't looking. Not only does wood gathering destroy the appearance of the campground and disrupt natural habitats of small animals but it also may stop formation of the travertine pools for which Havasu Creek is famous. The dams which contain the pools are formed when travertine deposits build up on sticks and brush washed into the creek.

Another problem is the souvenir hunter who removes crystals from the caves and mines in the canyon and breaks off travertine formations.

These natural things are not replaceable and it's a real problem.

The Park Ranger also talked about water pollution problems in both the creek and the campground citing the fact that in the previous summer several Boy Scouts had had such serious cases of dysentery that they needed to be flown out and hospitalized at Grand Canyon Village and when water samples from Havasu Creek and Fern Spring, the campgrounds water source were analyzed, they both showed contamination by fecal bacteria. This he attributed to the fact that the creek runs through the reservation above the waterfalls where there are "outhouses and horses [that] roam freely in and out of the water" (Rukkila 1970:12). This prompted the Park service to install a chlorinator on the campground spring and issue a warning to the campers to "swim at your own risk... and don't swallow the water" (Rukkila 1970:12).

Ironically, by Easter morning, itself, that year almost all of the 2000 individuals had left to Canyon by Saturday night leaving the campground "nearly empty" to the great disappointment of Reverend John Greenfield of the Supai Mission Church who "...had often hoped to have a crowd of campers who would attend an Easter Sunday service at Havasu Falls" adding that "most of the tourists usually arrive early in the week and leave a day or two before Easter" (Rukkila 1970:8)

Realizing that eventually something needed to be done to restrict the number of people overcrowding the campground during the holidays and on weekends, the Park Ranger sadly told the Arizona reporter:

Probably restrictions on the number of people will be necessary someday if people aren't responsible for themselves and the overcrowding gets worse.

That is a long way off due to the lack of funds and manpower. Havasu is a difficult place to manage. Crowd control would require a permanent ranger station and phone at the campground as well as at Hilltop. At present the park service will only be able to maintain a seasonal ranger at Havasu. (Rukkila 1970:12)

As already discussed in Chapter 1, the Havasupai had mixed feelings about this massive increase in numbers of tourists in spite of the fact that as early as the mid-60s, tourist dollars began supplying about one half of all the annual income flowing into the tribal economy (Martin 1968:452) and about one third of all direct and indirect personal cash income (Martin 1973a:154–155). However, the main problem with tourism was that the average resident of Supai derived very little direct economic benefit from it during those years (Martin 1973a).

And, as also discussed in Chapter 1, access to the major portion of the tourist dollar was only open to the fortunate few Havasupai males who controlled most of the reservation's small amount of good pasture land, for without good grazing land it was impossible to maintain the necessary saddle and pack animals that the present tourist industry demanded. This reality was in sharp contrast to the illusion held by much of the American public (unfortunately including many members of Congress) that Indian land and other resources are held in common for the equal benefits of all tribal members.[3]

Even though many tribal councils including the one at Supai in theory have the "right" to redistribute "unused" land and to seize land for tribal purposes, in practice these rights are seldom if ever enforced on most reservations. Supai residents, in particular, in a 1968 opinion survey (Zaphiris 1968:64), expressed extreme displeasure over the "seizure and reassessment" clause in their tribal constitution and were reported to be determined to prevent the practice of this procedure which they felt was "superimposed on them." As evidence of this resistance to the authority of the tribal council to reassign land, one researcher (Martin 1968:451,458) reported that in 1963 there were eight absentee landowners at Supai, some of whom had been absent more than 20 years from the reservation yet they still retained all of their original landholdings while at the same time there were 49 landless Havasupai men. It is thus not surprising that the majority of disputes at Supai were over land use rights.[4]

Those who did control land rights[5] shared the benefits of this privilege with those members of their immediate and extended family who were willing to be subservient to them. However, sons would often rebel at this control and thus compete with each other and their fathers in a desperate attempt to gain their own inheritance rights to a portion of their father's or mother's land. It was therefore not unexpected that the tribal council usually experienced great difficulty in obtaining land to be used for communal purposes. In fact, the first major campground to be built by the tribe as an attempt to handle overflow visitors to the waterfalls was built on such a hot, barren piece of ground that few if any visitors remained there for long.[6]

And in a follow-up attempt to accommodate more visitors, a newer campground established by the tribe on flood ravaged land near the first barren site contained only one or two campsites which had much appeal to the average white visitor even if he or she overlooked the results of the severely unrepaired vandalism that had destroyed the appearance and convenience of this new camping facility. Justly or unjustly, during my visits to Supai, many visitors blamed such vandalism and theft, especially at the more popular campground built originally by the Parks Service just below Havasu Falls, on Indian young people seen roaming through the area and occasionally observed scavenging for items left behind by departing campers who had abandoned items so that their backpack load would be lighter on their hot, strenuous climb back to their hilltop vehicles.

Also, despite the fact that the average family spent more than 70% of their very meager annual cash income on food, by 1964 when a survey was undertaken (Martin 1973a) only 5 acres of Supai was in gardens with an additional 3.2 acres in alfalfa even though with the available irrigation network, 170 acres a good fertile land could easily have been planted. To many tourists and "would-be-saviors" including older Mormon missionary farm couples now being sent periodically there to encourage the local people to do more gardening, these small utilization figures despite the lush growth seen on the few cultivated plots made possible by the long growing season, rich soil, and abundant water merely reinforced in the minds of many of these individuals "proof" that the average Indian would rather live on welfare handouts than work. Indeed, by 1964 welfare brought $20,000 into the local economy while horse rentals and basket sales provided only $18,000 in personal income. Much of the remaining $25,000 earned by the approximately 200 permanent residents of the canyon came from federal sources in the form of short-term federally financed wage labor during the winter months and salaried federally financed positions. Thus, of the total personal income of $63,000 earned by Supai residents in the 1963-1964 fiscal year only $22,450 came directly or indirectly from tourism while almost all of the remaining two-thirds came from federal sources (Martin 1973a:154-155).[7] Therefore, with an average per capita income of only $315 in cash and $4.78 in kind it is easy to see why many outside individuals and agencies during the late 60s and early 70s rushed in with various plans and schemes to help these "poverty-stricken" natives out of their misery. However, although everyone, native and non-native alike, agreed there was a serious economic problem at Supai, reaching a consensus about the source of the problem and the solution needed was another matter.

Although the success of the many earlier attempts by government farmers and teachers to achieve the transformation of the Havasupai Into successful agriculturalists had proven to be ephemeral, the "Mormon Church" (Now officially wanting to drop the "Mormon" nickname and only be known by its official name i.e., "The Church of Jesus Christ of Latter-day Saints")[8], launching at this time, an intensive national American Indian conversion effort[9], felt that it could now supply that which had been missing in these earlier government attempts to "civilize" and "Christianize" the Havasupai and other Native Americans.

While as seen in chapter 2, some of the earliest white visitors to the Havasupai were the Mormon explorers, Jacob Hamblin, John D. Lee, and Joseph C. Ives, the first major effort by the Mormons to obtain Havasupai converts to the Church came as mentioned in chapter 7 with its "Indian Placement Program" offer to tribal parents as an alternative to having their eight years of age or older children being sent away to the despised Fort Apache boarding school[10].

To qualify for this program, the student must have been at least eight years old[11] and be a baptized member of the church. He or she was then sent to live with an off-reservation Mormon family during the school year only returning to his or her tribal home during the summer months.

Major differences between the placement program and the earlier boarding school assimilation attempt by the government Include a mandatory return of the children to the reservation each summer and the placement of students individually in Mormon homes that contained similar age children that in the case of the Havasupai were in Utah and California (C.S. July 22, 1971:6). And since the parents of each Havasupai child would have to agree to have their child be baptized as a Mormon, the Church naïvely assumed that the returning child, hopefully growing stronger each away school year in his or her allegiance to the church's doctrine and lifestyle, would become an instrument in the conversion of his or her parents and reservation peer group to the church and its beliefs and practices.

However, as I have heard from many such students as well as from a number of the Mormon families that accepted such students, the desired Church conversion outcome did not often occur. Especially hard for the older returning students to resist was the power of their peer groups which would often entice them to break Church standards that forbid the consumption of alcohol and tobacco and to engage in sexual activity prior to marriage. And during the time I lived on the nearby Navajo reservation both as a visiting professor at Diné College and years later as a volunteer manager of an employment center, returning students often were under tremendous pressure from parents and other relatives to attend and engage in traditional Navajo or Peyote religious ceremonies and activities all of which were strongly condemned by the Mormon church.

That such a negative outcome had occurred at Supai was confirmed by the BYU farmer I talked with during my 1973 visit to the reservation who related that some of the returning students would throw rocks at him while he was plowing fields. And, a friend of mine who together with his wife and children had been the school year Mormon "parents" of a Havasu boy told me that things went well with him until one year as a teenager he returned after undergoing "some tribal ritual" after which he had completely changed his behavior, losing any interest in completing school assignments or interacting in a positive way with the rest of their family.

Despite such negative outcomes, later objections to the Church's placement program as seen in such articles as "The Mormons and Indian Child Placement:-- Is Native Culture Being Destroyed" that appeared in the influential Indian Journal, Wassaja in 1979 (Wood 1979:7,8; See also (Stucki 1979)) were not evident at Supai when in 1970 the tribe readily met with the Church's President of the Southwest Indian Mission and other Mormon leaders who had arrived at Supai to organize a new local branch of the church to be headed by Leon Rogers, a Havasupai pack animal owner, who was ordained an elder in the Church and set apart as branch president after only being baptized the previous February (Anonymous 1970:6).

During the "long" meeting with the Council that had been called to "consider … the business of the tribe," the President of the Southwest Indian mission made an offer to "help the [Havasupai] with their farms and businesses[12]" which offer "was taking under advisement by the council" (Anonymous 1970:6).

And at this meeting, members of the tribal council were given copies of "Meet the Mormons" and shown the movie "Day of Promise," that told the story of the Indian Placement program of the church along with "Man's Search for Happiness" and "For Time and Eternity" both films introducing the Mormon concept of marriage and family bonds continuing in heaven after death through special sacred rituals performed in Mormon temples (Anonymous 1970:6,7).

Following the showing of these movies all Supai residents were invited to a pot-luck dinner featuring spaghetti, fry bread, beans, and "a popular fruit flavored punch" prepared by several lady Mormon missionaries, an offer accepted by "nearly 60 persons" (Anonymous 1970:7).

After only taking a very short time to consider the offer from The Church of Jesus Christ of Latter-Day Saints (Mormon) Southwest Indian Mission President "to help the Indian people with their farms and businesses", Lee Marshal, the tribal chairman, in a letter to the Church wrote:

> Our needs here involve both business and agriculture. Would it be possible to find a couple to stay here for two years with knowledge in both fields?....
>
> We appreciate very much your offer to help us. We have many offers of help from others, but they don't show up, they just talk. We hope you can find someone for us real soon" (Anonymous 1970:6).

The church then "assigned" an older couple from Springville Utah "to help with the Supai projects and to guide the new branch as it grows" who would be joining the two younger male missionaries and two lady missionaries already there that summer (Anonymous 1970:7,10).

By this time there were 12 baptized members in the branch and an average attendance of 25 to 30 persons at the Sunday meetings. The two young male missionaries ("elders[13]") were raising an experimental small garden using water from the nearby stream, tilling it with a tiller that they had pulled by hand down the rough canyon trail, a five hour job. And it was reported that:

> They use the tiller, not only for their garden but to help the people of the village. Young Indian boys are also taught to use the machine and family gardens throughout are cultivated with the gasoline operated machine....
>
> The lady missionaries share the responsibility of teaching the Gospel with the elders. They work with the children in crafts, recreation and with the women in the homemaking skills (Anonymous 1970:10).

And by the time of my June 1973 visit to the reservation, I was told by the two young male missionaries there that there were 41 members of the Church[14] in the village out of about 300 people while the other Protestant missionary church had only about 15 members. An especially effective tool in these conversions had been specifically me targeted filmstrips and tapes that the church had developed using American Indian actors to portray the Mormon belief that all individuals had a life in heaven as spirit children of God before coming to earth and that all individuals through righteous living and temple rituals can, after death, together with their loved ones return to live with God. However, by the time of my visit the two young missionaries said that everyone in the Village had seen these special filmstrips and tapes so they were now using the same standardized missionary lessons as were used anywhere else in the world[15].

The missionaries went on to say that "there is no one in Supai who is unfriendly to them (except possibly the Protestant minister and his family) or who refuses to talk to them when he or she has time." Proof of this claim was easily seen by the fact that the missionaries were spending many hours playing with village children with no evidence of any parental concern. In sharp contrast, unfortunately for the Community Educator, Jay Hunt, who was also a Mormon, he had seen his approval rating fall from his successful last contract renewal by the Council in 1971 (C.S. may 12, 1971:3) to a unanimous decision by the Council at the July 22 meeting the following year "to have the BIA transfer him to another location as soon as possible" giving the following reasons:

  a) He generates resentments rather than accomplishing anything among the people of the village.
  b) His outside commitments seldom make him available for local work. The council noted that during the 10-month period preceding the meeting, Jay had been away 170 days.
  c) The council has received no adequate reports on the need for such excessive absence.
  d) He is not performing the job – community education – the tribe and the BIA hired him to do.
  e) He involves himself too closely with law enforcement, which the council emphasized interferes with his function as an educator.
  f) He had not informed all the Council members of his change in status from tribal employee to civil servant.
  g) He frequently uses government and personal horses to transport personal and church visitors, even though this robs local horse owners of a chance to earn needed income.

h) He brings in all sorts of animals that people do not request or want in the canyon. (C.S. July 26, 1972:2)

However, the feelings of community members toward his wife were not nearly as negative and there were no requests for her immediate transfer. Nor during my 1973 visit to Supai were there any apparent feelings of hostility toward the resident farmer and his wife except from a few unhappy returning placement students who sometimes threw rocks at him while he was plowing village fields. And in March 1974 (C.S. March 10, 1974:7,8) the tribal newsletter reported that:

> Last month a group from Brigham Young University brought several hundred young peach, apricot, plum and cherry trees to the canyon and helped individuals get them planted at a minimal charge of $1.00 per tree. In about three years most of the trees should begin to bear their first fruit. This was a very good thing for us....

Further details about this project are found in the Mormon Church's weekly news update (anonymous 1974:6,14) listing the number of trees planted as being "more than 400." And in describing why these new trees were needed, the article then goes on to state that: "several years ago during an extremely cold winter the tribe had cut down most of [their existing] trees for firewood in order to survive the winter." The article then goes on to state that the early Mormon explorer, Jacob Hamblin, had "visited them and [taken] them their first fruit trees and vegetable seeds." However, the tribal newsletter (C.S. March 10, 1974:7) gives a different version of where the earlier trees came from and how they had been destroyed stating that:

> Well, this year it looks as if Havasu Canyon may once again bloom with fruit trees as it used to. Once the canyon was full of orchards of peaches, apricots and other fruit, most of which had been brought to the Havasupai in 1780, when the Hopi came to escape a drought and stayed for several years among the tribe. The major part of these orchards was destroyed January 2, 1910, when a great flood destroyed nearly all the tribe's farmland. A further flood August 1, 1928 took many of the rest of the trees.

However, Mormon church attendance during my next visit to the reservation in 1977 had fallen almost to zero[16] during the annual Peach Dance Festival and the two young Mormon missionaries there were very discouraged as many of the Indians had fallen back into their old heavy drinking patterns and other "sins." (The Mormon church puts a heavy emphasis on abstaining from the use of alcohol, tobacco, tea, coffee, and stresses sexual abstinence except between husband and wife in a marriage). The training program in farming and household skills had also suffered a setback, and by this time the last older farm couple sent out by the church had departed and had not been replaced. However, this was no surprise to me since when I had last talked to one of these older missionaries during the summer of 1973, he was quite discouraged as he told me that all the Indians did was watch as he plowed their fields for them with a tractor that had been supplied by the church. (The tribally owned tractor had at this time been suffering from transmission troubles for many months without any attempt being made to repair it and was only being used to pick up the village garbage.)

This apparent lack of interest in learning how to increase their agricultural skills was also seen in the failure of a hydroponic farming experiment financed by the tribal Council. Knowing how expensive it was to provide feed for their horses, in October 1972 the Council "repeated its wish to go ahead and try hydroponic farming" (C.S. October 30, 1972:5). And soon after this meeting, they had purchased a grass-growing unit from Forrest Byers of Hydroculture Inc. that was capable of growing "a ton of feed from the unit, which is as much as 100 acres of rangeland could grow" in a week from "300 pounds of barley seed" (C.S. January 22, 1973:4). And at the January 22, 1973 meeting of the Council Mr. Byers:

> … talked to the Council about the grass-growing unit they had purchased and asked them to settle on a place for it and provide the water and power hookups. The Council set the site beside the new lodge. Mr. Byers told the Council his company was doing everything it can to bring in newspaper and magazine interest both for the hydroponic unit and to bring attention to the tribe's need for more land. He also said his company would be more than happy to fly Sen. Goldwater into the canyon January 27. (C.S. January 22, 1973:4).

However, by February of the very next year enthusiasm for this experiment had waned and the unit had been shut down even though Florence Marshall speaking at a meeting of the tribal Council said:

116

> ... the hydroponic farming unit can provide great benefit to the tribe and should be put into operation again. She said if people don't use it, they are just wasting money. (C.S. February 3, 1974:6).

At first glance, one might be tempted to agree with the frustration of both the older and younger Mormon missionaries and others who felt that many Supai residents preferred "welfare over work" but as Martin (1968, 1973a) has pointed out this apparent lack of industry is probably due more to structural rather than moral factors. Thus, the water table in the valley is quite high and by this time Bermuda grass, a plant which has the ability to reach this water, had spread throughout the valley creating a permanent pasture which required no irrigation.[17] Also, the senior males who controlled the packing industry and most land-use rights had no time during the busy summer tourist months to plant and care for gardens while those males who did have free time to garden, had little economic incentive to do so. For, not only was the economic return low for agricultural labor at Supai (an estimated $.16/hour given the then present level of technology and insufficient distribution of land) but, more importantly, these subservient males were not permitted to convert any produce which they grew into personal cash incomes. Instead, they were required by the resource controlling older males to share any food produced with all their close kinsmen. Therefore, in spite of the fact that the residents of Supai spent a major portion of their meager annual incomes on food which they themselves could produce, it would have taken a major restructuring of landholdings and society before much more irrigated farmland would be created in the canyon. That this was unlikely in the near future was documented by a survey taken by Zaphiris in 1968 when he found that 33 of 39 families surveyed said that they would be unwilling "to move their home to another location in the village so that all farm land could be farmed as one unit for the purpose of improving their crop" (p.57). Also, only two employed adults expressed their preference for farming as a vocation while 20 expressed their dislike for this profession "because of the amount of work required in such occupational activity and the non-guarantee returns of the same" (pp. 31-32). However, over one half of the families surveyed said that they would be willing and able to donate some of their time to improve the village irrigation system (p.42). Also, over half of the families owning horses and mules were willing to sell them to obtain cattle instead (pp. 97-98) if this could be arranged.

A much different conception of the action "needed" to solve the economic and social problems that plagued the Havasupai Indians was put forward by those individuals and groups that blamed government inaction and the Park Service-backpacker lobby for the poverty to be found at Supai. As discussed in the last chapter individuals like Martin Goodfriend, a California "do-gooder" begin publicly attacking the "paradise" image that many summer visitors had about life in the canyon by pointing out the poverty, sickness, and unemployment to be found at Supai which were often intensified during the winter months when the long dirt road to the hilltop would be made impassable by snow or rain for weeks at a time and when tourist income was nonexistent (Dedera 1967,1971). Goodfriend and others[18] tried to convince the canyon residents that with improved access to the outside world a massive tourist complex could be created at Supai that would easily make the tribe the wealthiest in the nation on a per capita basis. Put forward as the easiest way to accomplish this feat would be the construction of an aerial tramway from the canyon rim to the valley floor[19]. The nearby South Rim area of Grand Canyon National Park was already being over utilized by tourists even during many of the winter months and it was certain that large numbers of these tourists could be lured to the milder winter and spectacular waterfalls of Havasu Canyon. All of these visitors could be brought into the canyon below the central part of the village of Supai so that the Havasupai could actually enjoy more privacy than was now possible with the main trail winding past many of their houses. Increased numbers of visitors would mean increased employment and, as additional tribal members returned to Supai or the nearby canyon rim to share this new wealth, perhaps additional grade levels could be taught at the local school (or perhaps a new school that could be built on the nearby canyon rim) to reduce the number of long periods of lonely separation that children and parents must now endure when older students are shipped to boarding schools each winter. And with easier access to the outside world, it should be easier than in the past to recruit and retain qualified schoolteachers and staff especially if new housing was made available to them on the rim. Food prices at that time 140% of the level of retail prices in the nearest outside towns and cities would drop and the level of medical care would dramatically improve especially if a medical clinic could be built on the nearby canyon rim. Housing for the staff of such a clinic could be added to that provided for schoolteachers and staff as well as for the returning Havasupai. The water needed for such a development could be pumped to the rim for storage but only during the night to avoid damaging the daytime waterfall viewing experience for visitors.

Although many residents of Supai were not overjoyed at the prospect of massive numbers of tourists coming to their peaceful canyon, about one half of Supai's families in a 1968 survey (Zaphiris 1968:94) felt that the construction of a tramway or road to the village would help them economically and on March 21, 1969, the Havasupai tribal council passed a resolution supporting the construction of tramways in the Grand Canyon (Evans 1974:27). Opposition to the tramway or road came mainly from those heads of households who controlled the packing industry. They feared that a tramway or road would destroy their means of making a living as well as their dominant economic, social, and political status in village life (Zaphiris 1968:94-95). And, as anyone can easily see during the annual Peach Dance Rodeo when horses and riders are compared and either admired or jeered, it would not be an easy transition to a new way of life where horse ownership and control would lose their primary importance as symbols of power, wealth, and independence.[20]

However, one would be mistaken to suppose that the Havasupai wanted to reject the material comforts of the surrounding outside world in the 1970s since at that time there was much dissension over who should be the first to receive new homes under a federally assisted program and all families welcomed the arrival of electricity from the new plant that was built on the rim just above the village. In fact, I was told that so eager were certain members of the tribe to receive this electricity that the lines were quickly strung across Park Service land one night without asking for or receiving the "necessary" permits. As a statement appearing in National Geographic magazine emphasized (Garrett 1978:29), the Park Service was often viewed as being the "enemy"

119

by the Havasupai who had always resented the land use restrictions placed upon them by these government officials. I well remember my own irritation that I shared with these people on my first visit to Supai with my wife and young daughter when I unexpectedly had to make many difficult trips up and down a steep trail from the top of Havasu Falls to the main campground lugging heavy pieces of camping gear and supplies because the Park Service had forbidden all Havasupai packers from entering the campground due to a "serious fly problem" that they blamed on the pack animals.

Rightly or wrongly, many of the Havasupai by the 1960s felt that the U.S. government was more concerned about the welfare of the backpacking tourists than of the permanent inhabitants of the canyon. And by 1969, they seemed resigned to their fate as they accepted the payment of 124 million dollars from the Indian Claims Commission as a "final" settlement for the land which had earlier been taken from them although they did at this time manage to retain use rights to 173,400 acres of the barren land surrounding Havasu Canyon (Hirst 1976:231).[21]

At this point in their history the people of Supai were badly divided and seemed to have given up hope for a better future as relatives fought each other continually over the remaining land and horses (Zaphiris 1968:102). Zaphiris (1968) in a comprehensive survey conducted at this time found that alcoholism was rampant (p.53), community spirit was lacking, (p.106) the communication system and remaining acres of farmland were deteriorating (p.40) and that members of the tribal council were accused by over half of the Supai families of not representing their interests and of such other things as being secretive, not helpful, untrustworthy, cruel, exhibiting favoritism, and only interested in their own personal gain (p.86). Most residents felt that their personal incomes were insufficient to meet even their minimum daily needs although they had some hope of obtaining additional amounts from an increased emphasis on tourism and government aid programs (pp.22-24). To make ends meet almost three quarters of the male heads of households reported that they at one time or another had worked outside of the village (p.34) but most perceived the possibility of permanent relocation as emotionally detrimental in spite of its economic advantages (p.108). Parent-child separation was blamed for the 50 percent dropout and expulsion rate among Supai high school students who were being forced to attend schools outside the canyon (p.96).

However, at about this same time the isolation that had long separated the Havasupai from the battleground of national American politics broke down suddenly with the controversy that began with the completion of the controversial Glen Canyon dam upstream on the main Colorado River. River running had by now become a popular American sport creating a major wilderness lobby against the construction of further dams along the Colorado.

Opposing this lobby were members of a powerful political coalition from the Phoenix-Tucson area who were fighting for what they believed to be their fair share of the water from the already over-utilized river. A key component in the proposed Central Arizona Project to obtain this water was the construction of a dam on the Colorado just above Lake Mead. Revenues from this dam were to be used to pay back the construction costs of the remainder of the project. The second benefit would be the creation of a new recreational lake that would please not only Arizona sportsmen but also the Havasupai's neighboring tribe the Hualapai who for economic reasons enthusiastically supported the construction of the dam.

Opponents of this proposed project quickly pointed out that not only was the storage capacity of this new dam not needed for the Central Arizona Project but also that it would back water up into the Grand Canyon National Park (a claim that proponents of the dam pointed out that in the **currently existing boundaries of the Park** was false). And sensing that National Park protection would be their best bet against further dam construction on remaining free-flowing sections of the Colorado, they were able to persuade their supporters in Congress to sponsor a bill to enlarge the boundary of the park, thus injecting the Havasupai with their large grazing permit areas into the middle of the controversy as basic human rights were pitted against the need to protect the natural flora, fauna, and scenic values of the canyon and surrounding plateaus.

As this battle began, some of the Havasupai tribal leaders sensing that this was perhaps an opportunity to unite the tribe, greatly enlarge their reservation, and throw off the yoke of the National Park Service[22] sought congressional support for their cause and found it in a rare coalition of liberal and conservative senators and representatives including among many others such well known individuals as Senators Barry Goldwater, Ted Kennedy, and Hubert Humphrey and Representative Morris Udall. Even President Nixon, perhaps, it is suggested, because of his need for support from key senators and representatives during his Watergate troubles, became a firm supporter of the Havasupai cause (Bernstein 1974; Lovett 1978). The Havasupai, their tribal lawyers and the above coalition of congressmen in a brilliant campaign beat out the combined opposition of almost all national conservation groups and the National Park Service.

Perhaps the best source of information about the early events in this chaotic period of time can be found in the issues of *Canyon Shadows*, a tribal newsletter revived on October 20,1967 by Steve and Lois Hirst who had just come to Supai to operate a Head Start preschool.

Thus in the February 18, 1971 issue of *Canyon Shadows* the Tribal Council Chairman "cited the case of Taos Pueblo who had 48,000 acres additional land restored to them" as hope for a victory in their long struggle to regain control of the National Park Service campground and other traditional use areas despite having accepted Government compensation for their earlier losses (p.2). However, "After hinting they might change plans to help the tribe get more land, the Park Service has decided to stick to its original master plan…[leaving] the Havasupai In danger of losing Hilltop, Long Mesa and upper Havasu Canyon" (C.S. May 12, 1971:1).

And in the June 1, 1971 issue of *Canyon Shadows* we learn of the senate bill to Congress to triple the size of the Grand Canyon Park to 2.14 million acres most of which would be preserved as an "undeveloped, natural area" (p.1) and addressing specifically Havasu Canyon the master plan draft states:

> The charm and beauty of Havasu Canyon is attracting more and more people, who threaten the area with results of their heavy impact on the limited, rather fragile environment. With extensive development on the reservation, the Havasupai may lose the charm and beauty of their environment and ultimately the qualities that attract the visitor (C.S. n.d.:4).

Reacting to this Senate bill, Joe Babbitt, the tribal lawyer, quickly opposed it saying, "it would keep the tribe from becoming self-supporting to surround the reservation with a wilderness area" (p.1) as did also Tribal Chairman, Lee Marshall, who "insisted that no one has the right to restrict to primitive or non-mechanical means reasonable access rights the Havasupai must have to their land" (p.2).

Especially objectionable to Marshall and the other tribal leaders was that;

> ... the master plan proposal is directed at preserving the Grand Canyon as a sort of vast outdoor museum, keeping it in as nearly as natural state as possible. This is commendable except where it impinges on the Havasupais' efforts to build a better and freer life for their children....
> The people of the tribe are not interested in serving as museum pieces (C.S. n.d.:4)

Realizing that they were fighting an uphill battle against the extremely powerful conservation lobby, in May the tribal Council had sent "letters and Information to influential Senators and newspapers (C.S. July 22, 1971:1). Aiding this effort was a new would be "Savior, " Edna Christ, who began "a one-woman campaign to persuade the government that the Havasupai need land" (C.S. July 22, 1971:1). Positive offers of assistance to the tribe were also received from Sen. Edward Kennedy, Rep. Sam Steiger, and Sen. Fred Harris, who had helped restore Blue Lake to the Taos Pueblo and although both Senators Fannin and Goldwater favored the park expansion, Goldwater said that he would introduce a bill "authorizing the Secretary of the Interior to assist me Havasupai Indians develop their tourist and recreational economy" (C.S. July 22, 1971:1).

However, Goldwater's apparent support for the Havasupai cause came with a important caveat, since he strongly opposed building a tramway from the rim into the canyon and efforts to pipe water to the dry plateau pastureland above (C.S. August 14, 1971:3). Thus, in that same issue (p.3), although the Council said it had "no immediate plans to build a tramway, just as it [had] no immediate plans to pipe water to the top [that] does not mean the tribe could agree never to do it."

Going on (C.S. August 14, 1971 p. 3), the Council stated that:

The tramway would provide the only cheap and practical way to bring food and supplies to the village and could mean a dependable source of income for the tribe and many jobs for its people. The Council said it had to think of the tribe's future. The tribe's only assets are in its water and its tourist attractions; to agree not to make money from them would guarantee the tribe would remain poor.

By January 18, 1972, *Canyon Shadows* reported that "After nearly a year of negotiating, the final shape of the Havasupai reservation and of the Grand Canyon National Park still [was] not clear" but time was quickly running out before Goldwater would be submitting his bill to Congress (p.2). The Park Service said that it would not give up its campground and the Forest Service said that it would not give up any of its land without a land trade, an impossibility given the fact that the Havasupai had no land left to trade with. Also, the Park Service did not want to give back lambing areas for the mountain sheep that they felt "would become extinct under Indian management" (C.S. January 18, 1972:2). Thus, a map prepared by the Park and Forest Services on December 14, 1971 would add "roughly 40,000 acres" to the present reservation but would not include the National Park campground nor anything on the east side of the reservation "where so many Havasupai people used to live and farm" (C.S. January 18, 1972:2-4). However, the tribe would continue to "have free use permits in this [eastern] area, as in the past" (C.S. January 18, 1972:2).

Rejecting the Park and Forest services December 14, 1971 proposal as being inadequate, Chairman Lee Marshall at the March 11, 1972 Council Meeting "reminded that the tribe had offered a counterproposal with their own hopes for a larger reservation [and] wondered what had happened to this proposal and why it had apparently received no consideration" (C.S. March 11, 1972:2). He then advised the Tribal Council that it should act on its own and submit its own proposal to Congress. However, having decisively lost his bid for continued membership on the Council at the Christmas dinner and Council election in 1971[23], his power to influence the decision the Council would make that day was greatly diminished although he received strong support from Tribal Lawman, Daniel Kaska, who "urged people to stick to what they needed and repeated his believe that tribal representatives should go to Washington" adding that "we can't just sit here and rot! "(C.S. March 11, 1972:2).

Countering Marshall and Kaska was Supai Community Educator, Jay Hunt who:

...then spoke at length of his role in the community and ensured the tribe that he and the BIA were on the tribe's side but that the people should be realistic. The Havasupais would not have a chance of getting what they want for the reservation, he assured them, because they are nothing compared to the rest of the country. He advised them going to Washington would be a waste of money, as Congress would not help them either (C.S. March 11, 1972:2).

This was followed by an additional warning from Grand Canyon National Park Superintendent Robert Lovegren that:

Sen. Clifford Case is sponsoring a bill for the Sierra Club which would expand the Grand Canyon Park even more than the master plan and would leave the tribe out in the cold. If the Havasupais insisted on their own proposal, the Case bill would likely win in Congress and leave the tribe with nothing (C.S. March 11, 1972:2).

And another ominous warning from Kabab Forest Supervisor Keith Pefferle was that:

... the Forest Service will hold hearings April 21 in Williams on whether to designate upper Havasu, Coyote and Beaver canyons as wilderness areas. Though he would try to postpone such a decision, the tribe would run a chance of having these canyons turned into wilderness unless the Council could first take them into the reservation under the joint Park-Forest proposal (C.S. March 11, 1972:4)..

Even the tribal lawyer, Joe Babbitt "reminded the Council that Goldwater would apparently pattern his Congressional bill after the wishes of the Park and Forest Services in spite of his empty promise to the council in August 1971" (C.S. March 11, 1972:2) and "advised the Council they may never get another chance like this and the tribe would have nothing to lose by agreeing to the joint proposal" (C.S. March 11, 1972:4).

At this point the newly elected Tribal Chairman, Alfred Hanna reluctantly:

...urged the Council to go ahead and accept the joint proposal as the best the tribe could get under the circumstances. The Council resolved 4 to 1 to accept the joint proposal if [certain] mentioned adjustments would be included" (C.S. March 11, 1972:4).

Following the vote, Superintendent Lovegren "reminded the Council that the tribe would still have to agree to the Park Service's conditions on using the land before achieving complete agreement but advised the Park could work that out with lawyer Joe Babbitt" (C.S. March 11, 1972:4). (As would soon become obvious such a caveat would block any further effort to build a tramway into the canyon.)

As a final comment as he closed the meeting that day, Tribal Chairman, Alfred Hanna, said that "he expected he would have to resign, as the people would not be satisfied with the agreement made with the Park and Forest Services" (C.S. March 11, 1972:4).

Not wanting a repeat of the social and environmental chaos such as that which had, as earlier described, occurred during the 1970 Easter weekend, the Park Service decided to limit the campground to 100 persons after May 1, 1972 (C.S. March 4, 1972:2). And, giving the Havasupai some informal power to enforce this limit, from this time forward visitors were urged "to call ahead to the Havasupai tourist office and make reservations for any future visits" (C.S. March 4, 1972:4). Also, a warning to those coming without a reservation "if 100 persons are already in the campground you will be turned away. Save yourself a long trip for nothing" (C.S. March 4, 1972:4). And in another concession to the tribe the Park Service informed the Tribal Council that it would be hiring a GS-5 Ranger for the campground with preferences being given to Havasupai, three of which were "already under consideration" (C.S. March 4, 1972:2).

Still, Council interest in the possibility of constructing a tramway from the canyon rim to Supai continued throughout the remainder of 1972 as seen when, in September, Chairman Oscar Paya asked Supt. Pitrat:

> ... when the BIA planned to prepare the resolution on studying the feasibility of the cable car, as they had requested him to do June 22. Supt. Pitrat said he knew of no such request but he would look for it. The Chairman later produced a copy of the request (C.S. September 15, 1972:6).

And after the Council had passed Resolution 15-72 on September 19 "requesting a study of whether a tramway into Havasu Canyon would be practical to build" (C.S. October 30, 1972:4), in a November planning session meeting held in the BIA Phoenix area office (C.S. December 11, 1972:3) during a discussion on access into the village:

"Martin Goodfriend felt the tribe ought to study the use of a tramway to see if it could reduce some of the present transportation difficulties. He and others pointed out the noise and dirt the use of helicopters causes. Former community worker Bill Willoughby reminded the village would again be dependent on packing when the construction [of new houses] is over, so the tribe should take this into account in discussing a possible tramway.

Knowing that Sen. Barry Goldwater would soon be presenting his Grand Canyon bill to Congress, on December 12, 1972 the Tribal Council sent the following urgent invitation to him by telegram:

We must meet with you personally before you complete wording on the Grand Canyon expansion bill. We propose a delegation of our leaders meet you in our Tribal Council office on our reservation within the next few weeks if possible. We offer our complete hospitality for this visit, as we feel your long familiarity with our area and its people enables you to understand the urgent needs we must explain. Please contact us as soon as possible if such a meeting is feasible or if an alternative location is necessary (C.S. January 22, 1973:1).

Worried after not having received a response from him by January 10th of the new year, Lois Hirst sent him a letter "questioning why the Council had received no response to their telegram" but the very next day, the Tribal Council received a long distance phone call from the office of Senator Barry Goldwater saying that the senator "wished very much to meet with the tribe's leaders and learn their wishes before presenting his Grand Canyon bill to Congress" (C.S. January 22, 1973:1). His office then informed the tribe that he would be free to meet with them on January 27 in the morning. And in a personal reply to Lois Hirst that she received on the 19th, Sen. Goldwater said in part that the Havasupai:

...are a wonderful people... I would be happy to meet with them relative to helping them expand their Reservation... I am planning to include a provision in the Grand Canyon boundary changes bill that will be to the benefit of the Tribe (C.S. January 22, 1973:1).

This positive response offering a chance to "present the tribe's needs for some of its old lands" was very welcome news to tribal leaders since the feeling was:

> Sen. Goldwater is finally the man who holds in his hands the power to help the tribe; he does not have to run and check with his boss to see if it is all right. On this, Goldwater is the boss. What he writes up for a bill is pretty much what Congress will vote on (C.S. January 22, 1973:1).

Rather than having tribal leaders meet with him in his Washington office, Goldwater agreed to come to the reservation on January 27, arriving in the village "just before 11 a.m." (C.S. February 7, 1973:1). After listening to the tribal Councilmen and their lawyer Joe Babbitt explain the importance of the various areas of land they wanted back, Sen. Goldwater:

> …inquired how much land the tribe is asking for and learned it comes to perhaps 170,000 acres. He then said, "We are in better shape to get the land back than we have been in many years."
> That word "we" stopped everybody; Goldwater was in it with them. The councilman had convinced him and won him over. He went on to tell the Council that he could make a good case for what they wanted and would put it into his bill. (C.S. February 7, 1973:1,2).

Then after asking the Council if they wanted the falls, he said that he felt "the tribe should control the falls in order to improve its tourist income" and would look into "extending the reservation down Havasu Canyon to the Colorado" (C.S. February 7, 1973:2).

However, terrible news came to tribal leaders on February 16 as they met for an emergency meeting in the Tourist Office. A phone call has arrived from Terry Emerson, Sen. Goldwater's assistant saying that:

> … the Sierra Club was taking a stand against returning any land to the Havasupai end that the senator was under a great deal of pressure because of this. He had called advising the tribe to begin efforts to inform the public about the tribe's case (C.S. March 24, 1973:7).

Added to this were "letters coming in" that because the Havasupai had already received compensation which they had accepted for their lost aboriginal land, they now had no legal right to regain any of it (C.S. March 24, 1973:7). To answer these critics:

The Council members said indignantly they had been given no choice. They did say they were ready to refuse compensation at [$.50] an acre for whatever lands they could regain by this refusal. They said that they stood ready to notify the Senate to this effect (C.S. March 24, 1973:7).

At this point Steve Hirst tells Council of the several letters he had sent to wire services and newspapers explaining the tribal situation but that "only the Flagstaff Sun had paid any attention to this" (C.S. March 24, 1973:8). He then suggested that they needed to hire a public relations firm "to get the tribe's words to the people and get public backing," recommending an Indian PR firm based in Washington (C.S. March 24, 1973:8). To his suggestion the Council "decided they had better try anything they could [and] asked him to look into the cost of doing this" (C.S. March 24, 1973:8)

From this point on Steve Hirst and his wife Lois play an increasingly important role in the Havasupai battle to regain ownership and control of their former land. Thus, Steve and Lois had arrived in Washington a few days before the first day of congressional hearings on the Grand Canyon bill "In order to do some historical research for the tribe" (C.S. July 10, 1973:1). This followed an earlier offer at a special May 24, 1973 Council meeting by Hirst "to put a book together on the Havasupai effort to get the tribes land back," an offer they eagerly told him to begin (C.S. August 29, 1973:4).

And for the second House of Representatives hearing on the Grand Canyon enlargement bill to be held on November 12, Steve paired up with Lee Marshall to be witnesses for the tribe, both arriving a few days early so that they could spend some time with members of the Subcommittee on Parks and Recreation to present the tribes viewpoint before the hearing itself would take place. (C.S. November 21,1973:1). (Lois came along also as a recorder of the hearing proceedings.) At the hearing, Steve was called as a witness followed by Lee, both giving very powerful long statements that were published in Canyon Shadows in their entirety (C.S. November 21,1973:2-6). And during their speeches, Lois noticed that the Sierra Club representatives in the front row "were going over their maps and shaking their heads [looking] very upset" (C.S. November 21,1973:2).

However, In both of his books (Hirst 1976, 2006), in contrast to the many other would-be "saviors" documented in this book, completely leaves out any mention of the crucial role both he and his wife played in the successful battle by the Havasupai tribe against formidable opponents. Also, he never mentions Martin Goodfriend and others both in and outside the tribe for their initial very strong support of a tramway from the canyon rim to the village. Thus to win their battle against the powerful environmental lobby, the Havasupai had to portray themselves as being "super ecologists" opposed to any kind of 20th century "progress" that would damage the flora, fauna, or "wilderness" aspect of the proposed enlarged reservation that would now include the formerly National Park Service protected spectacular waterfalls. They quickly renounced their earlier tribal resolution supporting the construction of tramways in the canyon and stressed they were completely opposed to any massive tourist development at Supai.

Thus, facing the opposition of such powerful opponents as the Sierra Club and many other by now very strong "environmentalists," Steven Hirst using the pronoun "we" instead of his own name writes:

> It is a great mistake to think the tribe wishes return of these lands in order to make economic developments there. Anyone who has bothered to know anything about the Havasupai people knows these lands are precious to them, more precious then they could be to Sunday hikers....
> If these environmentalists wish all commercial activity in the area to stop they have better realize this means the closing of Havasu Canyon to all further visitors (C.S. March 24, 1973:3).

He then urges the readers of *Canyon Shadows* to write to members of the Senate Subcommittee on Parks and Recreation as well as to Sen. Goldwater seeking their support for the return of their former lands. And hoping to change the attitude of two individuals from the opposing side, he urges the readers of *Canyon Shadows* to write to them telling them "you believe the tribal wishes correspond with their own and that they should support rather than oppose the return to the Havasupai of what is rightfully theirs" (C.S. March 24, 1973:3).

And Hirst, in the July 1973 issue of *Canyon Shadows* (pages 1-3), reporting on the points that he and his wife along with tribal leaders, Clark Jack, Augustine Hanna, and tribal lawyer Joe Babbitt made on June 20, 1973, the first day of Congressional hearings on the Grand Canyon bill, writes:

> As you have probably heard by now, when we're going to have tourists in our canyon, it should be under our control on our land. We'd welcome them that way. Not too many of you would stand the humiliation we stand every day; we live in a Park Service zoo; we have to open our house to somebody else's guests. Remember we used to own the whole place....
>
> "Now we come to the big trouble for this bill: these so-called conservation groups who keep saying we want to get this land to make some kind of big development on it. That's just crazy. We don't have any way to do that and we don't even want to. They're just saying that so they can get it away from us. Look at what these people have done to our lands already. We can do a lot better without their so-called protection.
>
> "We have a little tribal tourist business which just lets hikers and horse riders come visit our lands. This is our only income, and we're going to keep it going. But we're not talking about anything more than that; none of us wants anything more than that. Some big business operation would change us into white people, and we like our way of life the way it is. We think it's better than yours.

A major turning point in their battle against their environmental opponents occurred at the end of that year (1973) when a group of Sierra Club people representing the Prescott, Phoenix, and Tucson groups of the club made a special trip to the Canyon on December 29–31 "to speak with tribal people and see at first hand the problem the Havasupai have in being restricted to the canyon bottom" (C.S. February 3, 1974:1). Meeting with the Tribal Council and other Supai residents on the 31st, in explaining their visit, they said they had come to see if they, too, could find a reason to join the Flagstaff group that had already decided to split from the National Organization's bitter opposition to any transfer of government land to the Havasupai (C.S. February 3, 1974:1).

At this meeting:

> "Steve Hirst proposed that Grand Canyon Park would be better managed if it were entirely staffed by Havasupai, from the superintendent on down. This would guarantee a real commitment to the Park, because the administration would live in the area for their whole life rather than just four or five years. He said that the Grand Canyon would still be a Park operating as it does now but it would be run by people who really care about it. He recommended this plan for all National Parks where Indians still live. It would provide permanent, meaningful employment to people in their own homeland (C.S. February 3, 1974:2).

131

Then, very cleverly, the Tribal Council:

> ...registered some specific complaints about the present management of the Park. They felt tourism there was out of hand. Tourists should travel into the Park by rail, bicycle, horse or on foot, they felt; cars should stay outside. The number of buildings at the rim should be reduced (C.S. February 3, 1974:2).

As a reaction to these comments *Canyon Shadows* then reports that "The Sierra Club people agreed very much with these views" (C.S. February 3, 1974:2). Thus, it was not surprising that soon after this meeting the Arizona chapter of the Sierra Club voted to "now support the return of government-owned land to the Havasupai" (C.S. February 3, 1974:1).

Obviously, this was no longer a time to promote any of the earlier tramway proposals that would bring thousands of tourists into the canyon but in an interview with Oscar Paya, the tribal chairman he stated:

> Our young people do not stay here.... They go to school beyond the fifth grade and when they finish they stay outside. There is no future for our tribe. All that is left are old people and the very young....
> We must have more cattle. We must establish a tribal herd and we must form associations. We must become independent. We can't live on welfare (Cowgill 1974:G1).

However, to make this dream become a reality the tribe felt that they must be allowed "to pump 40,000 gallons of water per day from Havasu Creek to plateau lands above for irrigated pasture" (Cowgill 1974:G1), a proposal that tribal leaders were forced to abandon to avoid losing support from key U. S. senators and representatives who were facing strong opposition from the Park Service and the conservation lobby to allow any further commercial development of the plateau land in an expanded reservation.

Although any hope of getting permission for expansion of commercial development on any returned land to the tribe was soon to be abandoned, on the 8th of January 1974 at a land-use planning meeting attended by representatives from the Indian health service, Arizona State Government, National Park Service, the Bureau of Indian affairs, the Sierra Club, and two Havasupai tribal leaders the possibility of building a tramway to haul only freight from the rim into the canyon was still being considered (C.S. February 3, 1974:5). However, based on a study that had already been made, such a tramway would cost at least a half million dollars to build and would have to haul people as well as freight "to keep from being a loss." At this point, Oscar Paya, one of the tribal leaders present at the meeting while not rejecting the idea of a tramway to at least haul freight into the canyon said that "the tramway should wait then" (C.S. February 3, 1974:5). He was clearly well aware by now that bringing visitors into the canyon by a tramway would be a losing argument in any hope of defeating the tribe's environmental foes.

However, just prior to the critical October 10, 1974 debate and vote on S. 1296, the Grand Canyon enlargement act, by the U. S. House of Representatives:

> .... the Sierra Club, Friends of the Earth and several other conservation groups began circulating reports that the Havasupai had entered into agreements to build a road and two tramways into Havasu Canyon, dry up the falls and build a railroad to Topocoba Hilltop. According to these spokesmen the Havasupai were going to link all these developments with a huge amusement park in Havasu Canyon (C.S. October 21, 1974:1).

And, "On the day of the vote people were stationed at every entrance to the voting chamber telling each congressman that the Havasupai tribe had signed a contract with the Marriott Hotel Corporation" (C.S. October 21, 1974:1).

This enormous distortion of the earlier tribal support for a tramway and for a modest amount of the creek's water to be pumped to the very dry plateau above (probably only at night to avoid any daytime visible change in the in the volume of water going over the falls), both of which ideas they had by now abandoned, "finally angered some of the environmentalists' usually staunchest supporters," such as Morris Udall, John Rhodes, and Sam Steiger and by a vote of 180 to 147 the House voted to pass the Grand Canyon enlargement act even though to the continuing anger of the environmental lobby, the spectacular waterfalls and campground would no longer be part of an enlarged National Park (C.S. October 21, 1974:1).

However, before the enlargement bill could become law, "a Senate-House conference committee was required to meet to iron out the differences between Senate bill S. 1296 which provided only a study of the Havasupai question, and H.R. 5900, the bill the House had just passed (Hirst 2006:233). But such a meeting would be delayed by the October 18 to November 18 Congressional recess during which the 1974 election was held (C.S. January 6, 1975:4). Further delays occurred as Congress "faced many large national issues, including an energy bill, the Soviet-American trade agreement, the Strip Mining Act, and the confirmation of Nelson Rockefeller as vice president" (Hirst 2006:233). Still, despite delaying tactics by "certain elements of the House Interior Committee" on December 12 and 13, "the conferees were finally able to meet and discuss S. 1296" (Hirst 2006:233) and "on Friday the 13th … the conferees finally approved virtually the exact wording of the Udall measure which had passed the house two months earlier" (C.S. January 6, 1975:4).

Further delaying tactics by the House Interior Committee "held up submission of the conference report until 6:30 PM December 17 … only the fact that [two Havasupai tribal leaders] Leon [Rogers] an Ethel [Jack] sat in the committee room the entire day and would not budge until the report was submitted saved us" according to the *Canyon Shadows* (C.S. January 6, 1975:4).

Now only one day remained "for a confirmation vote in both houses of Congress since Thursday, December 19, the House of Representatives would devote to the nomination of Nelson Rockefeller as vice president" after which they would adjourn for the remainder of the year (C.S. January 6, 1975:4). Thus on Wednesday, December 18 after John Rhodes gained a special suspension of the House of Representatives rules, Morris Udall presented the conference report at about 6 p.m. after which Carl Albert, the Speaker of the House:

> …called for a voice vote; by a large margin the ayes had it.
> The report was rushed over to the Senate immediately, and Senators Paul Fannin, Barry Goldwater, and Henry Jackson, without difficulty, obtained final congressional confirmation within the hour (Hirst 2006:236).

Now all that was needed was President Gerald Ford's signature. On December 24, 1974 the bill was presented to him giving him until January 4, 1975 "to sign the measure to prevent its defeat by pocket veto [vetoing a bill by failing to sign it within 10 days of presentation from Congress] (Hirst 2006:236).

After days had gone by with no assurance that Pres. Ford would sign the bill, on January 1, the Havasupai legal representative, Joe Sparks, " learned that an examiner in the Office of Management and Budget would recommend that President Ford veto S. 1296 on the grounds that the Havasupai land return would upset the work of the Indian Claims Commission" which recommendation was made official on January 3 (Hirst 2006:236). A defeat now for the Havasupai would be especially disastrous for the tribe since they would then have to start their efforts all over again in 1975 with the added disadvantage of having lost nineteen of their House of Representatives' supporters in the November 1974 election.

Fortunately for the Havasupai cause, last minute repeated contacts to the White House by Congressman Rhodes and Senator Goldwater combined with a personal visit to President Ford by Sectary of Interior, Rogers Morton, persuaded the President, probably reluctantly, to sign the bill into law the evening of January 3 which he announced the next morning on a call to John Rhodes (Hirst 2006:237).

Undoubtedly, "white guilt" and a certain romanticism many Americans have always felt toward their "own noble savage" played an important part in the Havasupai "victory" over the conservation lobby. Certainly, many members of such groups as the Sierra Club had mixed feelings about the controversy as evidenced by the internal split which had occurred in that particular group over this issue (Hirst 1976:272-275). However, in retrospect, one wonders if it was not in reality the conservation lobby not the Havasupai who had won this final round of the battle. Certainly, this seemed to be the case by the time of my visit to Supai in August 1977.

During the long campaign for the return of their land, tribal spokesmen and lawyers had promised away almost everything that would have made an improved living standard for the Havasupai possible. They already had use rights to almost all the land to which they gained title as the bill was signed into law but now they were prevented from developing the economic potential of this barren property. Overgrazed and short of water it barely supports small herds of horses and a few cows in good years and in 1974, twelve Havasupai pack animals out of a herd of about 100 died of starvation caused by drought (Thomas 1974). Not only had the Havasupai gone on record in opposition to massive tourist development but also against the diversion of creek water to irrigate their parched acreage above the canyon if a feasible economic way could have been found to pump the water up the high canyon walls, an option many Supai residents had earlier strongly favored (Zaphiris 1968:66).

One tribal member confided to me in late 1977 that "nothing had really changed" since the 1975 land transfer. The legislation had even directed the Secretary of the Interior Department to seek input from the National Park Service and Forest Service in addition to the tribe as he prepared a land use plan for the Havasupai and that "no uses shall be permitted under the plan which distract from the existing scenic and natural values of such lands" (Senate Bill 1296(1974); Goldwater 1974; Sparks 1974).

Just off the trail, near the scenic splendors of the waterfalls, above the grave of a small child, in 1973, I sadly observed a weather-battered doll lying in a decomposing crib. This grim reminder of the terrible price that the Havasupai people continued to pay for their wilderness isolation was not even noticed by the average backpacking tourist. In fact, conditions for the weekend backpacker were never better than during my 1977 and 1980 visits. The campground was less crowded than usual and the splendid waterfalls and "noble savages" of Supai had been saved "forever" from the evils of exploitation.

Few campers remember that their own ancestors often fled from the wilderness to the cities to escape from poverty or that today it is seldom the lifelong rural resident who advocates further expansion of our national wilderness areas. For city dwellers, a brief wilderness experience is a welcome change of pace especially when buffered by expensive boots, freeze dried foods, tents, sleeping bags, and other technological gadgets. However, most such adventurers after their brief encounter with the wilderness eagerly anticipate their reunion with the luxuries of urban living, an option that in 1977 no longer appeared to be available to most permanent residents of Supai unless the land use limitations imposed upon them by the restrictive land transfer bill of 1975 were to be circumvented in the future.

Notes Chapter 8

1. Kolb, Ellsworth and Emery, 1914 Experiences in the Grand Canyon. *The National Geographic Magazine*, Vol.XXVI, No.2 August, 1914; Breed. Jack. 1948. Land of the Havasupai. *National Geographic Magazine,* Vol.XCIII(No.5):655-674 (May).

2. Hirst (1976:4,5) talks about the "growing number of tourists" coming to the reservation being "nearly 8000 visitors a year" adding that "Most of them hike into Havasu Canyon, but about a quarter of them prefer to ride the trail." However, in the March 24, 1973 issue of *Canyon Shadows* (C.S. p.7) the number of visitors for the year 1972 was reported to be about 9,000, "about 8,000" of these being hikers and "some 1,000 riders." Obviously, the decision by the Park Service to limit the campground to 100 persons after May 1, 1972 (C.S. March 4, 1972:2) had prevented a repeat of the 1970 overcrowding disaster. For some unknown reason, Hirst fails to talk about this planned reduction but instead gives the impression of a steadily increasing growth of visitors to "nearly 8,000." Also, the 1972 report contradicts his statement that "about a quarter" of the visitors are riders.

3. It is ironic that perhaps one of the most extreme example of this rich-poor class division on reservations is found on the Eastern Cherokee reservation not too far from our lawmakers in Washington D.C. See Stucki (1984).

4. Zaphiris (1968:72) States that out of a total of 82 disputes reported to him, 46 were over land, 6 over "living space", 2 over "trespassing", 20 over horses, 2 over irrigation and 6 over drinking.

5. In 1971, in an attempt to address the many disputes that were coming to the Tribal Council over who had control over the granting of new home sites on the reservation, the Tribal Chairman "...explained that the tribe's constitution and bylaws give the council authority over all tribal territories … the council assigns land and not individuals of the tribe." He told people to stop willing land because they do not own it individually. If the people want to change the law they may do so; In the meantime, the council must enforce the existing law which does not recognize willed land. (C.S. 4/21/71:2)

6. In 1973 I and a group of my students from the University of Nebraska were assigned to set up our tents in this treeless, barren campground on an extremely hot summer day. Although I was willing to "tough it out" my students were not so we quickly retreated to a shadier nearby severely flood damaged and now abandoned campsite closer to the creek.

7. The value of garden produce grown during this year was only estimated to be an additional $955.

8. The current Church Prophet strongly wants to have all members and outsiders to stop calling the church, "the Mormon Church" but instead always refer to it as "The Church of Jesus Christ of Latter-day Saints."

9. During this time period the special films were created for American Indians using Native American actors as a direct result of the Book of Mormon's assertion that American Indians are direct descendants of ancient Israelites that had come by boat to the Americas but that through sin their ancestors had fallen into darkness and moral decay. It was now the duty of the missionaries to teach these "fallen" people their "true" heritage and bring them back into the light of their glorious past. Now, perhaps due to largely (but not totally) unsupportive DNA evidence, the Church has acknowledged that larger non-Israelite populations were present in the New World before the arrival of the Book of Mormon Israelites. Thus, any remaining Israelite genetic heritage in today's Native Americans would be fairly uncommon.

10. Although as Beth Wood (1979:7) points out, "Very little public information is known about the LDS Indian Placement Program. As with their other affairs, Mormons are reluctant to give any data or hard facts about their program," however, Martin (1966:188) records that in 1963 during an eight month period when there was not a replacement for the departing Protestant missionary, "visiting Mormon missionaries made a series of visits and succeeded in getting the parents of all the boarding school students, save one family, to designate the Mormon church as the church they wanted their children to attend while in school. Reportedly, the children liked their newfound faith as the Mormons have many social events and parties while the Protestant missionaries 'just preached.'" According to Martin (1966:187) such other missionary effort in the canyon became common starting in 1927 when the Episcopal church begin sending missionaries on infrequent visits to the village and in 1939 began holding monthly meetings aided by a local convert. However, unfortunately for the church "this man thought that because of his faith he and his family would be protected from misfortune. He subsequently lost three children in two weeks to measles. He lost faith in everything and left the canyon to spend the better part of the next ten years in the bars of Williams and Flagstaff." Martin (1966:187 footnote 61). Since that time, even though in 1948 using a helicopter they flew in a Quonset hut to serve as the mission building (Martin 1966:187-188), their efforts including 20 years spent by one couple translating the new Testament into Havasupai (Ettenborough 1998) have not produced very many converts.

11. No child can be baptized until he or she is at least eight years old.

12. The Church's offer of humanitarian help came as a key part of its efforts to be allowed to continue its missionary conversion efforts in the village.

13. Male missionaries do not use their first names on their official badges. Instead, a man whose name is John Smith would have as an identification the name Elder Smith on his badge

14. . Many of these would have been former school-age children who had been required to be baptized before they would have been allowed to be placed in off-reservation Mormon families during the school year.

15. This set of missionary materials specifically targeted to Native Americans was abandoned (as was also the conversion materials specifically designed for the Los Angeles Jewish community during the time I attended UCLA in the 1960s) soon after the church "introduced in earnest a more consistent approach to the faith that became to be known as correlation. [This] sweeping effort attempted to make every congregation, class and calling the same across all regions, climates and cultures" (Anonymous 2018). This change occurred at least in large part to prevent the loss of centralized leadership control over its worldwide congregations as had happened much earlier in the case of the Catholic Church. (See (Stucki 2009:Chapter 10) for more details about this important change.)

16. The only member of the tribe attending the Sunday service during my visit that year was a very old woman. The only other Native Americans at the meeting were a visiting Hualapai Church leader from Peach Springs who had been sent by the Church to preside over and lead the service and his teenage son. After my last visit to the reservation the last set of full-time missionaries had been pulled out of Supai not to be replaced until "More than 20 years" later in 2006 (Lee 2007:6). This renewal of effort by the Mormon Church began in the spring of 2004 when Doug Angle, first counselor in the Peach Springs, Arizona Branch of the Church started organizing some service projects "helping Supai Residents fix up their homes and yards. It was then that church members begin identifying themselves in the village. Others expressed interest in hearing church lessons and some had been involved in the old American Indian placement program. He estimates there are 40 church members in town" (Arave 2004). Then, after obtaining a lease on an old rundown house at the south end of Supai which was then demolished except for a 30' x 30' cement foundation slab by his son and friends as part of an Eagle Scout project, he and 80 outside volunteers built a small Church chapel that included "a large meeting room and a bedroom for missionaries" whom he hoped would soon be sent there (Arave 2004). This time instead of sending a farmer and his wife for the estimated 60 Havasupai baptized Church members in Supai, the Church sent an older urban missionary couple in 2006 to conduct weekly Church services in the chapel with an attendance that ranged "from four to 18 each Sunday." (Lee 2007:7). During the week they also spent much of their time tutoring children to improve their English language skills. They also would occasionally teach missionary lessons, but these were usually done by a pair of young "elders" who would arrive "about once every other month … to proselytize for a day."

17. However, this has also created a serious weed problem when other crops are attempted

18. I joined this effort in1970 when as a young professor of anthropology at California State College at San Bernardino. (See Appendix C for more details.)

19. An earlier 1969 proposal by Recreational Railroads, Inc., of Washington, D.C. "to construct a tramway and scenic railroad from the reservation to Grand Canyon Village" would have ended the railroad at the Topocoba Hilltop where a 6,500-foot aerial tramway would be built to "take passengers down about 1 mile into Lee's Canyon with the drop of about 1000 feet in elevation from the hilltop" and from there "passengers going to or coming from Supai village would have to walk or ride horses about 13 miles" (Cowgill 1969:B1).

20. However, proponents of the tramway pointed out that although this device would eliminate the need for long distance pack animals, many tourists would still elect to ride the long hot trail from the village to the waterfalls and campgrounds on horseback and have their camp gear and supplies carried on pack animals. Also, Half or full day horseback trips to other scenic viewpoints in the area could easily be established.

21. It was this final payment that made President Ford very reluctant to sign the later land transfer bill. He and his advisers feared that this could lead to new challenges from many other Indian tribes who had also accepted monetary settlements (Hirst 1976:280). Conservation groups and lumber interests also shared this concern especially about federal park and forest lands being claimed by other Indian tribes (Towell 1974:24).

22. The enlarged reservation would now remove the spectacular waterfalls from the enlarged Grand Canyon National Park and end such imposed restrictions as that which my wife, young daughter, and I had experienced on our first trip as described earlier in this chapter.

23. There were three vacancies to be filled on the council during this election. All three of the outgoing council members ran again for the positions and lost. Of all the nine candidates seeking the positions, Lee Marshall fared the worst receiving only eight votes, nine votes fewer than the individual just above him in the vote totals and 20 to 22 votes lower than the winning three individuals (C.S. January 18, 1972:2).

Chapter 9

The fulfillment of their long-held dream had come with a very heavy price since the expansion agreement would require them to forever severely restrict any attempt to greatly expand tourist visitations and accommodations over those few that were already present at Supai. Especially forbidden would be such things as the construction of the original tramway or road proposals to the village and the pumping of water from Havasu Creek to the canyon rim. Thus, in contrast to their neighbors, the Hualapai, who without such restrictions would after eight years of the opening of its extremely popular tourist attraction, the Grand Canyon Skywalk, in 2015 record its 1 million[th] paying visitor that year[1], no such option would be available to them. Instead, the Havasupai on their official website have recently decide to capitalize on the growing numbers of "adventure tourists" who are willing to pay a high price to spend a few days in "Shangri-La." Therefore, beginning in 2019, the tribe required a stay of a minimum of three nights with a camping and reservation fee of $100 per person per night Monday through Thursday, and $125 per night Friday through Sunday. And in 2020 for those staying in the lodge, the charge is $440 per night, each room accommodating up to 4 persons, each of which will be charged an additional $110 entrance/environmental fee. And for those hikers willing to pay extra to have their backpacks carried by Pack Mules to the campground or lodge and then at the end of their visit back to the hilltop parking lot, the price is $400 round-trip per Pack Mule, each one of which can carry up to 4 bags. The charge for emergency Pack Mules (if available) is $400 one-way and campers on the day they will be hiking back to the hilltop who bring their packs to the "campsite drop off point" later then 7am will be charged an extra $300. Daytime hiking to the waterfalls and back to the hilltop in one day is now forbidden.

So far, this steep hike in fees has not led to a decreased number of visitors seeking to obtain, as early in the year as possible, the highly coveted entry permissions even though the average income level of the visitors is probably much higher than it had been previously. However, despite this tremendous increase in tribal income many of the societal problems that the earlier tramway proposal had sought to alleviate still remain.

Especially troubling were major floods that occurred in 1990, 1993, and 1997. Of these the 1997 flood was especially disastrous when 3 to 4 inches of rain fell on the watershed area of Havasu Creek within two-and-one-half hours Sunday morning August 10th (Anonymous August 11, 1997b; CNN August 11, 1997). "About a dozen homes had been flooded with a foot or two of water" according to a B.I.A. spokesman and up to 400 tourists who had been camping and attending the reservation's annual Peach Festival were described as being "trapped ... but basically safe" (Anonymous August 11, 1997b; CNN August 11, 1997). By nightfall that day about 60 people had been flown out of the canyon by helicopter and by the next afternoon "some 300 people" most who were tourists had been airlifted out to a shelter being set up in a school gymnasium on the nearby Hualapai reservation (CNN August 12, 1997; Anonymous August 12, 1997c). And by Wednesday it was reported that "more than 350" village residents along with "more than 300 tourists" had been evacuated from the canyon by helicopter (Anonymous August 13, 1997d).

To help the displaced residents, U.S. Interior Secretary Bruce Babbitt announced that the government would provide $300,000 in emergency assistance funds to meet the immediate needs for food, shelter, and clothing for the residents who had been airlifted from their homes (Hanna and Sweeney August 12, 1997; Anonymous August 13, 1997d). Additional money would be needed to repair major damage to the village's sewer system that sustained several pipeline breaks and one 400-foot section that was washed away. This was a especially serious since the sewer line damage had contaminated the water system, meaning that clean water to village residents wouldn't be restored until the sewer was repaired (Anonymous August 13, 1997d).

As bad as this flash flood was, the damage it caused to the Canyon and the tribe's tourism industry was vastly overshadowed by the flood of 2008 when the breaching of an earthen dam and three days of heavy upstream thunderstorms on August 15, 16, and 17 "increased the flow of Havasu Creek from a normal 66 feet per second to nearly 6,000 feet per second" (Witt 2010:69). A group of Utah hikers vividly described how they narrowly escaped the rushing waters that "sent a rush of water through parts of the canyon, uprooting trees, washing out trails and footbridges" trapping them while it "swept away tents, rafts, packs, food and supplies" (Gehrke 2008:A1). In all:

> …1600 feet of trails were obliterated or damaged. Navajo Falls, a favorite playground for visitors, was suddenly sucked dry. Naturally, creation accompanied destruction as the rerouted creek carved a deep new channel, revealing a plunging red canyon and three new waterfalls (Witt 2010:69).

The damage was so extensive that it was uncertain by late October if it could be repaired before the beginning of the following spring's tourist season even though about 100 tribal members starting in mid-August had been working to clear debris from and rebuild the campground and trail (Fonseca 2008:A19).

As it turned out the work to restore the campground and trail was only completed in time to reopen the canyon for visitors on June 1, 2009 (Witt 2010:70) and would have been even later had it not been for a very generous $1 million dollar donation from the California-based San Manuel band of Serrano Mission Indians on October 23, 2008 (Fonseca 2008:A19). In explaining why his tribe had made such a generous donation to the Havasupai, Chairman James Ramos said that after his band members had watched TV footage showing hundreds being evacuated via helicopter:

> … the tribe can relate to the hardship. In the 1980s, A flood washed out their sewer lines, And it was months before the lines were repaired.
> "We feel very good about helping our brothers and sisters, the Supai people…. We believe this needs to happen. Who knows when we might be on the other side of the fence?" (Fonseca 2008:A19).

Also, the neighboring tribe, the Hualapai, donated 10 percent of the money it received for the four weeks it provided shelter for those evacuated from the canyon by helicopter (Fonseca 2008:A19).

Ten years later, just before dark on July 11, 2018 and again before sunrise the next morning two periods of extremely heavy rain sent floodwaters through the campground:

... forcing the evacuation of about 200 tourists. Some, wearing only their swimsuits, had to abandon their camping gear.

Footbridges collapsed, tents were buried in sand and debris strewn about as water rushed over the landscape. Campers sought refuge on benches, in trees and in caves. The existing waterfalls turned a muddy brown, and new ones emerged from the steep walls of the canyon (Fonseca 2018:C9).

Fortunately, the flooding was not as severe as it had been in 2008 and all but 17 of the tourists were able to hike uphill to the community center in the village where they spent the night followed the next morning after the waters had receded by the remaining 17 (Fonseca 2018:C9). And to help these unfortunate campers:

The tribe opened a small store in the village for tourists and didn't charge for food or water. Tourists and tribal members gave out socks and shoes.... A lodge on the way to the canyon offered free showers and breakfast to the evacuees (Fonseca 2018:C9).

And a year later a "News Brief" in the *Navajo Times* December 5, 2019 reported:

A popular tourist spot deep in a gorge off the Grand Canyon known for its blue-green waterfalls will make repairs after heavy flooding over the Thanksgiving break sent tourists scrambling to higher ground.

About 170 people were at the Havasu Falls campground when water rushed through early Friday raising the creek that flows through it by about 1.5 feet (half a meter), tourists said.

No one was injured in the flooding on the Havasupai Reservation, And the water receded within hours. The extent of the damage is unknown.

The tribe soon plans to send crews to survey the 10-mile trail and the campground which closed for the season this week (News Brief 2019:C7).

Another continuing problem that resists a permanent solution (given the severe land use restrictions that the tribe had to agree to before Congress and the President would allow the passage of a bill to greatly expand their reservation) was brought to national attention when on January 23, 2017, the *New York Times* reported on a federal lawsuit filed against the government by members of the Havasupai Tribe saying that the United States had reneged on its legal duty to educate their children citing a recent evaluation that students there were performing well below every other school on Indian reservations which in turn were already among the worst in the nation. (Santos 2017:A-9). Thus, as seen in the earlier chapters, despite the many attempts beginning in the

1890s by very motivated teachers any progress initially made proved to have been ephemeral.[2] This continuing failure was visibly demonstrated when zero percent of Havasupai elementary students tested "proficient" in both English and math during the 2014-15 school year (Woods 2018).

Important clues for this long-term failure can be found in the story by Woods and Cano (2017) of "a former Havasupai teacher who hoped to help students in a Grand Canyon Village [but] instead found a school that appeared to be failing a community." Thus, even compared to native students in other BIE schools where only 53 percent go on to graduate from high school, a rate far below the national average, things were much worse at Supai where only 20 percent continue on to high school graduation according to Woods and Cano who then add:

> The tiny Havasupai Tribe's only school is the worst in the Bureau of Indian education system that Congress once called a "national disgrace." It has few textbooks and only a small library. There are no clubs or sports teams, no choir or art programs. Students with learning disabilities are often just sent home. Classes end at noon most Fridays so teachers can leave the Canyon early....
> The 2015-16 school year had started three weeks late because the school staff was even thinner than usual. When classes finally began, students arrive to classrooms led by teachers who sometimes rotated in and out of Supai on two-week assignments. The school janitor and secretary each covered a class. There was no principal, so [a teacher] filled in but kept teaching.... So began another year in which Havasupai children learned almost nothing.... The seventh and eighth grade teaching job was still open in March. (Woods and Cano 2017:3,4)

Mary Beth Burke, the new teacher that year was especially concerned about the fact that "About half of Havasupai Elementary's students have recognized disabilities, and yet few received any services to address them," (Woods and Cano 2017:7)

A year later, the lawyers pursuing the lawsuit against the government said that "... the case from a small, remote school at the bottom of the Grand Canyon could send shockwaves throughout the BIE system" (Pineo 2018:A11) adding that:

> We're not saying that every school has the same exact issues that Havasupai struggles with, but the sorts of claims that we're bringing in [this case] are systematic to bureau schools across the country.

The conditions include classes limited to the basics of math and English, a lack of special education resources and understaffed classrooms ... throughout the school.

And despite attempts by the attorneys representing the federal government to dismiss the case, a federal judge in Arizona ruled that spring that the case could continue (Woods 2018).

As seen in many other national problems, spending additional huge amounts of dollars alone will never solves this failure although such things as building repairs and the provision of computers and improved internet connections do need increased funding. A far worse problem on most reservations is the problem of attracting and retaining fully qualified teachers. This is especially true at Supai where:

> The school is constantly understaffed. Administrators combine classes and have assigned school secretaries and a janitor to cover classrooms. Teachers who do move into the Canyon rarely stay more than one year, and employees who push for change are often forced out (Woods 2018).

In retrospect, had federal legislation not been passed that prohibits any revival of the original tramway proposal with the possibility of building a school on the rim of the canyon above the village, it is quite possible that the tribe would have a much easier time attracting and retaining qualified teachers who would then have much easier and faster access to the non-reservation outside world since few such teachers have the financial resources to pay for frequent expensive helicopter rides in or out of the reservation. Thus, as two young teachers told an Arizona Republic reporter in 1972 (Thomas 1972:C1):

> "It's quite a chore to just to get out of the canyon. You have to plan ahead. It really takes a three-day weekend. We manage maybe once a month to get out." Sue said.
> "We ride a horse the 8½ miles up to hilltop, where the road ends, and usually hitch a ride with the mailman into Peach Springs. We can always get someone to drive us to into Valentine [where their car was parked]. So far our car has started right up even though it has been sitting a long time."

Trash removal also remains a problem despite rules that all backpackers are required to leave no trash behind as they depart the canyon. Several visitors to the

Canyon since the year 2000 have told me that trash can still be seen along the trail, in the village, and in the campground and that not all of it, especially alcoholic beverage containers, had been left by backpackers who are especially forbidden from bringing alcohol into the canyon. And one scout leader who had had his scout troop clean up the campground of trash left behind by other backpackers, despite the rule forbidding such behavior, became very angry when the tribal official at the tourist office, instead of thanking the scouts, insisted that they pack out of the canyon not only their own trash but all of the additional campground trash that they had collected as a favor to the tribe. Reluctantly, they left the office with the extra trash but then quickly ditched it at a location just before leaving the south end of Supai.

Also troublesome to the tribe, I strongly suspect, are the accusations on the Internet, especially by PETA, that Havasupai pack horses and mules are being abused as well as complaints from visitors about the lodge, its condition, and the person running it. On the other hand, tribal residents continue to have their own complaints about the bad behavior of many visitors, especially troubling being the unwelcome taking of photos and videos. Thus, effective November 3, 2018, in "CHAPTER 18, TOURISM" of the document "HAVASUPAI TRIBE LAW AND ORDER CODE" whose purpose is "to protect the community and environment of the Havasupai Reservation, and to ensure the safety of tourists, by regulating the activities and practices of tourists visiting the Havasupai Reservation and of companies who bring tourists to the Reservation" in Section 18.7 states:

> Supai is a living community and the privacy of its residents must be respected at all times. Tourists or outfitters taking pictures or video of tribal members, their homes, or the village is strictly prohibited, unless advance written permission has been granted by the Tribal Chairperson or Tribal Council. Cameras must be put away between the first home south of the village and the last home on the trail to the waterfalls. Pictures of Tribal members or their animals on the trail may only be taken with the permission of the individual pecker. Camera used for taking video or photos in prohibited areas may be confiscated, and persons who violate this Section may be liable for a civil fine of $250.00 and expulsion from the reservation.

The serious nature of these and many other remaining problems that cannot be solved merely by increasing the fees charged incoming tourists merit a re-examination of Martin Goodfriend's massive June 1, 1976 analysis entitled <u>The Havasupi Indian Reservation: An Economic Profile</u> in which he states (p. 38):

> This report has shown that Supai is imprisoned by remoteness. Its lifelines are frail. If helicopter service is curtailed, or if parcel post service is discontinued, or if less freight is brought in by horses, Supai will face a crisis almost overnight.
>
> Even if the present services continue unabated, Supai is paying dearly for them. Its costs of bringing in freight, either by helicopter or horse … would be considered outrageous in any other town. These costs render many everyday problems almost insoluble….
>
> These problems must be faced. There is only one solution: a cable car, to be used only for hauling freight – never passengers.
>
> Environmentalists may object. Probably they are unaware of the damage done by the dust and air-blasts of incessant helicopter landings and takeoffs (1,200 of each last year). To people in Supai, the helicopter is becoming intolerable, but this may not disturb environmentalists who live elsewhere.
>
> A cable car is the only way to ease the packers' burden. To feed the present number of horses, packers will have to buy a minimum of 300,000 pounds of pellets each year. There is no other way they can keep their horses working. And they must spend thousands of hours of otherwise unproductive time merely bringing the pellets in.
>
> As long ago as 1963: a study made by consultants showed that Supai's supply system is wasteful, inefficient, and precarious. Supai residents can never live a normal life until they are free from this slow, costly, 19th-century way of moving goods
>
> Of the money paid for helicopter service, not a dime stays in Supai.

That such a proposed solution might still be acceptable to key allies in the environmental community can be seen when the possibility of building a tramway to haul only freight from the rim into the canyon was still being considered on the 8th of January 1974 at a land-use planning meeting attended by representatives from the Indian health service, Arizona State Government, National Park Service, the Bureau of Indian affairs, the Sierra Club, and two Havasupai tribal leaders (C.S. February 3, 1974:5). However, at that time based on a study that had already been made, such a tramway would cost at least a half million dollars to build and would have to haul people as well as freight "to keep from being a loss." At this point, Oscar Paya, one of the tribal leaders present at the meeting while not rejecting the idea of a tramway to at least haul freight into the canyon said that "the tramway should wait then" (C.S. February 3, 1974:5). He was clearly well aware by then that bringing visitors into the canyon by a tramway would be a losing argument in any hope of defeating the tribe's environmental foes.

However, since the tribe has now put its emphasis on attracting visitors willing to pay a relatively high price to experience a wilderness adventure, an example from Zion National Park provides an important clue about how to make a visit to Havasu Canyon more exciting than ever while at the same time providing a way to keep a non-tourist, freight tramway from becoming a financial loss.

Thus, in Zion, in addition to such wilderness adventures as wading the Virgin River narrows and hiking to the "subway," the most exciting and extremely popular activity is the climb to the top of Angels Landing giving the visitor the same sort of thrill that one gets climbing down the cliff to Mooney Falls in Havasu Canyon. And to explain why such a comparison has any value in an attempt to solve the remaining societal problems at Supai given that it does not appear that in the foreseeable future any water from Havasu Creek will be allowed to be pumped to the plateau above Supai to permit the construction of such things as pastureland, a school, housing for Havasupai families, teachers, health clinic workers, etc., here is the following proposal:

1. Repair and extend the road that for many years until 1957 (Wampler 1959:109) was used by the mail bus on Tuesdays and Fridays as well as by such occasional visitors as National Geographic's Jack Breed that at the time of his 1948[3] visit still provided an eastern access link between Supai and the outside world (Breed 1948:655). This road extends 35 miles from Grand Canyon Village through Rowes Well to Topocoba Hilltop that is the trailhead for a 14-mile horse and foot trail to Supai. Although this older road was replaced in 1938 by a "new graded road … built to Hualapai hilltop from a point near Peach Springs" (Hughes 1967: 161) as the main access road to the reservation, the reasons for the replacement have nothing to do with the older road itself, except for not being graded, but instead include the following: 1) The trail distance from the new hilltop

to Supai is only 8 miles as opposed to a distance of 14 miles from the Topocoba Hilltop. 2) The 14-mile trail passes through canyons with greater drainage areas than the shorter 8-mile trail in its side canyon before entering the reservation and "suffered periodic damaging floods" (Hirst 2006:163) probably more severe than those that are now occurring on the shorter trail. 3) I also strongly suspect that such a change was part of the continuing attempts by the National Park and National Forest Service to greatly diminish the control or return of any land within their boundaries to the tribe as has been documented in earlier chapters in this book. Thus beginning in 1935 "the government began improvement of the hazardous western trail down Hualardoi Canyon at a cost of some $10,000" (Hirst 2006:163) and in 1938 built a new graded road to Hualapai Hilltop from a point near Peach Springs (Hughes 1967:161). And beginning in 1967 work began to widen and straighten this road as it was being prepared for hard top surfacing (Wampler 1959: added material on 1971:112).

2. However, the last stretch of the older road instead of ending at Topocoba Hilltop should be extended to end at a point on the plateau above the upper end of Schoolhouse Canyon where there would be a simple shelter and parking lot for Supai residents' vehicles, postal/supply/repair vehicles, shuttle busses (for schoolchildren, reservation holding tourists, and Supai residents), and other vehicles holding Tribal Council permits..

3. At the end of this road a tramway would be built down Schoolhouse Canyon to Supai possibly ending somewhere near the tourist lodge. However, the **primary** function of this tramway will **not** be to transport visitors in or out of the canyon. Instead, there will be a new adventure trail leading from the end of the road to the upper end of Carbonate Canyon that will follow that canyon down to the campground at the base of Havasu Falls.

4. There will probably be sections on of this trail that will require the same sort of solution that the early miners used to create a safe but exciting way to descend from the campground to the base of Mooney Falls that are also similar to the National Park's use of safety chains to make the climb to the top of Angels Landing not only safe but exciting.

5. For those few visitors too fearful to use the trail, a much higher fee should be charged to be allowed to travel to or from Supai on the tramway.

6. In order to avoid any new opposition to this proposal from the tribe's former environmental opponents there should be no attempt to increase the numbers of visitors allowed into the reservation over those numbers presently allowed.

7. Although there will be some hikers who could make it through such difficult trail sections carrying heavy backpacks, most might have trouble so the best approach, for comfort and safety reasons, would be to **require** the visitors before starting down the trail to leave their backpacks to be sent down on the tramway to Supai where they would be carried by packhorse down to the campground.   And for the trip back the reverse sequence would occur. For this service each visitor would be charged as least as much as is now charged them for having their backpacks packed by horse into and out of the canyon.

8. For those departing from the campground, a set time to bring backpacks to a pickup point will be required as it is at the present time.

9. For safety reasons hiking the trail up or down should only be done during daylight hours. This should be strictly enforced.

10. The tribe should purchase or perhaps lease land in or near Tusayan to build a dormitory for its school children so that they could attend the nearby public elementary and high schools. (An alternative might be the purchase of an existing hotel. Any extra rooms not needed for the school students could then be rented out to tourists or used to house Havasupai individuals and families employed in the Tusayan area.) The combination

of the tramway and a school bus on an improved road to Tusayan would make it possible for the children and Havasupai working adults to come home on weekends, leaving Tusayan on Friday afternoon and returning Sunday evening. This same bus would also be used throughout the week to shuttle tourists holding reservations for either the campground or the lodge as well as Supai residents and others holding Tribal Council permits to and from Supai.

11. One of the main benefits of this proposal would be that it would provide, as in the old days, a much better way to enjoy the freedom of spending winter days on the sunnier plateau instead of remaining for months confined to the dark, damp, dreary canyon bottom. There, on this important part of former tribal plateau lands, as a substitute for the old days when families would make a living doing such things as hunting deer and other hunting and gathering activities, Havasupai could now make a living working in the winter tourist industry or helping with the boarding school or, if a hotel had been purchased or built, the many tasks associated with running and maintaining it. Also, it would be possible for individuals or families to continue living in the canyon during winter weekends, if they wished, but commute to and from employment in the Tusayan area, living there during the work week in a hotel or other tribally owned or provided housing (perhaps sharing it there with their school-aged and other children). And if enough families chose this latter option there might be no need for a boarding school at all, perhaps the best of all alternatives. I still vividly remember during my days as a professor at California State College at San Bernardino hearing about the dismal state of the educational instruction occurring at the nearby BIA Riverside boarding school from one of my returning war veteran students. His class assignment had been to spend a week at the school interviewing both the teaching staff and students. He quickly found that very little class instruction was actually occurring there. Most instructors had given up

even trying to teach anything to the students. Classroom behavior was completely out of control in many of the rooms he visited but as long as the teachers could prevent students from actually leaving the classroom during the class period that was all that administrators required them to do to keep their employment. One instructor even invited him to try to teach the scheduled lesson for the day to his unruly students, an experience that my war veteran student would never forget. Thus, I can greatly empathize with the ongoing efforts of Havasupai parents to avoid having to send their school-age children to any boarding school especially the far away Fort Apache one where I suspect conditions were not that much different from what I learned was occurring in 1970 at the Riverside boarding school.

12. On this land the tribe would also construct a new Havasupai parking lot/shuttle bus pick up point for all tourists holding reservations for either the campground or the lodge (or use an existing hotel parking lot). Enough spaces in the parking lot should be reserved for the vehicles of those holding reservations for either the campground or lodge and such visitors before being allowed to board the shuttle bus would have to verify their reservations, making sure that all required fees had been paid,

13. All such visitors would be required to leave their vehicles in this parking lot during their visit to the reservation. They would not be allowed to drive their own vehicles to the tramway and new trail.

14. On the road to the tramway and the new trail, at the reservation boundary would be posted an enormous warning sign telling all motorists that from this point on, the road is only open to Supai residents, the "Supai Transit System" shuttle bus, postal/supply/repair vehicles or other vehicles holding valid entry permits from the Havasupai Tribal Council. All others would be subject to arrest and/or fines.

15. A similar warning sign should be placed on the road to the Hualapai Hilltop at the reservation boundary telling motorists that from this point on, the road and the 10-mile trail to Supai are only open to Supai residents or

others authorized by the Tribal Council such as the nearby Hualapai. All others would be subject to arrest and/or fines. Closing this entryway to Supai and its waterfalls for visitors would give the residents of the village the long desired privacy that has been denied them by the seemingly endless number of picture taking backpackers passing by their houses at all hours of the day and night on their way to and from the campground and waterfalls.

16. In order to lower the cost of operating the tramway there is no need for the tramway to be operated on a continuous basis. Instead, a schedule for its operation should be determined on the basis of the transportation needs of Supai's residents and its suppliers coordinated with runs to carry visitor backpacks up or down. Supai residents would not have to pay any fee as long as they used it during the time it was operating for other purposes e.g., the transport of the tourist backpacks up or down, mail, incoming goods or supplies, schoolchildren coming in or out, etc. Nor would they have to pay any fee on any additional Tribal Council approved "bus-like" scheduled runs in and out of the canyon.

Although there may be some in the environmental community that would object to both the extended road and the tramway, I'm sure they, especially along with the residents of Supai, would welcome a drastic reduction in the number of helicopter flights in and out of Supai with all their accompanying noise, dust, and air blasts. Also, with a more dependable and easier way to obtain food for their horses, there would be far fewer, if any, "half-starved"[4] horses for PETA members to secretly photo but openly share on the Internet. And, the often crowded, unsanitary camping that, at least in the past, has occurred at the present hilltop parking lot would cease[5].

This new proposal would also solve the current enormous waste disposal problem. Although there has long been a "pack-it-all-out" policy in effect for backpackers, not only have many left ordinary types of trash behind in the campground but also items of camping gear in order to lighten their backpacks to make the, at times difficult, hike back to their cars easier[6], a choice they will no longer have to make. Also, Supai's residents given their very few landfill options, would appreciate this better way to deal with ordinary household waste as well as a way to get rid of no longer useful larger items such as I and other visitors would sometimes see in the yards of some of the houses we passed by as we walked through the village on our way to the campground.

Now returning to the two major problems addressed in the beginning of this chapter, in light of the increasing frequency of floods in recent years necessitating the emergency evacuation of tourists from Canyon, a tramway would be a far cheaper alternative than the current transport by helicopter. Also, since both the new trail and the tramway would not be located in the main flood prone Canyon there will be much less damage to repair after a flood, which damage in the 2008 flood shutdown destroyed visitation income to the reservation for about nine months,

And Goodfriend (1976:38) gives the following examples of why a cable car (tramway)[7] would be a far superior and enormously cheaper way than the current helicopter to solve everyday problems facing the residents of Supai:

> An example: the store's refrigerator stops functioning. What can be done? If it is to be sent back to the supplier, a container must be found for a 14-foot object; elaborate arrangements must be made for a helicopter flight and trucking pick-up. Or if a mechanic is to come in, he will insist on being ferried by helicopter. The helicopter must wait while he works. The round trip would cost hundreds of dollars – for a minor repair.
> Such complications confront anyone in Supai when a window is broken, a door warps, a pipe leaks. Repairs or replacements are not easily available.
> Another example: whenever a member of the tribe dies outside the valley, the body is brought down by helicopter, costing the family around $500. If the family cannot pay, it must borrow from the Tribal Council, and may never be able to repay its dept.

Turning now to the school situation at Supai, throughout the entire history of the school at Supai although it has been able to attract a number of adventuresome young teachers, few of them remain for more than a year or two after facing the types of problems described earlier in this chapter. Thus, I feel it is now time to reconsider the "acceptable compromise solution" described in chapter 7 when "during the summer of

1961 the Bureau of Indian affairs explored the possibility of sending Supai children to the public school in Grand Canyon where the children would not be as far from home as they would be if they continued to attend Fort Apache" (Meador and Roessel, Jr.1962:30). Although, at that time this attempt was dropped after the National Park Services refused to be willing to provide the necessary land on which a dormitory could be built, the possibility of purchasing land or a hotel in the Tusayan area for a school dormitory should now be seriously reconsidered.

This "compromise solution" would be a win-win opportunity for the students who would now have access to a wider variety of school offerings and any needed special-education needs and the teachers who would no longer feel the social and emotional stress of living in Supai. And the new proposed road would also provide a much cheaper way than paying for a helicopter ride out for many Havasupai having medical conditions that need to be treated but are not immediately life-threatening or any others seeking such aid to enter or leave the canyon. Certainly, having far fewer noisy helicopter landings and takeoffs, creating dust and air-blasts, would be welcomed not only by the residents of Supai but also by their visiting tourist guests who come to the reservation seeking a brief wilderness escape from the outside world.

Another, much less likely, possibility for obtaining the necessary property for a school dormitory and visitor parking lot would be to obtain permission from the National Park Service to build such a structure on the 160 acres set aside in 1926 for a Havasupai Indian "camp" about two miles west of Grand Canyon Village as part of the continuing effort to rid other areas of the Park of Havasupai Indians beginning in 1903 when President Roosevelt rode down into the canyon where he found the Havasupai Yavñmi' Gswedva (Dangling Beard) living at his family home and further down the trail Burro and his family in what is now called Indian Garden and urged both of them through an interpreter to vacate the area so that their lands could become part of a new national park (Hirst 2006:81,83, 157).

Though now confined to this new camp "a considerable number of Havasupai Indians found employment in Grand Canyon Village" despite the fact that they were not provided with "adequate medical attention, proper housing or adequate water" (Hughes 1967:161) until 1936 when:

> the National Park Service provided new cabins, and the Indian Service made arrangements with the resident physician to give medical care. Later, the older shacks were torn down, And Havasupai children began to attend the Grand Canyon school (Hughes 1967:161).

However, by 1976 having lost control over the Havasupai campground and waterfalls, the National Park Service was determined to eliminate this last 160-acre remnant of Havasupai occupied land within the national park boundary. At first all of the remaining four families in the camp "said that they'd be happy to move" out of the cabins, "built in the 1930s that had no plumbing and were "lighted by bare electric bulbs" and with wood stoves used for both heating and cooking, to concessionaire housing in the Park but, Steve Hirst, listed in a news article as being the "tribal spokesman," (Anonymous January 21,1977a:B2) was able to obtain a delay in the Park's plans to tear down the remaining houses for at least another year (Anonymous January 21,1977a:B2) after successfully arguing that:

> "The area has a lot of symbolic meaning to the tribe…. It's kind of the last hold of the tribe to an area where they used to live. They've been there for a thousand years or more."
> "I think the Park Service is aware of the special meaning but they'd like to make the Havasupais like everyone else in the park. We have a sort of moral claim, and that's what they're trying to resist." (Anonymous January 21,1977a:B2).

And to the relief of Hirst and the Tribal Council, three of the four families now sided with the position of the Tribal Council and decided they did not want to move to the offered concessionaire housing in the Park. However, when a relative of one of the remaining three families asked to be allowed to occupy the now, "boarded up and adorned with a condemned sign," house vacated by the fourth family, "his request was denied" because "the relative was not employed at the park and park policy is for housing to be provided by employers" (Anonymous January 21,1977a:B2). However, despite the Park Service being "uncomfortable about extending police authority over the people living there," repairs on the remaining three occupied houses were made and the Park Service continued to pick up trash and provide other services at the camp in return for $20 a month rent from each of the three remaining families. (Anonymous January 21,1977a:B2).

Since that time, it has not been easy for the author of this book during the current Corona virus pandemic to discover the fate of this camp. However, at the beginning of May 2020, when I made a phone call to Grand Canyon National Park, the Park Ranger answering told me that there was no Havasupai Indian camp in the park and he was not even aware that there had ever been such a camp in the park. And even page 157 in Hirst's 2006 book in which he states that an unknown number "still reside" there is merely a reprint of page 201 in his 1976 book.

I now feel that even if the National Park Service would be willing to transfer the old camp's 160 acres to the tribe for a school dormitory and visitor parking lot, a most unlikely possibility, the Tusayan location would still be a better choice for the following reasons:

1. Even if permission to build the boarding school and parking lot on the old Havasupai camp land were obtained there would still remain the difficulty of providing adequate quantities of water to this site.

2. This would give the tribe much more freedom to add such features as a gift shop, visitor center, museum, restaurant, or visitor lodging that would provide much needed revenue for the tribe during the winter months when their canyon campground is shut down.

3. Such features would open up more and often better paying[8] full time jobs for both male and female Havasupai workers as well as part-time jobs for older Havasupai high school students

4. Even the possibility of a gambling casino could be considered.

5. This would become a place to create and sell Havasupai handicrafts and possibly those of other tribes in a location that even in the off-season winter months is still visited by large numbers of tourists.

6. Most importantly, this property would give the tribe legal ownership of a small but very important portion of its former land, a toehold that Steve Hirst feared would be lost forever as he argued against the National Park's decision to shut down the old Havasupai "Indian camp" saying: "The area has a lot of symbolic meaning to the tribe.... It's kind of the last hold of the tribe to an area where they used to live. They've been there for a thousand years or more." (Anonymous January 21,1977a:B2) and would enable them in a visitor center to inform tourists through exhibits, a short film documentary, and the sale of such items as Stephen Hirst's excellent book "I AM THE GRAND CANYON: The Story of the Havasupai People" to learn why this area has always been so important to them and also portray the key role that Havasupai workers played in the development of the trails, bridges, and water/sewer lines of the modern National Park (See Chapter Note 8 on page 161).

Turning now to the question of how to obtain the fairly large amount of money needed to finance all parts of this proposal, there are many extremely wealthy individuals as well as federal and state politicians in recent years that are seeking opportunities to publicly show their support for a worthy cause. Thus I am certain, given the tremendous support that the Havasupai received from many such individuals during their bitter struggle to regain control of a large chunk of their ancestral land, that such an individual or group of individuals would be more than willing to supply or help obtain the needed funds in exchange for the public honor or political advantage such support would bestow upon the donor.

Another source of needed funds might be the Navajo tribe or perhaps the Hopis who in return for tribal economic support could be given not only a guaranteed share of any revenue generated but also preferential job placement and an additional place to create and sell their own Native American handicrafts in a location that even in the off-season winter months is still visited by large numbers of tourists. And perhaps the Navajos might be willing to purchase an existing hotel in Tusayan to lease to the Havasupai as an investment possibility if the Havasupai chose to create a mini-casino on the property especially if they, the Navajos, using their Twin Arrows casino expertise would be allowed to share or take over control of such a casino.

Another major advantage for the Navajo Nation, even if the casino option was not chosen, would be that a Twin Arrows reservation center could be located in or by a Havasupai museum or gift shop that would offer special lodging deals to tourists on their way out of the National Park who would otherwise seek lodging for the night in a closer Flagstaff hotel or motel.

Notes Chapter 9

1. (Region Briefs 2015:C-5)
2. The ephemeral nature of these attempts can be easily seen in a 1957 table listing the percent of Havasupai Indians "6 years of age and over who read English and who speak English" (Meador and Roessel, Jr. 1962:14) where although the percentage of those who could speak English increased from 27% of those 45 or older to 94% of those between ages 18 and 44, it dropped to 82% among those ages 6 to 17. And although the percentage of those who could read English increased from 11% of those 45 or older to 81% of those between ages 18 and 44, it dropped to 68% among those ages 6 to 17.
3. An exact year for this visit is not given in the 1948 article.
4. Martin (1966:41,42) explains the reason for the existence of such animals at Supai in the following passage from his 1966 Ph.D. Dissertation: "… the way, land is distributed results in the situation where not enough feed is grown in the canyon to support the number of horses maintained there…. And, for cultural reasons as well as because they cannot afford it, the packers do not buy sufficient feed to make up the difference between what their pack animals require and what is locally available. Without the availability of the rangeland on the plateau, the Havasupai tourist packing system would thus be constricted by a lack of feed. This situation is avoided, however, through the use of several strings by each packer and the practice of bringing in feed "on the hoof." This practice amounts to no more than the practice of bringing in a grass fattened string of pack animals from the plateau and working them, on inadequate feed, until they are so thin that they are barely able to walk back up the trail to the plateau again. At this point they are released, and a fresh string of grass fattened horses is brought down and the process is repeated. Thus, a packer, by switching his pack strings two or three times during his summer, may get by on the inadequate local supply of animal feed without having to buy supplemental hay or grain."

5. On several of my trips to the reservation, the portable toilets were completely filled to the top with human waste and were unusable forcing people to relieve themselves by the sides of their cars.

6. The final last mile of this hike is especially difficult after the sun has arisen on a hot day since the trail becomes much steeper and there is no shade in which to rest.

7. Perhaps Goodfriend is wise using the term "cable car" rather than "Tramway" since the primary purpose of this aerial transport system is not to transport endless numbers of tourists up and down on a continuous basis. Therefore, to break this misleading public misconception it might be shrewd to choose a different name for the tramway/shuttle bus combination (e.g., my suggested "Supai Transit System.")

8. For many years the work skills of the Havasupai were highly valued for such tasks as the 42 who were hired to carry ten steel cables each 550 feet long and one and one half inch in diameter and weighing 2320 pounds down the Kaibab trail to complete a new bridge across the Colorado River (Hughes 1967:139,140). Compared to members of other tribes in the area the superior size and strength of Havasupai males made them especially desirable for heavy pipeline work (Hirst 1976:202). Thus they were hired to work on the new sewer line and the water line from Bright Angel Creek. They also worked on the new Kaibab Suspension Bridge across the Colorado River and the maintenance of Bright Angel Trail (Hirst 1976:201:2006:157). "Havasupai women worked for the most part as maids, kitchen helpers, and laundresses at Grand Canyon" while after "the trails and building construction of the 1920s were completed the men were left with more menial jobs like washing and bussing dishes" (Hirst 2006:158).

Excerpts from a class report by a female student as a participant in a 1973 class field trip to study tourism development on several Indian reservations.

...The museum exhibits in Grand Canyon National Park and the slide projector show given in the park at the theater present a very romanticized view of the Havasupai. In one exhibit it was stated that the Havasupai are irrigation farmers and proud their yields are usually greater than their neighbors when in fact, agriculture is on the decline there, and has been for years. If it was not, there would be no need for Brigham Young University to send people there to encourage the Havasupai to raise more than the little they do. The statement was also made that the Havasupai raise cattle, when in fact they do not have any cattle at all[1]. During the slideshow, it was stated that the Havasupai live in harmony with their surroundings, when a walk through the village with trash visible on the trails would suffice to show the idea of the noble savage repairing and preserving his land is nothing but a myth. People are often very disappointed when they arrive in Havasupai and actually see how they live.

A week was spent on the Havasupai Indian reservation on our field trip. As mentioned earlier, it was evident the romantic ideal of informal leadership and coercion among Indian groups does not work well in terms of getting community repairs and development done. The trail just prior to the village could be improved, but has not been. We observed a broken canal pipe, and two bridges you crossed over the stream before entering the village were nothing but a few logs hastily nailed together.

Observation of tourist behavior show the Havasupai have good reasons to feel hostile towards white tourists, who were often patronizing, and snobbish. One incident we observed in the cafe involved a photographer who asked a girl working there if he could take her picture. She shook her head no, but he backed up and took one anyway. An old Indian woman became very angry over this. She shouted, waving her arms in the direction of the campground and falls, "Scenery yes, people no." A Havasupai man requested the photographer to leave, which he did, but commenced taking more pictures of children in the street. He was observed still taking pictures out of the helicopter door as it took off.

More and more of the young men are unwilling to take the pack mules in and out for the tourists. The tourist manager stated there used to be sixty animals a day on the trail, now there are only twelve. But the Havasupai still want the money derived from tourism. They just do not want the contact with them. A dislike is especially felt for long-haired people, for they tend to hang around the village a lot to gain a sense of "Indianism." Perhaps a solution could be found whereby the tourists could be rerouted along a different trail skirting the village....

[1] **A point of clarification:** she Is referring to the fact that in Supai itself there were horses but no cows being fed or watered and as Martin pointed out In his Ph.D.

dissertation (1966:70) that during his stay in the canyon the estimated 100 head of cattle that roamed the dry plateau and canyons surrounding Supai "are of no commercial value; they are seldom sold, although some are occasionally slaughtered and the meat is packed into the canyon," a situation that had not changed by 1973.

Appendix B
Excerpts from a class report by a male student as a participant in a 1973 class field trip to study tourism development on several Indian reservations.

The Save-An-Indian-A-Month-Club …

One of the severest plights brought upon the Havasupai Indian is a malady called the "tourist." These tourists flock down upon the Supai village with their cameras, their stares, their rudeness but most of all, with the firm belief that they alone have the only true cure for all the Havasupai's ills and problems.

With a very small exception in my dealings with the tourist, I can share, as much as any "tourist" could, the frustration and the animosity that Havasupai feel toward the tourist.

When the tourist comes to the Supai village, he leaves his manners and his tact on Hilltop with the rest of his possessions. It is my impression that it is not the Havasupai, their village or their culture that the average tourist is really interested in when he comes to the Supai village. The tourist is attracted to the "back-to-nature" primitiveness offered by the long hike from the civilized world, the good campground sponsored by the National Park Service, and the splendor and beauty inherent in the area's three waterfalls. This theory is somewhat supported by the fact that only a small percentage of the tourists ever visit the village except on their way to campgrounds and then on their way out of the campgrounds. Most of the tourists are not interested in the Supai village or their culture so they will not walk two and one-half miles from the campground through the canyon to the village.

The tourist, in general, is subconsciously opposed to any progress for the Havasupai. The tourist does not think the white man should allow the Havasupai to "ruin" themselves with the progress that we have ruined our lives with. The tourist who comes to Havasupai is really interested in an escape from his fifty week-a-year world: a place to spend his two-week vacation and forget all his troubles and failures of his own little world. The tourist does not take into consideration the fact that the Havasupai Indian, being an equally human being, should be allowed to decide his own fate. The Havasupai, although isolated from most of the world, do travel outside the village and they are aware of things like televisions, radios, etc., and, naturally, they would like to have these things just as we do. Why should the Havasupai be deprived of these things just to accommodate a tourist during his two week need to get "away from it all?"

I encountered a prime example of the tourist attitude towards the Havasupai one morning while talking to three teenage Havasupai girls who work in the village Snack Bar which is practically the only regularly used tourist-oriented facility in the main part of the village; the tourist lodges being the only other. The typical attitude of many of the tourists is shown by the example of one man who flew into the village by helicopter. He apparently was sent to the Supai Village by a tourist agency to take pictures of the Havasupai. The photographer, loaded down with several different kinds of cameras, came into the Snack Bar to get a drink. After a short rest from his "strenuous" helicopter flight, he walked to the counter and asked the girls if he could take their pictures. Not one of the girls wanted to have their pictures taken, So each of them told him "NO" in very definite terms. The photographer decided that it didn't really matter whether the girls wanted to have their pictures taken or not. So, with the true tourist spirit, He took their picture, regardless of the feelings or wishes of the girls.

This active rudeness aroused the anger of all of the Havasupai patrons of the Snack Bar. The oldest resident of the village, old Mamie Chick, was so aroused by the photographer's bad manners that she spoke out for the first time since I was there, and it was in obvious anger, which is not common practice for a Havasupai Woman to do in public. Mamie Chick told the man to get out of the village and get back to the Campgrounds with the rest of the impolite tourists. The Havasupai Indian tourist manager, who was in the Snack Bar at the time, told the photographer that it was not considered polite for the tourists to take pictures of the Havasupai people but that he could take pictures of the buildings in the village.

Despite all the trouble that he had caused in the Snack Bar and all of the warnings that he had been given, The photographer, in the tradition that has caused the Havasupai to dislike all tourists, went to the main street and stood around there trying to take some more pictures of the Havasupai as they tried to go about their business. After causing many bad feelings among the villagers, he got back into his helicopter and flew down to the waterfalls area. It is people like this that have caused so much trouble for the Havasupai tribe. Much dissent among the tribal members is a direct result of the lack of consideration that seems to be so prevalent among the tourists....

The Havasupai have developed a tribal bureaucracy much in the same way as the whites have (Too many chiefs and not enough Indians). Many of the adult Havasupai males are actively involved in tribal politics and most of the others are ex-councilmen or have served some other political function in the tribe at one time or the other....

The council is divided four to three on the subject of progress. It is no wonder that the tribal council is not very effective with a division like that. Unfortunately, it is not very effective [in matters concerning] tourism either. The tribal Council is just so divided that it cannot function effectively for either side of the controversy.

The Havasupai also have a large following in the Mormon church. Along with the two young white missionaries, there are two members of the Havasupai who are ministers of the Mormon church. This could be classified as a real achievement by the Havasupai in that one of the ministers, Leon Rogers, has reached a level of Mormon president [i.e., ordained leader of the Supai Branch of the Church] a very high attainment in their church.

The Havasupai have their own tribal police force. There is one full-time policeman, and two part-time deputies. They are involved with enforcing the various tribal laws and in trying to keep the tourist and tribe members from getting out of hand.

For those who do get out of hand, there is a tribal judge. Although she is not a Havasupai by birth (she's a Hualapai), Nanny is a Havasupai by marriage…. This is a source of irritation for the Havasupai. They do not like being judged by an outsider….

The economy of the Havasupai tribe is dependent for a large part on tourism. The remainder of the economy is from government welfare payments. With the growing opposition to the tourist business, more of the Havasupai are becoming dependent on welfare to provide them with the necessities of life. Because the tourist season is only four or five months long, many Havasupai are on welfare for most of the year.

Although the land is excellent for agriculture, the Havasupai are not very active or very skilled farmers. There is very little land developed for agriculture at this time and what farming is done is primarily used as food for the farmer and his family. This family farming is only done by a very few of the Havasupai. The Havasupai do not know much about modern techniques in farming. Brigham Young University has sent a retired Utah farmer and his wife to Supai to try to teach the Havasupai modern methods to farm their land and get the best possible production for their efforts. This man and his wife are a generous couple who have volunteered their services to assist the Havasupai people in improving their poor conditions through self-help. At the present time, their success would have to be called minimal…. This farmer will plow anyone's field for just the cost of the gas used. He does not charge for his services….

The Havasupai operate a tribal mule team. These mules and horses are used for tribal business such as the mail and for bringing supplies in for the village. The tribal team is also available to bring tourists into the village to take them back out again. The mule team is handled by Ervin Crook who receives a flat salary from the tribal council. It was reported to me that the mule team is presently operating at a loss each month. The explanation for this was that the cost of Ervin Crook's salary and the price of feed for the animals is amounting to more than it is making each month. And after tourist season ends, the mules become a liability because they must still be fed, although they bring in no income at that time. It should be added that, although the mule teams are an expense to the tribe, they are necessity in order to provide the specific services that benefit the tribe as a whole.

The Havasupai who own the horses used in the tourist trade command a strong hand in tribal economic affairs. They are, for the most part, opposed to any progress in the tourist trade. Their opposition in this matter is an economic one, not against

166

progress in general. Any step forward, such as the proposed tramway system, would take money away from the horse owners....

Upon arriving in Supai, one could not help to notice the large number of children playing throughout the village.

The children are deeply affected by the tourist business. Most of the Havasupai children have learned the art of panhandling and many of them are very good at their trade. During my time at Supai, I had many more contacts with the children because it was much easier for me to approach them or to have them approach me.

My first real contact with a child was with a little firebrand named Tony. His father is one of the Indian ministers of the Mormon Church. Little Tony, who is five years old, was just as cute as he could be and he employed this factor to his best advantage. He was a panhandler, par excellence. He seemed to know just how far he could go without angering anyone. I was in the Snack Bar one morning when he came in and sat with me. He saw that I had a drink and without asking my permission he helped himself to my drink. He drank most of it but he was sure to leave a little bit in the bottom of my cup. He did the same thing with my cheeseburger and my pickles and he was careful to leave a little bit of everything he tried, no matter how small it was. Tony was not the least bit shy but he could come on a bit too strong and he could quickly wear out his welcome. Tony's parents were separated and he lived with an aunt who already had several children of her own. It was easy to see the influence that Tony had on his cousins but it was even more apparent in the youngest boy. Gaylen is two and one-half or three years old and he did not talk too much. But when he did say something, it sounded like a tape recording of Tony's panhandling routine. Although Gaylen was strongly influenced by Tony, he was a player, a cuddler, who liked to have someone's attention almost as much as their coke or cheeseburger. He never tried to panhandle anything from me even though he knew that he could have gotten almost anything he wanted from me very easily. His sisters were always very quiet and much more restrained then either Gaylen or Tony. I found that to be a general rule among the Havasupai: the Havasupai girls were generally less aggressive than the boys.

I did get acquainted with four little girls one morning while we were talking to the two Mormon missionaries. These girls were very playful and they seem to be enjoying themselves very much. Their play seemed to be directed toward the young missionaries, who the little girls were well acquainted with. Although the children were friendly to us, it was only because we were with the two missionaries. One of the Mormon missionaries told us that the Havasupai parents do not show much affection towards their children and that is one of the reasons that the children are so anxious to take up with anyone who shows them attention.

Several times while I was playing with a child, one of the parents would come up to us and spirit his child away. Sometimes I felt that it was because they did not want their children playing with a white tourist but mostly, it seemed that the parents were truly concerned that their children might be a nuisance. It was extremely hard for the parents to realize that one could be enjoying himself by playing with the children because the parents very seldom played with their own children….

One interesting side note about the children was that I hardly ever saw an Indian child without a can of soda in his hand. This was not pursued but it is obviously an influence of the tourist trade. The children are also influenced by the little quirks of the tourists. They pick up little things like colloquial sayings that the children hear the tourist saying. Although there is no television anywhere in the Supai village most of the Havasupai children know the often-repeated expressions which come from the television such as the Campbell's Soup song or the exclamation, "Yaba daba do" from the Flintstone Comedy Hour. It would seem that the children would have to get these sayings from the tourists who are passing through the Supai village [or as I, the class instructor, pointed out to the student submitting this report perhaps more likely from older children who had left the village during the school year]….

There is also some evidence that there is sexual activity between the Havasupai boys and a few of the female tourists. An example of this would be the case of Miss Mooney Falls, 1973, so named for the topless act that she put on for everyone while sunbathing at Mooney Falls. She was part of a group of the "cool people" who came to Supai "to groove" with the Havasupai teenagers. In the short time that she was there, she managed to make quite a reputation for herself by sunbathing topless, walking around braless and almost shirtless, enticing a few of the Indian boys who were obviously interested in only one thing, sharing her marijuana around the village and angering many of the older residents of the village with her attitude. It would have been interesting to have seen who was the next patient to request an examination for a venereal disease a couple of days after we left the village.

I had a talk with the Protestant minister's wife who was the nurse at the Health Clinic. She told me that many of the Indian girls in Supai are pregnant by the time they are sixteen years old. It seems to be an accepted fact of life among the members of the tribe. It does not carry the stigma that an unmarried pregnancy carries in our culture….

[One older girl] told me that there is quite a lot of sexual activity among the other girls, not only with the tourists but also with a few of the Havasupai boys as well. Although, she said, that there was more prestige in "doing it" with a white man. I think that the avid participation in sexual activity among the Havasupai young is due to the lack of anything else there to keep them busy. In addition, I think that there is a direct correlation between the number of tourists who visit Supai and the sexual activity of the Havasupai youth. But I think that their sexual activity might be more apparent in Supai because of the closeness in which everyone is living. In our own society, there may be as much sexual activity, proportionally speaking, as there is in Supai, but because of the size of our society, it is just not apparent to us. We don't know everyone within our society whereas the Havasupai society is small enough that everyone knows each other. Also, with the small size of the Supai village and the lack of privacy, everyone is aware of everything that goes on in the village....

In comparison with the tourism efforts of the [other] Indian tribes [visited during this field trip]...the Havasupai are far behind them. But there are many factors that could explain the lack of development of the tourist trade among the Havasupai.

The Navajos and the Utes are both located in the mainstream of tourist travel. with those ideal locations, They are able to get a tourist business unavailable to the Havasupai. Many tourists who are not particularly interested in the Indian reservations, stop at the reservation trading posts while they are traveling to wherever else they are going.

The type of tourist most likely to come in contact with the Havasupai are campers who want to use the National Park Service campgrounds. This particular type of tourist is not like those who do most of the business with the Navajos or the Utes. The Havasupai tourist is carrying all his gear for camping on his back or on a pack horse and because of this, he is less likely to buy souvenirs that will break easily or take up a lot of space. Also, the Havasupai tourist is less likely to carry large amounts of cash with him as a safeguard against theft.

The most important difference between the Havasupai tourist business and the other tribes' tourist business is the type of trade offered. For the most part, other tribes offer the tourists beads, artifacts and Indian folklore while the Havasupai tourist trade deals with services, not sales. This is what the Havasupai feel is demeaning in their encounters with the white tourists. But due to their location and circumstances, an Indian trading post, such as those on Navajo or Ute reservations, would not be profitable for the Havasupai. Thus, out of necessity rather than choice, the Havasupai feel that they are thrust into a servant-style tourist business with which they are not happy.

Appendix C

Confessions of a Would-Be "Savior"

Having long been a lover of wilderness experiences ever since as a Boy Scout and later as a college student I was one of the fortunate few to be able to, by raft, explore and photograph Glen Canyon four times before its most spectacular scenery and archaeological sites were destroyed by the rising waters of Lake Powell. Thus, in the bookstore at UCLA, when I saw and immediately purchased a copy of the special July 1963 issue of Arizona Highways with its description and glorious color photos of Havasu Canyon's stunning waterfall wilderness, I knew immediately that I must find a way to get there. And such an opportunity did arise four years later when, during the completion of my Papago (Tohono O'odham) research needed for my PhD degree, I and my adventuresome young wife and two-year-old daughter were able to make arrangements for a pack animal to carry our backpacks and tent from the hilltop to the Park Service campground and a few days later back to the hilltop.

Although by this time I had observed a few examples of the serious problems facing Native Americans on the Papago reservation and such nearby off-reservation locations as Tucson, the company mining town of Ajo, and farm labor camps, on this first visit to Supai I was naïvely unaware of similar and very serious additional problems facing tribal members there. In fact, other than the apology that the packer gave us for having to unload our camping equipment before the descent to Havasu Falls and the government campground, I had no additional hint of the hostility that tribal members had long felt toward the government's control over the major waterfalls and campground.

However, this ignorance of the many severe problems facing the Havasupai would disappear In 1970 when as a young professor in charge of organizing a new anthropology program at California State College at San Bernardino, I tried to arrange a field trip for some of my students to Supai but because of a very dry season the tourist agent wrote me that the pack horses that I had requested were not available. Instead, I then volunteered to lead a troop of Boy Scouts who needed no pack animals to the reservation. The boys had a great time there but on this trip while the boys were enjoying playing in the water, I was meeting with the Tribal Chairman and the local BIA

170

official, Community Educator Jay Hunt, about the many problems facing the residents of Supai at that time which improved access to the outside world might help alleviate. During this conversation the possibility of building a tramway from the top of the canyon on the east side of Supai to the floor of the canyon was discussed, one similar to the one that my family and I had just a short time earlier ridden to the top of Mt. San Jacinto, the Palm Springs Aerial Tramway.

Although at that time I was unaware of Martin Goodfriend's possibly earlier support of such a tramway I, too, felt that not only would this greatly increase the wealth of the tribe but also give them a much cheaper way to import food, building materials, and other necessities into their community. And, it would give them a much less costly alternative than evacuation by helicopter when a tribal member or tourist was seriously injured or sick. I also left with them a copy of the tourist development plan that Roger Neilson, a faculty associate of my father, had prepared for the Ute tribe east of Salt Lake City. They seemed very interested in my proposal and promised to get back to me after they had discussed it with the full tribal council. Apparently, unbeknownst to me, they did get back to me as I was later told during my next visit to Supai in 1973 when Jay Hunt asked me why I had not replied to an employment offer to become their tourist manager they had sent to me sometime after the summer of 1971. However, by then I had left San Bernardino to take a year-long Research Associate position at the Boreal Institute at the University of Alberta where I was put in charge of studying the effect that a proposed multi-billion dollar natural gas pipeline would have on the Native American populations of Northern Canada's NWT but for some unknown reason the letter with the offer was never forwarded to me.

There, too, in Canada were many Native American communities with no dependable year-round access to the outside world except by air that were even more dependent for income on welfare than the residents of Supai. Thus, my duty was to determine whether the proposed pipeline would provide enough employment opportunities to ease this poverty. Another parallel to Supai was the perception of many Canadians that these villagers actually preferred living off welfare payments rather than seeking other employment options now that their traditional hunting and gathering way of life had been severely disrupted by outside forces beyond their control.

In an effort to determine the truthfulness of this commonly held belief not only in Canada but also here in the United States (unfortunately, sometimes by certain visitors to Supai), I soon welcomed the opportunity to visit the town of Hay River in the Northwest Territories where there was an opportunity to learn about the "Work Arctic" experiment, an attempt to see if the local native men when given the opportunity would choose work over welfare. ((See (Gemini North 1972) and (Sigvaldson 1972) for more complete details about this very important social experiment.)

Hay River is located in the midst of a pine forest on the southern shores of Great Slave Lake. And, contrary to what I had earlier believed, much of the Arctic receives less annual precipitation than the deserts of Southern Arizona. This creates a major problem especially in the very dry fall when the fire danger becomes extremely high.

The previous fall, a massive wildfire had come dangerously close to the edge of town. Because of this event, a very altruistic local businessman developed a proposal to clear a firebreak around the town using local Native American workers. He felt that this would be a win-win situation both for the town and for the natives almost all of whom were unemployed and on welfare.

This experiment proved to be remarkably successful with almost all of the native workers choosing work over welfare even though they would not be getting any financial advantage by working rather than relying on welfare payments. Furthermore, to get the same amount of money they had received on welfare, on bitterly cold mornings, they had to walk across a major frozen river to be on time to catch a bus to the worksite. In addition to offering proof that unemployed natives did not prefer living off welfare payments rather than seeking employment perhaps an even more important discovery was that, especially during the workweek, there was a remarkable enormous decrease in levels of drunken behavior, spouse abuse, and other violent behavior in the Indian community and in the adjacent town of Hay River.

In particular, one of the worst drunken offenders sobered up and was quickly promoted to lead the tree cutting crews. Sadly, when I met this man much later that winter, he and his crew had become so skilled and productive that the firebreak had been completed in much less than the anticipated time so that the Canadian government had decided to prematurely end the program.

And, even though this man was scheduled to remain on the payroll while the project was being shut down, when his fellow workers had been laid off, he too quit and quickly resumed his earlier heavy drinking pattern. I'll never forget his final words to me: "The government always does this to us. They make promises which they never keep."

Applying this example to Supai, I predict that the combination of having winter employment instead of relying on welfare payments (as occurred during the Hay River social experiment) as well as not having a long school-year separation from their children would greatly decrease winter levels of Havasupai drunken behavior, spouse abuse, and other violent conduct. And, since in past years there have been a number of times when jobs have provided an alternative to welfare on the reservation doing such things as trail repair after a flood or working in a mine to support the war effort, it would be interesting to see if, in Supai, there is also evidence of a correlation between such times of employment and a decrease in levels of drunken behavior, spouse abuse, and other violent behavior.

Now, as I approach the end of my life, in completing the research needed for this manuscript, I have come to greatly admire the work that Steve and Lois Hirst provided to help overcome the tremendous opposing forces the tribe faced in its bitter struggle to regain ownership of its waterfalls, campground, and much of its surrounding pre-European contact land. I only regret that while in Canada my efforts were not nearly as successful as theirs was in my failed attempt to help achieve a beneficial outcome for the Northern Canadian indigenous population facing a massive unemployment problem.

Although the oil and gas industry had spent large sums of money on how to solve the permafrost problem where heat from a flowing oil or natural gas pipeline needed to be kept away from the frozen waterlogged soil on which it was laid or buried, the only satisfactory solution found, even though it would greatly increase the cost of the project, was to elevate the pipe above such ground. This in turn could create a serious barrier for annual wildlife migrations so the industry felt the need to fund studies to solve this additional problem. In addition, they were also facing great political pressure to show how they would be able to include individuals from various indigenous communities along the pipeline's route into the project's workforce. And to study possible solutions to this latter problem, the industry gave the Boreal Institute a relatively small grant that was then divided into creating a program to train native workers to become pipeline welders that another University of Alberta professor was put in charge of and a study to determine other possible ways to include native northerners into the project workforce, a task I agreed to lead.

Unfortunately, it was not long before I determined that there was very little likelihood that the project would do much to solve the large unemployment problem in the native population. And this pessimism was confirmed when I examined what had happened during the construction of the Pointed Mountain gas pipeline in nearby Northern British Columbia where only 45 natives had been hired on a temporary basis, which for many was only a few weeks, to clear brush, etc. Furthermore, by the time I left Canada only a very small handful of natives was still employed doing menial tasks at the site.

Since I had undertaken this research only under the condition that I would be free to publish my results whenever or wherever I felt I should after I had submitted my report to the Northwest Project Study Group, I became greatly alarmed when in the middle of my research an attempt was made by the Northwest Project Study Group to get the University of Alberta to sign a contract that would effectively "seal the lips" of myself and others associated with the project <u>until after the Canadian government's gas pipeline hearings were completed</u>. Fortunately, largely through the combined efforts of several members of the Anthropology department aided by other faculty members, this attempt was thwarted.

Even then, up until the latter part of August, my report probably didn't contain enough "bad news" that would lead to its outright rejection by the various oil and gas companies funding our research. In fact, they seemed to be satisfied to at least have a documented study to demonstrate their concern about unemployment problems in communities along the pipeline route especially since there had been severe internal difficulties within the Boreal Institute before and during the life of the project so that much of the scheduled research had been delayed or not completed at all by the first part of September.

However, there seemed to be little support from the oil and gas industry to continue funding my research for another year, so I left Canada to accept a faculty position at the University of Nebraska. But, I did not forget the plight of the many "First Nation," Inuit, and Métis individuals I had met especially after gaining access in the latter part of August and during September to the draft of a study prepared by four Queen's University professors, a professor from the University of Saskatchewan, and a researcher for the Canadian National Railway (Macdonald et.al. 1972) as well as a paper prepared by a Virginia Tech mechanical engineering professor (Whitelaw 1972) that presented a highly convincing, data-driven argument that a far better and cheaper way of transporting oil and gas southward would be by rail rather than by pipeline. And since I was already scheduled to present a paper on the very successful Hay River social experiment at the American Anthropological Association meeting to be held that year in Toronto Canada), I secretly prepared a substitute paper (Stucki 1972) comparing the benefits of this alternative railroad proposal made by the scholars at two major Canadian universities and the mechanical engineering professor in Virginia to the pipeline plan of the oil and gas industry. Then, having heard stories of strange things happening to whistleblowers, I cautiously sent several advance copies of this paper to reporters who would be covering this meeting.

In this paper using research data provided by the university professors, I listed the following major advantages that transporting natural gas from the Arctic southward by rail in a liquefied form rather than by pipeline would have:

1. It would be much cheaper to build especially since a pipeline whether carrying oil or gas in Arctic regions generates too much heat to be buried or even laid on top of permafrost soil so for much of its length it must be elevated above such soil. A rail line would have no such problem.

2. Such an elevated pipeline would create a major barrier for the annual migration route of such animals as caribou. Again, a rail line would have no such problem.

3. The railroad option, as opposed to the pipeline, instead of merely being built to drain an Arctic resource for the benefit the people much farther south would provide on the return trip of the trains to the north a way to provide much cheaper goods and services especially to the many communities along the route which, at that time, at least in certain seasons of the year were only connected to the outside world by air.

4. On the basis of my analysis of what had taken place on a similar type of pipeline project in northern British Columbia, only a very brief time of employment had been provided for 45 indigenous laborers who mostly cleared brush from the pipeline route and by the time of my departure from Canada only a handful remained employed doing menial tasks. (I was not able to obtain an exact count since my research assistant I had tried to send there was diverted by my supervisor for another task.) In sharp contrast, the railroad option was estimated by the university data to provide "4,500 direct jobs in the north" (Macdonald 1972:i) far more than those required to supply decades of permanent employment for any native Northerner needing it, even unskilled workers who could quickly be trained to repair or replace railroad ties. In fact, additional workers from southern Canada would be needed even if all native Northerners signed up for such employment. The university professors then go on to document the many other highly important advantages that the railroad option would provide over the planned pipeline for many other Canadian workers and the national economy.

5. A larger part of the grant given to us by the oil and gas industry was to develop a training program to allow some Northern natives to become pipeline welders. However, a major problem with this would be that once this project was completed such individuals to continue working with the

industry would have to be willing to relocate to whatever region of the world a new project would be taking place, a sacrifice that judging from the reluctance of most of these people to even spending much time in cities farther south such as Edmonton, would be very hard to make.

6. Once the oil and gas deposits of the Arctic were depleted such a pipeline would serve no further purpose. However, a railroad would still be useful to continue to supply goods and services to Northern communities as well as possibly being used to exploit other Arctic resources such as a large, fairly rich iron deposit that had been discovered along the proposed route.

The response to this plan and my analysis was very encouraging. I was especially pleased with the backing for my report and recommendations that I received from many Northern native people including their elected representative to Parliament as well as from many members of the academic world in Canada and the U.S., many Canadian politicians, many Canadian government personnel, a Northern federal judge, the president of the Canadian Wildlife Federation, several major Canadian labor unions, spokesmen for the Canadian railroad industry, and many others.)

This led to a number of live and recorded radio and TV interviews which were broadcast in Edmonton, Calgary, Toronto, Yellowknife, and nationally in Canada, including several times the NWT and Yukon territory and I presented guest lectures at the University of Alberta (Dept. of Anthropology) and at the Grant MacEwan Community College in Edmonton as one of their featured speakers in a series of public lectures on Northern Canadian development problems.

However, it was at this public lecture that I began to feel the real wrath of the oil and gas industry when at the end of the meeting as I started answering questions from the audience suddenly a man who with a small group of others had been standing in the hallway outside of the meeting room burst into the meeting room loudly declaring that he had come to tell everyone there how incompetent I was as a researcher. Caught off guard, (in retrospect I should have asked him who he was especially since the Edmonton Journal the next day reported him as being a visiting anthropologist), this was an unanticipated surprise to me as well as to the faculty members of the University of Alberta anthropology department present at the meeting who had never seen or heard of him anywhere in Canada. Doing a quick investigation, they learned that he was not an anthropologist and not even a Canadian but had been flown in from United States specifically to attack me. And though the Edmonton Journal did not print a retraction of his identification as an anthropologist, the University of Alberta student newspaper, widely distributed in Edmonton, did later print a feature article on this deception (Stucki 1974).

Other attempts were made to silence me but, luckily, I had never signed a secrecy agreement thus I was glad to be back in the United States by this time. My brief moment of "fame" or "infamy" has now been almost completely erased in Canadian history. Thus, even though I had supplied a copy of my 1972 paper for use as a document to be considered in the official government "Mackenzie Valley Pipeline Inquiry" at the request of Judge Berger, the Canadian government official in charge of the inquiry, many years later, upon finally being able to examine a copy of his final report, I was greatly discouraged to learn that in the extensive listing of the many documents he had examined, there was absolutely no mention of my 1972 paper I had sent to him at his personal request.

In retrospect, I had vastly underestimated the power of the opposition I and the other advocates for the railroad solution faced. For a while I had been puzzled by why the industry would not choose an initially cheaper and more environmentally friendly way to transport not only natural gas but also oil from Arctic regions southward not only in Canada but also in Alaska, but then I realized that in the industry's overall long-term strategy, except in these permafrost areas, pipelines offered several major advantages:

1. Once constructed, only a very small in number of nonunionized specialists would be needed to operate and repair a pipeline in sharp contrast to a fairly large labor force that would still be needed to maintain a railroad. (Although in such permafrost regions as the Mackenzie River valley, even with the expense of paying the wages of large numbers of low-skilled native workers

for the projected lifespan of the project, the railroad alternative would still have been far cheaper.)

2. The construction of pipelines is very dependent upon having a large highly trained and loyal workforce that is willing to relocate to any part of the world. Thus, if the railroad solution had been adopted requiring the services of a much different type of workforce while possibly then greatly slowing down the funding or stopping of other pipeline projects in other parts of the world, the carefully constructed bond between the oil and gas industry and its highly mobile, specialized pipeline workers would be severely threatened.

Why am I including this Canadian experience in this book? Having failed completely at this attempt to help solve the continuing extremely high unemployment rate of the indigenous population of Northern Canada and only being marginally successful in solving similar extremely high unemployment problems as the volunteer manager of an employment center on the Navajo reservation, in my retirement years, I am hopeful that the proposal I have offered in this book may be at least considered by the Havasupai Tribal Council as a way to lessen the damage of the altogether more frequent economic and employment catastrophes facing the Havasupai by the increasing numbers of floods in recent years as well as by such unexpected events as the ongoing coronavirus crisis described in Appendix D. And in sharp contrast to the immense unemployment problems facing indigenous populations both in Canada's far North and on the nearby Navajo Nation that will continue to defy an easy resolution, I strongly believe that such a solution as that proposed in chapter 9 is now possible for the Havasupai where they would regain not only ownership but also control of a small but extremely important portion of their pre-European-contact plateau land. There, as in their ancestors' time, they would be able to spend much of the winter engaged in permanent productive economic activities.

Also, if the tribe would consider the option of providing not only weekday lodging for the school-age children in Tusayan but also for their parents, the ill effects of the boarding school environment on their children would forever be a thing of the past. That such effects can have long-lasting lifetime detrimental effects upon children became vividly obvious to me while visiting the town of Inuvik in Canada's far north. As usual throughout my many visits to other Northern towns about the only place I could meet to talk to officials and other local residents was the town bar. Fortunately, I had chosen as my native assistant a young man who had long since given up the urge to order any alcoholic beverage during all of our previous visits to other towns. In fact, he told me that he didn't even like the taste of beer anymore, a claim that seemed to be verified during these earlier visits. However, one of the largest boarding schools was located in Inuvik where he had spent most of his formative years as one of its students and it was not long before he met some of his old classmates. Never before nor since have I seen such a radical change in behavior that I witnessed for the next two days when he spent all of his time in the bar drinking one beer after another with his former school friends and it was only with great difficulty I was able to pull him away from them in time to make our flight southward.

As I have documented in this book, I doubt that there would be any Havasupai family who would not welcome the end of having to send their school-age children to a boarding school for their education where, as was in the case described above in Canada, they often begin emulating the many life destructive behaviors of the peer group. Thus, the adoption of my proposal by the Tribal Council would at last make this long-held dream possible.

In both the Canadian and Havasupai cases the destruction of the aboriginal hunting and gathering lifestyle was hastened by the well-meant actions of government and other "do-gooders." Thus, in Canada, children instead of being taught the skills needed to survive in the harsh Arctic environment during the winter months, were being taught the skills and way of life of Southern Canadians. Similarly, many attempts through the years have been made to show the Havasupai how to become good farmers and acquire the educational skills needed for life as ordinary assimilated Americans even though as discussed in Chapter 5 there is no way that agriculture would ever provide a sustainable economic base for the tribe unless they would be allowed to pipe water from Havasu Creek to irrigate some of their recovered barren plateau land, a possibility now federally forbidden.

Also, in both cases, well-intentioned government actions led to the destruction of a viable hunting economy. Thus in Canada's NWT, in an attempt to prevent the starvation of bands of natives that had misjudged the migration route that the caribou would take some years in their annual spring migration to the Arctic, the government instigated policies and programs that while ensuring that such starvation would never again take place led to the consolidation of most such natives into larger communities where the surrounding wilderness areas were then quickly depleted of huntable wildlife. Far less altruistically motivated, especially for Havasupai, were the severe limit and seasonal restrictions placed on the hunting of deer in the government-controlled lands surrounding the reservation where even after the end of an 1890's territorial law that "[made] it a crime … for anyone to kill deer for the next five years" in the Grand Canyon area (Chapter 4, p.41), they were then treated as if they were ordinary American hunting sportsmen subject to severe poaching penalties (Chapter 4, pp.41-43). The government was in no mood to grant a special exemption to the tribe even though the decline in local deer numbers was mainly the result of large numbers of incoming ranchers, miners, and other Americans. This was especially tragic for the Havasupai since one of the main pillars of their aboriginal economy had been the trade of highly desirable tanned animal skins to many other tribes "living as far away as the Rio Grande" and " to nearby whites, at first to obtain such items as tobacco and matches but later demanding such things as iron tools, clothes and money" (Chapter 3, p.16). Especially important to the Havasupai was the trade they established with the nearby Navajo from whom they "obtained horses, blankets, guns, and ammunition giving in return buckskins as well as such food items as dried corn, beans, and squash" (Chapter 3, p.16).

I strongly feel that perhaps now Is an especially opportune time to reestablish a trading relationship with the Navajo Nation since if the Havasupai Tribal Council decides to pursue the purchase of land or a hotel in the Tusayan area, in return for funding and management help from the Navajo, they could offer a prime location to divert tourists leaving the South Rim area who plan to spend the night in Flagstaff hotels or motels to instead sleep that night at the nearby, but financially struggling, Navajo Twin Arrows hotel and resort. The Havasupai could also offer space in their newly purchased property for information and artifact sales for other nearby tribes, thus once again, as in much earlier times "[serve] as 'middlemen' in the trade of a multitude of desired items from east to west and west to east" (Chapter 3, p.15).

I write this book fully aware then it will be up to the tribe itself to determine whether or not the proposal in chapter 9 is worth pursuing. But if they decide it has merit then I would hope that other readers of the book would consider providing them with the financial and political support they will need. I also write it to document the incredibly important help given by Steve Hirst and his wife, Lois, to the tribe in the battle to gain passage of Senate Bill, S 1296, that in his two books (Hirst 1976, 2006) he drastically minimizes. And, I also felt it important to tell the story of other well-intentioned "do-gooders" such as Martin Goodfriend.

Appendix D

The Coronavirus Pandemic

Just when the Tribal Council's decision to embrace an economic model based upon attracting adventure tourists willing to pay relatively high fees to enjoy access to its waterfalls, campground and lodge seemed to be highly successful, an even more serious problem than flooding now threatened to destroy the tribe's continued economic prosperity. Thus, on its official website as of Monday April 6, 2020, it was announced that: "

> All Havasupai tourism will be suspended for the Campground and the Lodge through May 14, 2020 in response to the continuing coronavirus/COVID–19 pandemic.
> Reservation holders with Campground Reservations that have arrival dates between March 16, 2020 and May 14, 2020 will have the opportunity to reschedule their reservation for dates within the 2021 season

Obviously, the tribe had hoped that by May 14, control measures would have been put into effect by the health industry and government agencies that would have been sufficient to allow the safe entry of visitors to the reservation without endangering the lives of Supai villagers, an optimism not shared by many health experts given the lack of a vaccine against the disease or a proven drug to treat it. Sadly, the more pessimistic forecasts proved to be accurate, so that on **June 29, 2020** the tribal website declared:

> Today is **June 29, 2020** and all Havasupai tourism remains suspended. It is not currently known when tourism will resume.

> As of today, Reservations with dates between March 15, 2020 and **July 13, 2020** are considered affected by this closure and are eligible to be rescheduled to the 2021 season.

Tribal leaders were now facing a much more difficult problem than that which confronts the airline industry that also offers rescheduling rather than cash refunds to those that paid in advance for flights. Thus, although the airline industry can more easily add additional flights to accommodate any increase in the number of daily passengers once the pandemic ends as rescheduled individuals boost the normal daily total, the Havasupai will lose income each time a rescheduled tourist takes the place of a paying guest once the pandemic ends since there is a rigidly enforced cap on the daily number of allowed campground and lodge occupants.

Thus, it will probably not be too much longer before tribal leaders will be forced to again let in paying visitors to avoid an enormous economic loss either in this year or next despite the serious health risk they and fellow villagers would then be facing.

And, since in our increasingly interconnected world this pandemic may not be the last one that the tribe might have to face in future years, there is another reason they should consider the proposal I presented in chapter 9 which gives most villagers much better privacy and physical isolation from the incoming tourists thus decreasing the likelihood of disease transmission from an infected visitor to the village's residents. This is especially important when dealing with viruses such as the present one which can be easily spread by individuals who are not even aware that they have become infected but who would be spreading tiny droplets of the virus into the surrounding air not only by coughing but also by merely breathing, speaking, or singing. And since these tiny droplets on a calm day can linger in the air for a fairly long period of time, one or more infected backpackers walking through the village on his or her way to or from the campground could thus endanger any villager also walking or riding along the main trail through the village.

Furthermore, since adopting much larger campground, lodge, and packing fees, more of the arriving high income "adventure tourists" will have also been visitors to various foreign countries in their never-ending search for a fresh "tourist activity that includes physical activity, a cultural exchange, or activities in nature[1]" thus increasing the risk of bringing a new foreign disease into the village.

1. This is the official definition of "adventure tourism" as defined by the **Adventure Travel Trade Association**.

References

Anonymous

1898 "A job lot of Supais were in Williams Friday selling deer and lions skins" (A news item in the column "Arizona Day by Day") *The Arizona Republican* (July 6, 1898:3).

1910 Supai Village Destroyed by Flood. *Native American* (January 15, 1910:17).

1972 Indians in Canyon Start to Prosper. *New York Times* (November 25, 1972).

1974 Fruit Trees for Indians. *Church News* (*Deseret News*, week ending March 30, 1974).

1997a Indians to keep Canyon cabins. Arizona Daily Star (January 21, 1977:B2).

1997b Flood forces hundreds of tourists, residents to flee Arizona canyon. *The Detroit News* (Monday, August 11, 1997).

1997c More tourists, residents evacuated from Havasupai reservation. *Las Vegas Review Journal* (Tuesday, August 12, 1997).

1997d Cleanup of flooded Indian village begins. *Las Vegas Review Journal* (Wednesday, August 13, 1997).

2018 'Mormon Land': Historian examines 'correlation,' the program that made the church what it is today. Is it helping or hurting the modern faith? *The Salt Lake Tribune* (October 3, 2018).

Appendix A

1973 Excerpts from a class report by a female student as a participant in a 1973 class field trip to study tourism development on several Indian reservations.

Appendix B

1973 Excerpts from a class report by a male student as a participant in a 1973 class field trip to study tourism development on several Indian reservations.

Arave, Lynn

2004 Grand design: LDS Church renews efforts in remote Arizona town. *Deseret Morning News* (November 13, 2004).

Bauer, R. C.

1895 Report of School Among Supais. (June 30, 1895). In "Report of the Commissioner of Indian Affairs." Annual Report of the Secretary of the Interior 1895 (p. 358). Washington: U.S, Government Printing Office.

1896 Report of Teacher in Charge of Yava Supai Indians (June 30, 1896). In "Report of the Commissioner of Indian Affairs." Annual Report of the Secretary of the Interior 1896 (pp. 111-112). Washington: U.S, Government Printing Office.

1897 Report of Teacher in Charge of Yava Supai Indians (June 30, 1897). In "Report of the Commissioner of Indian Affairs." Annual Report of the Secretary of the Interior 1897 (pp. 104-106). Washington: U.S, Government Printing Office.

Bernstein, Peter J.

1974 Conservation Groups in Arms over Nixon-backed Plan for Grand Canyon. *Phoenix Gazette* (July 25, 1974).

Birch, J. Neil
    1985 Helen John: The Beginnings of Indian Placement. *Dialogue* Vol. 18, No. 4, Winter 1985:119-129.
Breed. Jack
    1948 Land of the Havasupai. *National Geographic* XCIII(No.5):655-674 (May).

Casanova, Frank E.
    1968 General Crook Visits the Supais as Reported by John G. Bourke. *Arizona and the West* Vol. 10, No.3.
Chemi, James M.
    1963 Carrying the mail to Supai. *Arizona Highways* (June 1963:40-43).
Colons. Arthur V.
    1955 Unpublished letter to G. H. Marshall dated January 12, 1955. Tucson: University of Arizona Special Collections. G. H Marshall Papers.
Coues, Elliot
    1900 On the Trail of a Spanish Pioneer: Garces Diary 1775-6. New York: Harper.
Cowgill, Pete
    1969 Tramway for Havasupai Would Bypass Settlement. *Arizona Daily Star* (August 15, 1969:B-1).
    1974 Barry Maps A Grander Canyon; The Havasupai Interest: Sierra Club Sees Flaws In New Plan. *Arizona Daily Star* (January 6, 1974:G-1).
CNN
    1997 Flooding triggers evacuation from Arizona canyon. Posted at 7:53 a.m. EDT on August 11, 1997.
    1997 Arizona Canyon Evacuated Due to Flooding. Posted at 15:13:52 GMT. on August 12, 1997.
C.S.   *Canyon Shadows* (Havasupai Tribal Newsletter revived in 1967 by Steve and Lois Hirst).
Cushing, Frank H.
    1965 The nation of Willows. Northland Press (Reprinted from two 1882 issues of the *Atlantic Monthly* magazine).
Dedera, Don
    1967 How Lucky They Are: But Is It Really So? (A Three Part Article). *Arizona Republic* October 1,2,3, 1967.
    1971 The Man Who Spoiled Paradise. West magazine (*Los Angeles Times*) January 24, 1971.
Dobyns, Henry F. and Robert C. Euler
    1960 Aboriginal Socio-Political Structure and the Ethnic Group Concept of the Pai of Northwestern Arizona. In Havasupai Indians (A reprint of the Indian Claims Commission docket no. 91). New York: Garland Publishing, Inc.
    1967 The Ghost Dance of 1889 among the Pai Indians of Northwestern Arizona. Prescott (Ariz.): Prescott College Press.
    1971 The Havasupai People. Phoenix: Indian Tribal Series (Northland Press).

Emerick, Richard
1954a Recent Observations on Some Aspectsof Havasupai Culture. M.A. Thesis: University of Pennsylvania.
1954b The Havasupais, People of Cataract Canyon. *Pennsylvania University Museum Bulletin* 18(No.3):32-47.

Ettenborough, Kelly
1998 Couple Translating Bible for Grand Canyon Tribe: For 20 years, a couple has labored to translate the New Testament for a tribe of only 670 members. *The Arizona Republic* (September 19, 1998).

Euler, Robert C.
1974 (1961) Havasupai Historical Data In Havasupai Indians (A reprint of the Indian Claims Commission docket no. 91). New York: Garland Publishing, Inc.
1979 The Havasupai of the Grand Canyon. *American West* (May-June 1979) pp. 12-17,65.

Euler, Robert C., George J. Gumerman, Thor N. V. Karlstrom, Jeffrey S. Dean, and Richard H. Herly
1979 The Colorado Plateaus: Cultural Dynamics and Paleoenvironment. *Science* Vol. 205, No. 4411 (Sept. 14, 1979:1089-1101).

Evans, Brock
1974 Let's Not Give Up the Canyon. *Sierra Club Bulletin* 59 (No.8): 27.

Ewing, Henry P.
1898 Report of Industrial Teacher in Charge of Hualapais and Yava Supais (July 30, 1898). In "Report of the Commissioner of Indian Affairs." Annual Report of the Secretary of the Interior 1898 (pp. 120-123). Washington: U.S, Government Printing Office.
1899 Report of Industrial Teacher in Charge of Hualapais and Yava Supais (Aug. 18, 1899). In "Report of the Commissioner of Indian Affairs." Annual Report of the Secretary of the Interior 1899 (pp. 154-156). Washington: U.S, Government Printing Office.
1900 Report of Industrial Teacher in Charge of Walapai and Havasupai (Aug. 1, 1900). In "Report of the Commissioner of Indian Affairs." Annual Report of the Secretary of the Interior 1899 (pp. 201-203). Washington: U.S, Government Printing Office.
1901 Report of School at Truxton Canyon, Ariz. (Aug. 18, 1899). In "Report of the Commissioner of Indian Affairs." Annual Report of the Secretary of the Interior 1899 (pp. 526-528). Washington: U.S, Government Printing Office.

Floren, Albert W.
1905 Report of Superintendent in charge of Havasupai (Sept. 25. 1905). In "Reports Concerning Indians in Arizona." Annual Report of the Department of the Interior: 1905. Washington: U.S, Government Printing Office.

Fonseca, Felicia
2008 Grand Canyon tribe tries to get tourism back on track after flood. *Salt Lake Tribune* (Sunday, October 26, 2008:A19).

2018 Flooding cancels hundreds of trips to coveted waterfalls. *Navajo Times* (July 19, 2018:C9).

Gaddis, John F.

1892 Report of Farmer for Yava Suppai Indians (June 7, 1892). In "Report of the Commissioner of Indian Affairs." Annual Report of the Secretary of the Interior 1892 (pp. 650-651). Washington: U.S, Government Printing Office.

1893 Report of Farmer for Supai Indians, Arizona (May 31, 1893). In "Report of the Commissioner of Indian Affairs" (p. 402). Annual Report of the Secretary of the Interior 1893. Washington: U.S, Government Printing Office.

Galvin, John

1965 A Record of Travels in Arizona and California 1775-1776: Fr. Francisco Garces. San Francisco: John Howell.

Garrett, W. E.

1978 Grand Canyon: Are We Loving It to Death? *National Geographic* 154:16-51.

Gehrke, Steve

2008 Utah hiker, friends escape flood by a hair. *Salt Lake Tribune* (Wednesday, August 20, 2008:A1, A4).

Gemini North

1972 Settlement Council Labour Pools: A feasibility study for the Government of the Northwest Territories and the Department of Indian Affairs and Northern Development. Vol. II: Appendix 1A: Work Arctic Review. Yellowknife, N.W.T.

Goldwater, Barry

1974 Letter to Editor. *Arizona Republic* (October 11, 1974).

Goodfriend, Martin

1976 The Havasupi Indian Reservation: An Economic Profile. Santa Monica, California (June 1, 1976).

Gregg, Flora J.

1901 Her report in the Annual Report of the Department of the Interior for the year 1901 reprinted in Flora Gregg Iliff's 1954 book listed below.

Griffith, Elisabeth

1963 Adventure in Havasu. *Arizona Highways* (June 1963: 8-39).

Hanna, Stephanie and Thomas Sweeney

1997 SECRETARY BABBITT TO DIRECT EMERGENCY FUNDS TO HAVASUPAI *TRIBAL RESIDENTS DISPLACED BY FLASH FLOOD.* U.S. Department of the Interior, Office of the Secretary. (August 12, 1997).

Harrison, W. H.

1906 Report of Superintendent in charge of Havasupai (August 11. 1906). Report of Superintendent in charge of Havasupai. In "Report of the Commissioner of Indian Affairs" (pp. 178-179). Annual Report of the Secretary of the Interior: 1906. Washington: U.S. Government Printing Office.

Henderson, Earl Y.

1928 The Havasupai Indian Agency, Arizona. Lawrence Kansas: Haskell Printing Dept.

Heslop, J. M.

1970 Grand Canyon Indian Branch. *Church News* (*Desert News*, week ending August 8, 1970).

Hirst, Stephen

1976 Life in a Narrow Place: The Havasupai of the Grand Canyon. New York: David McKay.

2006 I Am The Grand Canyon: The Story of the Havasupai People. Grand Canyon AZ: Grand Canyon Association.

Horwath and Horwath

1963 Tourist and Recreation Study: Havasupai Reservation (Supai, Arizona). A report prepared for the Bureau of Indian affairs, Phoenix Area Office.

Hrdlicka, Ales

1908 Physiological and Medical Observations among the Indians of Southwestern United States and Northern Mexico. Washington D.C.: *Bureau of American Ethnology Bulletin* 34.

Hughes, J. Donald

1967 The Story of Man at Grand Canyon. Grand Canyon Natural History Association Bulletin #14.

Iliff, Flora Gregg

1954 People of the Blue Water. New York: Harper & Brothers.

1974 Indian Claims Commission Findings on the Havasupai Indians. In Havasupai Indians (A reprint of the Indian Claims Commission docket no. 91). New York: Garland Publishing, Inc.

Ives, Joseph C.

1861 Report upon the Colorado River of the West. House of Representatives, 36th Congress, first session, Ex. Doc. No. 90. Washington D.C.

James, George Wharton

1899 The Yava Supai Indians and their Cataract Cañon Home. *Good Health* (August 1899:446-456, Battle Creek, Michigan).

1901 Down the Topocobya Trail. *The Wide World Magazine* (April 1901: 75-79).

1903 The Indians of the Painted Desert Region. Boston: Little, Brown, and Company.

1911 In and Around the Grand Canyon (Revised and Enlarged Edition). Boston: Little, Brown, and Company.

King, Duane H.

1979 The Origin of the Eastern Cherokees as a Social and Political Entity. In the Cherokee Indian Nation: a troubled history, Duane H. King, ed. Knoxville: U. of Tennessee Press.

Knobloch, Madge

1988 Havasupai Years. Billings, Montana: Council for Indian Education.

Kolb, Ellsworth and Emery

1914 Experiences in the Grand Canyon. *The National Geographic Magazine*, Vol.XXVI, No.2 August, 1914

Kroeber, A. L., ed.

    1935 Walapai Ethnography. Memoirs of the American Anthropological Association No. 42. Menasha, Wisconsin.

Lee, Brandy A.

    2007 Called to canyon: serving in Supai. *Deseret News, LDS Church News* (Week ending January 27, 2007:6,7).

Lee, Richard B.

    1969 !Kung Bushman Subsistence: An Input-Output Analysis. In Environmental and Cultural Behavior: Ecological Studies in Cultural Anthropology (pp. 47-79). In Andrew P. Vayda, ed. Garden City: The Natural History Press. (A reprint from Ecological Essays. David Damas, ed. Ottawa: National Museum of Canada.

Lightman, Herb A.

    1971 Filming in Shangri-La. *American Cinematographer* 52:1110-13, 75-77, 83-88.

Lovett, Vincent

    1978 Indian News Notes. *Cherokee One Feather* (June 7, 1978).

Macdonald, J.A., Baldwin J.R., Olley, R.E., Woods R.E., Lake R.W. and Law C.E.

    1972 <u>RAILWAY TO THE ARCTIC</u> (Supplementary Report No. 2) <u>THE ECONOMIC EFFECTS OF AN ARCTIC RAILWAY.</u> Canadian Institute of Guided Ground Transport, Queen's University at Kingston, Ontario (August 18, 1972 Draft)

Manners, Robert A.

    1974a Havasupai Indians: an Ethnohistorical Report. In Havasupai Indians (A reprint of the Indian Claims Commission docket no. 91). New York: Garland Publishing, Inc.

    1974b An Ethnological Report of the Hualapai (Walapai) Indians of Arizona. In Havasupai Indians (A reprint of the Indian Claims Commission docket no. ?). New York: Garland Publishing, Inc.

Manners, Robert A. and John Collier

    1972 Pluralism and the American Indian. In the Emergent Native Americans, Deward E. Walker, Jr., ed. Boston: Little Brown and Company. (A reprint of the original 1962-63 articles).

Manners, Robert A., Henry F. Dobyns, and Roberts C. Euler

    1974 Havasupai Indians. (A reprint of the Indian Claims Commission docket no. 91). New York: Garland Publishing, Inc.

Marshall, George H.

    1903 Diary entries, G. H. Marshall Papers. Tucson: University of Arizona Special Collections (unpublished manuscript).

    1907 The Three Longest Days of My Life. (Magazine Section Vol. 32, No. 232, p. 6) *St. Louis Globe Democrat* (Sunday January 6, 1907).

Martin, John F.

    1966 Continuity and Change in Havasupai Social and Economic Organization. Ph.D. dissertation, The University of Chicago.

    1968 A reconsideration of Havasupai Land Tenure. *Ethnology* Vol., No. 4, October 1968: 450-460.

1973a The Organization of Land and Labor in a Marginal Economy. *Human Organization* 32: 153-161.

1973b On the Estimation of the Sizes of Local Groups in a Hunting-Gathering Environment. *American Anthropologist* Vol. 75, No. 5, October 1973:1448-1468.

1985 The Pre-history and Ethnohistory of Havasupai-Hualapai Relations. *Ethnohistory* Vol. 32, No. 2:135-153.

1986 The Havasupai. *Plateau* Vol. 56, No. 4.

McCowan, S. M.

1892a Report on Yava Supai Indians (June 25, 1892). In "Report of the Commissioner of Indian Affairs." Annual Report of the Secretary of the Interior 1892 (pp. 649-50). Washington: U.S, Government Printing Office.

1892b Supplemental Report on the Yava-Supai Indians (July 20, 1892). In "Report of the Commissioner of Indian Affairs." Annual Report of the Secretary of the Interior 1892 (pp. 651-652). Washington: U.S, Government Printing Office.

McGregor, John C.

1951 The Cohonina Culture of Northwestern Arizona. Urbanna: University of Illinois Press.

McGuire, Thomas R.

1983 Walapai. In Handbook of North American Indians, Vol. 10, Southwest, William C Sturtervant, general editor, Alfonso Ortiz, volume editor. (pp. 25-37). Washington D.C.: Smithsonian Institution.

Meador, Bruce S. and Robert A. Roessel, Jr.

1962 Havasupai School Survey. Tempe: The Indian Education Center, Arizona State University.

Mooney, James

1973 The Ghost Dance Religion and Wounded Knee. (Reprint of the Ghost Dance Religion and Sioux Outbreak of 1890, pt. 2 of the 14th annual report of the Bureau of American Ethnology 1892-93, J. W. Powell Director). New York: Dover Publications Inc.

News Brief

2019 Flood damages Havasupai waterfall. *Navajo Times* (December 5, 2019:C7).

Olson, James S. and Raymond Wilson

1984 Native Americans in the Twentieth Century. Provo: Brigham Young University Press.

Perkins, J. S.

1902 Report of School Superintendent in charge of Walapai and Havasupai (August 14. 1902). In "Report of the Commissioner of Indian Affairs" (pp. 163-164). Annual Report of the Secretary of the Interior: 1902. Washington: U.S. Government Printing Office.

Phoenix area office, Bureau of Indian affairs et al.

1976 The Secretarial Land Use Plan For The Addition To The Havasupai Indian Reservation (draft), March 12,, 1976.

1979 The Secretarial Land Use Plan For The Addition To The Havasupai Indian Reservation (draft), July 23, 1979.

Pineo, Christopher S.
2018 Havasupai lawsuit could impact BIE's nationwide system. *Navajo Times* (February 22, 2018:A11).

R.C.I A
1889 Report to the Commissioner of Indian Affairs

Reel, Estelle
1900 Report of Superintendent of Indian schools (August 20, 1900). In "Report of the Commissioner of Indian Affairs" (pp. 417-436). Annual Report of the Secretary of the Interior: 1900. Washington: U.S. Government Printing Office.

Region Briefs
2015 Grand Canyon Skywalk records one-millionth visitor. *Navajo Times* (December 30, 2015:C5).

Rukkila, John
1970 Trouble in Shangri-La. *Arizona* (June 21, 1970:8-12).

S 1296 (Senate bill 1296)
1974 Amended version (September 25, 1974).

Santos, Fernando
2017 Tribe Sues U.S. Over School that Barely Teaches Two R's. *The New York Times* (January 23, 2017).

Schwartz, Douglas W.
1956 The Havasupai 600A.D. – 1955A.D.: A Short Culture History. *Plateau* Vol.28, No. 3&4:77-85.
1983 Havasupai. In Handbook of North American Indians, Vol. 10, Southwest, William C Sturtervant, general editor, Alfonso Ortiz, volume editor. (pp. 13-24). Washington D.C.: Smithsonian Institution.

Scott, Derek
1971 All the Best Camera Angles Were in Five Feet of Water. *American Cinematographer* 52:11, 22-25, 50, 66-67, 78-82.

Shufeldt, R. W., M.D.
1892 Some Observations on the Havasu-pai Indians. *U. S. National Museum Proceedings* 14:387-390.

Sigvaldson, Jack
1972 Work Arctic Proves Men Prefer Jobs to Welfare. Star Weekly (Canadian Panorama) May 20, 1972:5.

Smithson, Carma Lee
1959 The Havasupai Woman. *University of Utah Anthropological Papers* No. 38. Salt Lake City: U. of Utah Press.

Smithson, Carma Lee and Robert C. Euler
1964 Havasupai Religion and Mythology. University of Utah Anthropological Papers No. 68.

Sparks, joe P.
1974 Letter to Editor. *Arizona Republic* (October 12, 1974).

Spicer, Edward H.

1952 Resistance to Freedom: Resettlement from Japanese Relocation Centers during World War II. In Human Problems in Technological Change, E.H. Spicer, ed. New York: Russell Sage Foundation.

1962 Cycles of Conquest. Tucson: University of Arizona Press.

Spier, Leslie

1928 Havasupai Ethnography. *Anthropological Papers of the American Museum of Natural History* Vol. 29, Pt.3:81-408.

Stephen, Alexander M.

1969 (1936) Hopi Journal. Reprint of the 1936 original, edited by Elsie Clews Parsons, *Columbia University Contributions to Anthropology*, Vol. 23. (Reprinted by AMS Press, New York in 1969).

Stucki, Larry R.

1972 Canada's Unemployable Northerners: Square Pegs in Round Holes in the System to be Created for the International Transfer of Energy by Pipeline from Northern Canada to the United States. (A 199-page manuscript privately published at the University of Nebraska to meet the large demands for copies.)

1973 The Railroad Pipeline Argument: One Year Later. (Privately published at the University of Nebraska to meet the large demand for copies.)

1974 Pipeline or Railroad: How Best to Exploit the Mackenzie Valley Resources Route. *Poundmaker* Vol.2, No. 28:8-9; Vol.2, No. 29:28 (This is the same article as 1973 with the change of title. Portions of this article were reprinted in the *Ontario Naturalist and Newsletter*.)

1979 Mormonism: The Restorer or Destroyer of the "True" Heritage of the American Indian. (A revised version of a paper presented at the 78th annual meeting of the AAA in Cincinnati Ohio a copy of which is found in BYU's Library.)

1981 Supai: Wilderness Paradise or Prison?. Anthro Tech Vol. 5, No. 2:8-13.

1984 Will the "Real" Indian Survive?: Tourism and Affluence at Cherokee, North Carolina in Affluence and Cultural Survival, R. Salisbury and E. Tooker, editors. Washington, D.C.: American Ethnological Society.

2009 Copper Mines, Company Towns, Indians, Mexicans, Mormons, Masons, Jews, Muslims, Gays, Wombs, McDonalds, and the March of Dimes: "Survival of the Fittest" in and Far beyond the Deserts of Arizona, New Mexico, and Utah. Victoria, BC: Trafford Publishing.

2017 The Bitter Navajo Language Fluency 2014 Presidential Election Conflict. *Sociology and Anthropology* 5(10):841-861.

Thomas, Robert L.

1972 2 teachers find new life In canyon. *Arizona Republic* (April 9, 1972:C1).

1974 12 Havasupai Horses Die of Starvation in Drought. *Arizona Republic* (October 11, 1974).

Towell, William E.

1974 What's new at AFA. *American Forests* 80, No. 9:24.

Wampler, Joseph
  1959 Havasu Canyon: Gem of the Grand Canyon. (Also contains chapters by
        Harold C. Bryant and Welden F. Heald). (This 1971 reprinting contains some
        revisions that were apparently done in the spring of 1969 – see p.112).
        Berkeley: Wampler.
Whitelaw, Robert L. (Virginia Polytechnic Institute and State University)
  1972 The New Case for a Railway to Alaska: Oil and LNG by Unitrain from the
        Arctic. A paper to be presented at the A.S.M.E. winter meeting in New York
        City on November 28, 1972.
Whiting, Alfred F.
  n.d.   The Havasupai: a study of intertribal acculturation. Xerox copy of typescript
        draft of thesis in the Arizona State Museum Library (183 pages, probable date
        about 1950). Tucson, Arizona.
  1958 Havasupai Characteristics in the Cohonina. *Plateau*, Vol.30, No.3 (January
        1958).
Williams, George
  1971 Havasupai: People of the Blue-Green Water. *American Cinematographer*
        52:11, 14-17, 60-61.
Witt, Greg
  2010 Havasupai: Paradise Remodeled by Mother Nature. *Native Peoples*
        (January/February 2010: 68-70).
Wood, Ben
  1979 The Mormons and Indian Child Placement:-- Is Native Culture Being
        Destroyed. *Wassaja* (March 1979:7,8).
Woods, Alden
  2018 Lawsuit against feds over "dismal" Havasupai school can continue, judge
        rules. *The Republic/azcentral.com* (April 2, 2018).
Woods, Alden and Ricardo Cano
  2017 At Havasupai school in Grand Canyon, fired teacher paints a pattern of
        neglect. *The Republic/azcentral.com* (September 18, 2017).
Zaphiris, Alexander G.
  1968 The Havasupai Survey: A Study of the Socio-Economic Conditions of an
        American Indian Tribe. University of Denver Graduate School of Social Work.

CPSIA information can be obtained
at www.ICGtesting.com
Printed in the USA
LVHW061508200221
679498LV00042B/424